MAKING SENSE OF THE CENSUS REVISITED

MAKING SENSE OF THE CENSUS REVISITED

CENSUS RECORDS FOR ENGLAND AND WALES 1801–1901

A Handbook for Historical Researchers

EDWARD HIGGS

LONDON
INSTITUTE OF HISTORICAL RESEARCH
THE NATIONAL ARCHIVES OF THE UK

Published by

UNIVERSITY OF LONDON
SCHOOL OF ADVANCED STUDY
INSTITUTE OF HISTORICAL RESEARCH
Senate House, London WC1E 7HU

in conjunction with

THE NATIONAL ARCHIVES OF THE UK
London

ISBN 1 905165 00 5

Cover illustrations:
TNA, Copy 1/449, Funeral of Queen Victoria, Hyde Park (1901)
Board of Inland Revenue: Valuation Office: Finance Act 1910, Record Sheet Plans:
London Region: Tower Hamlets District (TNA, IR 121/20/25)
Cover design by Frances Bowcock, IHR

Contents

PART IV APPENDICES

Tables and figures

Tables

Figures

Appendices:

Introduction

This is the third handbook on the manuscript census returns for England and Wales in the period 1801–1901 released by The National Archives in London (formerly the Public Record Office). In 1989, while an archivist at the Public Record Office, I published a book entitled *Making Sense of the Census: the Manuscript Returns for England and Wales, 1801–1901* in the Office's handbook series.[1] Seven years later a second handbook, *A Clearer Sense of the Census: the Victorian Censuses and Historical Research*, appeared.[2] This second volume included new chapters on using the census enumerators' books in historical research, and shed much of the material in the earlier volume on the pre-1841 censuses. Both volumes are now out of print, while the demand for guides to the census returns has continued unabated.

The present work is, in one sense, a reissue of the second of these guides, although it re-integrates the 'lost' material on the enumerations of 1801–31. Chapter 12, covering the use of census material, has also been completely revised, and analyses of actual communities from the 1901 census have been included to show how some of the methodological tools discussed in Chapter 11 can be used. This reveals the stark contrasts that existed in the period between the declining, and stagnant, countryside and the restless immigrant communities of the East End of London. The whole text has been updated to include references to material published since 1996, and to the new forms of access to the material, especially to the online version of the 1901 census. Much has changed in terms of historiography and access since the original handbook was published in the 1980s but the records themselves have not. Much of the descriptive material in earlier versions of the handbook has, therefore, been preserved.

The present work, like its predecessors, is still based on the principle that to understand a historical text it is necessary to see it as the outcome of a process of construction. By recreating the ostensible reasons for taking the Victorian censuses, and discussing how the enumerators' books were put together, one can help to illuminate the nature of the data that they contain. This is not to say that their meaning is transparent. It is indeed a constant refrain of the handbook that the meaning of the data in the census returns can be obscure. Citizens were asked questions they did not understand, or which they did not have sufficient information to answer, or answered questions that they were not in fact asked. However, just because the use of language creates problems in all forms of human activity, this does not mean that human beings cannot use language successfully to organise purposeful activities, or to refer to aspects of themselves or their surroundings that

---

[1] E. Higgs, *Making Sense of the Census: the Manuscript Returns for England and Wales, 1801–1901* (London, 1989).
[2] E. Higgs, *A Clearer Sense of the Census: the Victorian Censuses and Historical Research* (London, 1996).

appear significant. The information in the census refers to something outside itself but not necessarily in the form that modern historians assume.

As with the earlier guides, the present volume is almost exclusively concerned with England and Wales. Because of differences in the legal, constitutional and administrative systems in Scotland, the censuses in the northern kingdom were always handled in a rather different manner. From 1861 onwards the census in Scotland was administered by a separate registrar-general for Scotland, and diverged from its counterpart south of the border in content and form. The separate Irish censuses, and the enumerations or headcounts taken in the colonies to coincide with the census of England and Wales in the course of the nineteenth century, are also beyond the scope of this book. This is not intended to imply that the returns for England and Wales are in any sense more important than those for other nations in the Victorian United Kingdom or British Empire; merely that my expertise lies in an analysis of the work of the General Register Office in London. The activities of the registrars-general in Edinburgh and Dublin cannot be tacked on to the work of their English counterpart; they require complete studies in their own right. This task is beyond my expertise and resources.[3]

Numerous people should be acknowledged as contributing to the genesis and writing of the present work, not least those mentioned in the preface and introduction to the previous handbooks. Special thanks should be given here to Aidan Lawes of The National Archives (TNA), who commissioned the present volume, and made numerous helpful suggestions for revisions. Thanks are also due to the staff of The National Archives' Family Records Centre (FRC), especially David Annal, for answering various detailed questions about the returns. Tom Gregan, Head of Archive Production at The National Archives, supplied information on the structure of the 1901 census returns. Paul Glenister, one of my research students at the University of Essex, expertly undertook the analysis of the 1901 census data upon which my description of the various communities in Chapter 12 is based. I would like to thank QinetiQ, who funded the transcription of the 1901 census and the 1901 Census Online website, for supplying me with this data. Matthew Woollard read the manuscript and, as ever, made numerous helpful comments. The editorial support of Jane Winters and her colleagues at the Institute of Historical Research has been invaluable.

I must also thank my wife Liz for her usual helpful advice and support, and for the photograph on p. 30.

---

[3] For a guide to the Irish censuses in the nineteenth century, see E. M. Crawford, *Counting the People: a Survey of the Irish Censuses, 1813–1911* (Dublin, 2003). The work of the Scottish General Register Office is currently the subject of a research project at the University of Glasgow under the direction of Professor Anne Crowther, and funded by the Wellcome Trust.

PART I

THE HISTORY AND STRUCTURE OF THE RECORDS

1 The history of nineteenth-century census-taking

The state and population surveys

The central state in England has long been involved in surveying its resources in terms of lands, goods and people. Domesday Book itself was an attempt to discover just such information for Anglo-Norman England. The records generated by later methods of taxation have also been used by historians to calculate population size and structure.[1] But such sources were never intended to give the authorities a comprehensive picture of the whole population. Domesday Book was essentially a survey of landholding; people were only mentioned as appendages to the land, and even then in an incomplete manner. The records of the poll and hearth taxes only related to people who paid the tax, or to households. In order to calculate the total population it is necessary to estimate the extent of the unrecorded population, or to estimate average household size to act as a multiplier. Such difficulties arise from using these records as surrogates for population censuses, and much the same could be said of similar records produced in other countries.

Such narrow pecuniary interests gradually gave way to broader considerations in the late seventeenth and eighteenth centuries. In this period European states and their colonies came to take stock of their military resources in an age of almost incessant warfare. Possibly the first attempt to count everyone in an area larger than a city, at successive intervals, was made in La Nouvelle France (Quebec) and Acadie (Nova Scotia), where 16 enumerations were undertaken between 1665 and 1754. A complete census was taken in Iceland in 1703. In 1749 the Swedish clergy, who had long kept lists of parishioners, were required to render returns from which the total population of Sweden (including Finland) was obtained, and a similar exercise took place in Denmark in 1787. In Austria, under the impact of Maria Theresa's population policy, partly a response to the effects of the Turkish wars, censuses were initiated in 1754. Various Italian states conducted approximately accurate enumerations in the eighteenth century: Sardinia in 1773 and 1795; Parma in 1770; and Tuscany in 1766. Enumerations also occurred in several German states from 1742 onwards.[2]

The association between warfare, census-taking and other forms of population statistics has led Michel Foucault, and other postmodernists, to see the development of such state activities in

[1] For some examples of attempts to do so, see E. A. Wrigley and R. S. Schofield, *The Population History of England 1541–1871: a Reconstruction* (London, 1981), pp. 563–87. See also A. Hinde, *England's Population: a History since the Domesday Survey* (London, 2003), esp. pp. 65–78, 163–76, 271–82.

[2] D. V. Glass, *Numbering the People: the Eighteenth Century Population Controversy and the Development of Census and Vital Statistics in Britain* (London, 1978), pp. 12–13.

terms of new forms of 'governmentality' associated with the need to foster 'biopower'. In a situation of constant European conflicts, states came to see the need to conceive of their subjects as 'population' that had to be fostered and expanded in the interests of military survival. Demography was thus another of the 'technologies of power' that it is necessary for postmodernists to unmask.[3] But this is too simplistic a model to explain census-taking, certainly in the Anglo-Saxon world, since neither Britain nor the USA had, or needed, a standing army in the eighteenth and nineteenth centuries. Despite this the first census of the USA in 1790 broke new ground. This was not only because of the size of the area enumerated, and the attempt to obtain information on certain characteristics of individuals in the population, but also because of the political purpose for which the census was undertaken: the apportionment of representation in Congress.[4] In the case of England, state information gathering in the nineteenth century needs to be put in the much broader context of creating liberal citizenship.[5]

Private estimates of the population of England date back at least to the works of William Petty, Gregory King and Charles Davenant in the late seventeenth century. A new population debate arose in the 1750s as to whether or not the population had increased since the Glorious Revolution of 1688. Conservative defenders of the agricultural interest agreed with political radicals in believing that the population of England had declined under the dominance of a Whig aristocracy and the rising commercial classes. Commerce and political jobbery were seen as having caused a general moral and sexual debauchment that had led to population decline.[6] Similar views were held by radicals such as William Cobbett in the early nineteenth century.[7] Others defended the rise of commerce and claimed that the population had increased since 1688. Much of this debate revolved around population estimates based upon taxation records and the ecclesiastical registers of baptisms, marriages and burials.

A new twist was given to the controversy by the publication in 1798 of Malthus's *Essay on the principle of population*. The full title of the 1803 edition was, in fact, an *Essay on the principle of population, or a view of its past and present effects on human happiness, with an inquiry into our prospects respecting the future removal or mitigation of the evils which it occasions*. The debate shifted from the effect of morality on population growth to the relationship between the latter and the available agricultural resources of society. If population grew according to a geometric ratio (2, 4, 8, 16, 32 ....), and agricultural production according to an arithmetic progression (1, 2, 3, 4, 5 ....), at what point would population pressure encroach on subsistence, and what would be the consequences in terms of checks to population growth?

---

[3] M. Foucault, 'The subject and power', in *Michel Foucault: Beyond Structuralism and Hermeneutics, with an Afterword by Michel Foucault*, ed. H. L. Dreyfus and P. Rabinow (Brighton, 1982), pp. 208–26; M. Foucault, 'Governmentality', in *The Foucault Effect: Studies in Governmentality*, ed. G. Burchell, C. Gordon and P. Miller (London, 1991), pp. 87–104.

[4] M. Anderson, *The American Census: a Social History* (New Haven, Conn., 1988).

[5] E. Higgs, *The Information State in England: the Central Collection of Information on Citizens, 1500–2000* (London, 2003), pp. 64–98.

[6] Glass, *Numbering the People*, pp. 11–89.

[7] William Cobbett, *Rural Rides* (Harmondsworth, 1983), p. 67.

In 1753 a bill 'for taking and registering an annual account of the total number of people, and the total number of marriages, births and burials; and also the total number of poor receiving alms in every parish, and extraparochial place, in Great Britain', was introduced into Parliament.[8] This may have been linked to the population controversy noted above because the aim of the bill was stated as being to establish the 'progressive increase or diminuition [*sic*]' of the population. In this the wording was surprisingly similar to that contained in the Census Act of 1801 (41 Geo. III, c. 15). The 1753 bill provided that each year the overseers of the poor (or the clerks of the kirk-session in Scotland) were to go from house to house in their parishes recording the number of people in each dwelling. They were to distinguish separately for men and women the numbers under 20 years, aged 20–59, and those 60 years and over. The numbers of married persons, those receiving poor relief in the previous 12 months, and the total amount of poor relief were also to be noted. The local clergy were to record in a special registry book baptisms and burials within the parish, whether of members of the Church of England or not, giving details of names, sex, age, addresses of next of kin, and so on. Abstracts of these were to be sent to the commissioners for trade and plantations, who were to produce national abstracts of the numbers of births and deaths from them, and of population numbers from the overseers' returns.

Glass, drawing upon *The Gentleman's Magazine* for 1753, argues that the bill's supporters hoped that these measures would allow the calculation of the maximum size of any army which could be raised in times of need; provide evidence as to the desirability of emigration to the colonies; and show the burden of the Poor Law on the country.[9] This may be true, but the bill itself reveals other concerns, which link the 1753 proposals more closely with later, nineteenth-century, developments. First, the bill argued that the registration of vital events was necessary since 'great inconveniences have arisen from the present defective manner in which parochial registers are formed, and the loose and uncertain method in which they are kept and preserved; whereby the evidence of descent is frequently lost and rendered precarious'. The need to underpin rights to title to property via recording lines of descent was also the main reason for the establishment of the system of civil registration administered by the General Register Office (GRO) under the 1836 Registration Act.[10] As will be noted, the GRO was to take over the administration of the census in 1840.

Similarly, the bill envisaged the data collected on population and vital events as being used to create a national system of Bills of Mortality, and Buck has linked the bill to political calculations respecting the insurance of lives.[11] Data on population, births and deaths was required to facilitate the drawing up of life-tables, and so relieve poverty through the creation of actuarially sound insurance and friendly societies. This was also a feature of the early nineteenth-century censuses, and of the early statistical work of the General Register Office.[12]

[8] D. V. Glass, *The Development of Population Statistics* (Farnborough, 1973) contains a copy of the bill.

[9] Glass, *Numbering the People*, p. 19.

[10] E. Higgs, *Life, Death and Statistics: Civil Registration, Censuses and the Work of the General Register Office, 1837–1952* (Hatfield, 2004), ch. 1.

[11] P. Buck, 'People who counted: political arithmetic in the eighteenth century', *Isis*, 73 (1982), pp. 28–45.

[12] Higgs, *Life, Death and Statistics*, chs. 2, 3.

The opponents of the 1753 bill argued that the proposed enumeration would be impractical and costly, and might be used as the basis of new taxation and conscription. This needs to be set in terms of eighteenth-century 'Country' opposition to the power of the 'Court'. Given the eighteenth-century perception of a standing army as the first step to the establishment of an absolute monarchy, the violence of the opposition to the bill is perhaps understandable. Memories of the attempt by James II to establish just such a government through an army loyal to the Crown, and to reintroduce Roman Catholicism, were still very much alive. Similarly, the proposal to register lines of descent through the state smacked of the manner in which the monarchy before the English Civil Wars had used the Court of Wards and *inquisitions post mortem* as a means of controlling the estates of minors for the purposes of pillaging them. Nevertheless, the bill passed through all its stages in the Commons and received its second reading in the Lords. It was, however, referred to a Committee of the Whole House, and before this could meet the parliamentary session ended and the bill lapsed.[13]

The origins of the 1801 census

The inception of decennial census-taking in 1801 can be seen explicitly in terms of the particular conditions in the country in 1800 when the first Census Act was passed. The period was one of war with revolutionary France, bad harvests and food shortages; a typical Malthusian crisis of subsistence. Large numbers of agricultural workers were also serving in the militia and so unable to work on the land. What could be more natural than the desire to enumerate the population in order to discover how many mouths needed to be fed, and how many people were working to feed them?[14] Aspects of the first census do indeed appear to confirm this hypothesis. Not only was an enumeration made of the total population, an attempt was also made to divide it into three groups: those working in agriculture; those in trade, manufactures and handicrafts; and those in other employments. At the same date a separate agricultural survey to be performed by the clergymen of the parish was also initiated. The results of this survey, known as the Acreage Returns, show the number of acres in each parish devoted to differing crops and now form the record series HO 67 at The National Archives of the UK in London (hereafter TNA).[15]

The 1800 Census Act (41 Geo. III, c. 15) was, however, explicitly called 'An Act for taking an Account of the Population of Great Britain, and the increase or diminution thereof', as were all decennial Census Acts until that of 1850. As well as an enumeration of the population, an attempt was made to obtain data on baptisms, marriages and burials for the whole of the eighteenth century. This indicates that the reasons for the inception of nineteenth-century census-taking should be sought in the general population controversies of the late eighteenth century. It could be argued, moreover, that the role of the agricultural crisis was to facilitate enumeration rather

---

[13] Glass, *Numbering the People*, pp. 17–21; A. A. Rusnock, *Quantifying Health and Population in Eighteenth-Century England and France* (Cambridge, 2002), pp. 183–8.

[14] Glass, *Numbering the People*, pp. 96–8.

[15] The National Archives of the UK: Public Record Office (hereafter TNA), HO 67, Acreage Returns.

than to instigate it. Since food prices were high in 1800/1, many of the poor were applying to the overseers of the poor for relief under the provisions of the Poor Laws. This was usually granted according to the number of children maintained by each applicant, and the overseers would thus be in an excellent position to know the total numbers of people in their parishes.

The history of the taking of the first census in 1801, and that of the next three enumerations, is intimately connected with the career of John Rickman. Rickman (1771–1840) was the son of a clergyman and ran the *Commercial, Agricultural, and Manufacturer's Magazine* for some time after his graduation from Oxford in 1792. In 1796 he wrote a paper showing that it would be administratively easy and profitable to take a census of the population. The manuscript was shown to Charles Abbot (afterwards Lord Colchester) by George Rose, MP for Christchurch. Abbot hired Rickman as his secretary, and employed him in preparing the first Census Act, which Abbot introduced into Parliament in December 1800. When the latter become chief secretary for Ireland in 1801, Rickman went with him to Dublin, and was made deputy keeper of the privy seal. He refused a permanent appointment in Ireland, and when Abbot became Speaker of the House of Commons in February 1802, Rickman continued to be his secretary and settled in London. In July 1814 he was appointed second clerk assistant at the table of the House of Commons, and in 1820 clerk assistant, a position he held until his death. Rickman organised the administration of all the censuses from 1801 to 1831.[16]

In a memoir on his father written in 1841, Rickman's son, William, emphasised his father's interest in acquiring information via the census on the mortality and life expectancy of the working classes. He linked this to his father's desire to improve the regulation of friendly societies – primitive insurance schemes designed to protect the families of workers against illness and death – through the provision of proper actuarial life-tables.[17] Such considerations also appear to have underlain the development of a statistical branch within the General Register Office, which was to take over the administration of the census in 1840.[18] The link between the census and life-tables may explain why, as will be discussed below, the enumerations undertaken by Rickman included enquiries into records of baptisms, marriages and burials as well as a population count.

The first four censuses carry all the hallmarks of central government prior to the 1832 Reform Act. The initiation of census-taking reflected the interest taken in the subject by an aristocratic grandee such as Colchester, and the enumerations depended for their organisation upon the work of one of his clients. The local administration of the census was based on the officers of the Elizabethan Poor Law system and of the Established Church. However, with the changes in the structure of central and local government in the 1830s, new administrative methods and preoccupations were to develop.

---

[16] *Oxford Dictionary of National Biography* (Oxford, 2004).
[17] William Charles Rickman, *Biographical Memoir of John Rickman* (London, 1841), p. 18.
[18] Higgs, *Life, Death and Statistics*, pp. 22–40.

Early census administration, 1801–31

Since the administrative machinery established in 1801 remained the basis of subsequent enumerations until 1841, a description of the taking of the first census can be taken as a proxy for that of all the early censuses.[19]

The schedule attached to the Census Act of 1800 (41 Geo. III, c. 15) contained the following questions:

1. How many inhabited houses are there in your parish, township or place; by how many families are they occupied; and how many houses therein are uninhabited?

2. How many persons (including children of whatever age) are there actually found within the limits of your parish, township, or place, at the time of taking this account, distinguishing males and females, and exclusive of men actually serving in his majesty's regular forces or militia, and exclusive of seamen either in his majesty's service or belonging to registered vessels?

3. What number of persons in your parish, township or place are chiefly employed in agriculture; how many in trade, manufactures, or handicraft; and how many are not occupied in any of the preceding classes?

4. What was the number of baptisms and burials in your parish, township, or place in the several years 1700, 1710, 1720, 1730, 1740, 1750, 1760, 1770, 1780, and in each subsequent year to the 31st December, 1800, distinguishing males from females?

5. What was the number of marriages in your parish, township, or place in each year, from the year 1754 inclusive to the end of the year 1800?

6. Are there any matters which you think it necessary to remark in explanation of your answers to any of the preceding questions?

In England and Wales the responsibility for answering the first five questions was divided. The first three were addressed to those responsible for making the enumeration by house-to-house enquiry on 10 March 1801, or as soon as possible after that date. This duty was placed upon the overseers of the poor or 'other substantial householders'. The fourth and fifth questions were addressed to the local parish clergy. The king's printer was instructed to send copies of the act and schedule to clerks of the peace and town clerks, who were required to distribute them to the local justices of the peace. They were also required to deliver enough copies of the schedule to high constables, or 'other proper officers', so the latter could ensure that one copy was received

---

[19] For a more detailed discussion of early census administration, see Office of Population Censuses and Surveys and General Register Office, Edinburgh, *Guide to Census Reports, Great Britain 1801–1966* (London, 1977), pp. 13–18.

by the overseer of the poor, or other substantial householder, and by the rector, vicar, curate or other officiating minister, in each parish, township or place.

All census returns had to be made on prescribed forms that were attached to the schedule of the act. These merely asked for raw numbers to be returned. In order to make the returns the relevant officers were authorised 'to ask all such questions of the persons within the said parish, township, or place, respecting themselves and the number and quality of persons constituting the respective families, as shall be necessary for stating the particulars required to be stated concerning them, in the said answers and returns'.[20] This led some overseers to draw up nominal listings of the inhabitants of their parish from which the final returns were digested. Wall, Woollard and Moring have listed no fewer than 791 such listings, with high concentrations in Yorkshire and East Anglia.[21] In some areas local printers produced printed forms for this purpose, presumably based on Rickman's schedules but not always following them directly. In London and elsewhere printed schedules were produced which were to be left with householders to fill up themselves. These subsidiary documents were retained locally among the Poor Law records, or in the parish chest. It is possible that some parishes were broken down into smaller districts and enumerated individually by differing parish officials, particularly in the north of England, where the township was the basic unit.[22]

The official returns made by the enumerators had to be attested or affirmed before the justices of the peace on a day which they were authorised to fix between dates specified in the act. In England and Wales the returns were then handed to the high constables or 'other proper officers' to be endorsed and submitted, together with a complete list of the names of enumerators, to the clerks of the peace or town clerks. These in turn were to send the returns to the Home Office not later than 15 May. There they were to be 'digested and reduced to Order by such Officer as such Secretary of State (for the Home Department) shall appoint for the Purpose'. Returns compiled from the parish registers had to be forwarded by the clergy to the bishop of the diocese, who was required to send them to his archbishop. Their final destination was the Privy Council. The preparation of the abstracts of the returns that were laid before Parliament was assigned to John Rickman, who signed the *Census Reports*. The overseers of the poor laid their accounts before the quarter sessions that could order their reimbursement out of the revenues collected by the receiver-general of land taxes.[23] These orders were sent to the Exchequer and can be found in the record series E 182 at TNA.[24] There appears to be some rough correlation between the number of families in a parish or township, as given in the *Census Reports*, and the amounts paid out to the overseers.

[20] Census Act (41 Geo. III, c. 15), s. 3.

[21] R. Wall, M. Woollard and B. Moring, *Census Schedules and Listings, 1801–1831: an Introduction and Guide* (Working Paper Series, 5, Department of History, University of Essex, Colchester, 2004), pp. 6–7. An updateable version of this will shortly be available at <www.histpop.org.uk/pre41>.

[22] P. Laxton, 'Liverpool in 1801: a manuscript return for the first national census of population', *Transactions of the Historical Society of Lancashire and Cheshire*, 130 (1980), pp. 76–9.

[23] Census Act (41 Geo. III, c. 15), s. 10.

[24] TNA, E 182, Receivers' Accounts of Land and Assessed Taxes, Subsidiary Documents.

In 1811 three important changes were introduced into the core questions asked at each census. The question concerning uninhabited houses was divided in order to distinguish the number of houses being built from the number uninhabited for any other reason, such as dilapidation. The distinction was intended to give an indication of the degree of prosperity of the districts. The question relating to the occupations of individuals was modified to read 'What number of families (rather than persons) are chiefly employed in or maintained by' work in the three economic sectors of 1801. In the first census some male householders had included their female relatives, children and servants in the same occupational class as themselves, while others expressly excluded them. Lastly, the clergy were now asked to record the number of baptisms, marriages and burials registered in each of the previous 10 years.[25]

Other questions were later asked on an *ad hoc* basis. In 1821 enumerators were asked to indicate, if the information could be obtained 'in a manner satisfactory to yourself, and not inconvenient to the parties', the number of males and females in five-year age bands up to 20 years, and in 10-year age bands thereafter. This attempt to gather information on age structure was partly in order to improve the life-tables upon which life insurance schemes were based, and partly to establish the number of men able to bear arms.[26]

In 1831 much more extensive questions relating to occupations were asked. These appear to have reflected a desire to amass data on the economy which would refute potentially subversive economic theories such as the labour theory of value. The latter implied that all wealth was created by members of the labouring classes.[27] The number of males 'upwards of twenty years' was to be given for seven economic categories. These were those employed:

1) in agriculture (sub-divided into occupiers of land who employed labourers, other occupiers of land, and agricultural labourers);
2) in manufacture;
3) in retail trade or handicrafts;
4) as capitalists, merchants and professionals;
5) as miners, fishermen, non-agricultural labourers;
6) those retired or disabled;
7) those employed as servants.

Enumerators were also asked to give the trades of those employed in retailing and handicrafts, and to indicate the numbers following them; the specific manufactures employing those in the second category; and the specific numbers in the various occupational groups in the fifth category.

---

[25] *1811 Census Report: Abstract of the Answers and Returns* (PP 1812 XI [316 & 317], pp. ix–x); Census Act (51 Geo. III, c. 6), Schedule.

[26] Census Act 1820 (1 Geo. IV, c. 94), Schedule; *Minutes of Evidence taken (Session 1830) before the Select Committee on the Population Bill* (PP 1840 XV [396.], pp. 6–7, 25–7).

[27] *Minutes of Evidence taken (Session 1830) before the Select Committee on the Population Bill*, p. 7; Census Act 1830 (11 Geo. IV, c. 30), Schedule.

In addition, the clergy were asked to indicate the number of illegitimate children born in their parish in 1830. A formula giving a list of 100 of the most usual occupations in the retail trades and handicrafts was supplied with each schedule. There are problems in comparing the results of this occupational enumeration with those taken in later years but Wrigley points out that the returns of 1831 and 1851 'bear an intelligible and consistent relationship to each other'.[28]

1841: the transition to modern census-taking

With hindsight the course of history can seem a logical and inevitable progression. The transfer of responsibility for census-taking to the General Register Office in 1840, and the establishment of the means of enumerating the population which have lasted more or less intact until the present day, can be seen in this light. A detailed examination of the circumstances under which the 1841 census was taken, however, reveals a far more complicated picture. Indeed, the 1841 enumeration was a rather *ad hoc* affair, and very much a transitional stage between Rickman's censuses and the mature Victorian censuses from 1851 onwards. This explains some of the peculiarities of the 1841 returns.

The 1830s certainly saw the development of the administrative machinery that was to take over the census in 1841. The Poor Law Amendment Act of 1834 established the Poor Law union as the general unit of welfare administration, and this new administrative unit was gradually adopted first for the civil registration of births, marriages and deaths, and then for census purposes. The Municipal Corporation Act of 1835 paved the way for the creation of a new order of local government officials who were to become the backbone of the enumerating class in the towns and cities. Finally, the Births and Deaths Registration and Marriage Acts of 1836, providing for the civil registration of births, marriages and deaths, created a new system of central and local administration which was to be the basis of census-taking from 1841 onwards. The gathering of information on vital events from the records of ecclesiastical registration had always been part of Rickman's censuses: what could have been more natural than that the rest of the census process should be undertaken by this new registration machinery?[29]

In the wake of the acts of 1836, a registrar-general was appointed as head of the national system of civil registration. This officer had a central staff in the GRO whose task was to maintain a central register of births, marriages and deaths, mainly to protect property rights through recording lines of descent. But the GRO also gradually developed a statistical function via the preparation

---

[28] *Abstract of the answers and returns made pursuant to an Act, passed in the first year of the reign of His Majesty King George IV, intituled, "An Act for taking an Account ..." Enumeration Abstract, Vol. I, 1831* (PP 1833 XXXVII.1, pp. x–xi); E. A. Wrigley, 'Men on the land and men in the countryside: employment in agriculture in early-nineteenth-century England', in *The World we have Gained: Histories of Population and Social Structure*, ed. L. Bonfield, R. M. Smith and K. Wrightson (Oxford, 1986), pp. 308–18. A version of Wrigley's essay is reprinted in E. A. Wrigley, *Poverty, Progress and Population* (Cambridge, 2004), pp. 87–128

[29] For a history of the GRO, see M. Nissel, *People Count: a History of the General Register Office* (London, 1987); Higgs, *Life, Death and Statistics*.

of reports and summary statistics on vital events for actuarial and public health purposes.[30] The whole country was divided up into registration districts, based upon the Poor Law unions, and a superintendent registrar appointed for each. These areas were further sub-divided into sub-districts and part-time registrars appointed to them. These officers, initially often local doctors, were responsible for the registration of births, marriages and deaths within their sub-districts, and the forwarding of this information to the GRO in London. All that was necessary to turn this into an administrative system for the collection of census data was for the registrars to divide their sub-districts into smaller enumeration districts and to appoint a temporary enumerator for each. The latter could collect the necessary information that would be sent via the registrar and superintendent to the GRO for central processing in the same manner as data on vital statistics.

There was certainly public pressure building up in the late 1830s for a much more ambitious census. The London (later Royal) Statistical Society had set up a committee to make recommendations on the 1841 census, and its report suggested a radical change in the organisation of the census to take advantage of the new Poor Law and civil registration systems. The members of the committee advocated the use of an official household schedule to list each individual by name, and to give various pieces of information about them. These were to be transcribed into books by the enumerators for dispatch to London. They also advocated a greater range of questions relating to age, sex, marital status, occupation, place of birth, religion and health. This 'blunderbuss' approach to data collection was typical of the statistical movement that was so widespread in this period. Eventually many of their recommendations were incorporated into the 1841 census, although the range of questions asked was somewhat diminished.[31]

In reality, however, the transition to the new system of census-taking was far from inevitable, or straightforward. John Rickman appears to have been fully involved in the early preparations for taking the census of 1841. In 1836 he had forwarded circulars to the local clergy for the purpose of gathering information from the parish registers as far back as 1570. He had abstracted the results and hoped to publish these in order to show population trends from the sixteenth century onwards. He was also responsible for drawing up a draft Census Bill on the lines of previous censuses, and had been examining the possibility of using the boundaries and officers of the new Poor Law to gather information. Rickman appears to have been in charge of these preparations until approximately 11 June 1840, when he fell ill from a throat infection from which he eventually died in August of that year. It was only in the last week of June that the Home Office discussed the taking of the census with Thomas Henry Lister, the first registrar-general.[32] If Rickman had not fallen ill there would, presumably, have been far greater continuity in 1841 with the pre-Victorian enumerations.

---

[30] Higgs, *Life, Death and Statistics*, pp. 1–44.

[31] M. J. Cullen, *The Statistical Movement in Early Victorian Britain: the Foundations of Empirical Social Research* (Hassocks, 1975), pp. 96–7; D. V. Glass and P. A. M. Taylor, *Population and Emigration: Government and Society in Nineteenth Century Britain* (Dublin, 1976), pp. 14–15.

[32] TNA, T 1/4573, 10 Feb. 1841, Wm. Rickman *et al.* to C. G. Trevelyan [presumably E. C. Trevelyan, assistant secretary at the Treasury]; TNA, RG 27/1, p. 1.

Lister drew up a new bill which was the basis of the first Census Act for the 1841 census (3 & 4 Vict., c. 99). This act, although containing many of the recommendations of the London Statistical Society, also had certain similarities with Rickman's enumerations. The local gathering of information was certainly to be the duty of temporary enumerators appointed by the local registrars. They were to gather a much wider range of data on the characteristics of the individual members of the population of their district. This was to be done on one night in the year rather than, as previously, over a period of time. The census was to be a 'snap-shot' of society at a single moment so as to avoid the problems of double-counting as people moved from place to place.

Initially, however, Lister envisaged that the enumerators would gather this information themselves by house-to-house enquiries, as in previous censuses. He did not like household schedules because he believed that most householders were too illiterate to fill them in properly. He only appears to have countenanced their introduction after a pilot enumeration in London had shown how many enumerators would have to be employed to gather the data by door-to-door enquiries. The use of household schedules had to be hastily authorised by a supplementary Census Act (4 & 5 Vict., c. 7) which was passed only two months before the enumeration was due to take place. The clergy were also to be asked to give the usual information from the parish registers, and a schedule for that purpose was appended to the act. The information eventually formed part of the 1841 *Census Report*.[33] Nor was the connection with the Palace of Westminster severed at this date. The 1841 census was to be administered by three census commissioners: Lister, Edmund Phipps (about whom little is known) and Thomas Vardon, who was librarian of the House of Commons and had some experience of census-taking in 1831. Lister died in 1842, before the end of the census-abstracting process, and it was left to Vardon and Phipps to sign the final *Report*.[34]

The rather *ad hoc* nature of the transfer of census-taking to the GRO, and the limited amount of time that Lister had to plan the 1841 census, are reflected in the somewhat idiosyncratic nature of the returns. They are certainly rather different from those of later enumerations. Lister was anxious to produce as simple a household schedule as possible, and kept the headings of information gathered to a minimum. These included name (forename and surname only, not middle names), age (rounded down to the nearest term of five if over 14 years), sex, 'profession, trade, employment or of independent means', whether born in the same county (yes or no), or whether born in Scotland, Ireland or 'foreign parts'. Later censuses sought additional information on relationship to head of household, marital condition, full ages, the parish and county of birth, and details of medical disabilities.

Nor were some of the 'problem' groups, for which special arrangements were made in later censuses, catered for in the administration of the 1841 census. The schedule designed specifically for the crew of merchant vessels, for example, only appeared in 1851. Similarly, no distinct instructions were

---

[33] TNA, RG 27/1, pp. 6–11; *1841 Parish Register Abstract* (1841).

[34] TNA, RG 27/1, pp. 11–18; TNA, HO 45/146, 10 Jan. 1845, Phipps and Vardon to Phillipps; *1841 Census Report: Abstract of the Answers and Returns* (PP 1844 XXVII [587.], p. 72).

issued on the recording of night workers in 1841. Also, many of the detailed instructions given to enumerators and householders in later censuses were not distributed. For example, although the enumerator was instructed to leave a household schedule with each householder, the latter was not told if lodgers and boarders were to be counted as part of his or her 'family'. As one might expect, the accumulation of practical experience led to the gradual perfection of the census-taking machinery.

A final difference between 1841 and the later censuses under the GRO was that in the former the population tables in the published *Reports* gave the population for each ancient county, and within these for the traditional administrative units: hundreds, wapentakes, sokes, liberties and parishes. This was plainly to make the tables comparable with those in the earlier *Census Reports*. From 1851 onwards the main units used were the registration counties (which were not always the same as the ancient counties), registration districts, sub-districts, parishes and townships.

All these factors make it difficult to compare information in the 1841 census with much of that collected in later years.

Taking a Victorian census

The nineteenth-century censuses from 1851 onwards followed a common administrative pattern, and a general description of this census-taking machinery helps to reveal its strengths and weaknesses.

The first step taken by the GRO was to approach its parent department (the Home Office prior to 1871 and the Local Government Board thereafter) to get the necessary Census Act passed by Parliament. This authorised the questions to be asked and the disbursement of central government funds for the establishment of the census-taking apparatus. Having obtained sanction for expenditure, the GRO had to remind local officers of their duties, design and print household schedules and instruction books, and set up a central Census Office for processing the local returns. This involved hiring temporary clerks via the Treasury, training them, finding a suitable building in which to house them, arranging with the Metropolitan Police for night security, and so on. All this had to be done from scratch every 10 years, since the nineteenth-century Census Acts only sanctioned expenditure for the local collection of data, its central processing and the publication of reports. This operation only took three or four years, after which the census-taking apparatus was wound up. The Census Office did not become a permanent institution until the early twentieth century. The work also had to be done at great speed since the Census Acts were usually passed only some seven or eight months before the night of the census.[35] This process of negotiation with other departments and outside bodies over the information to be

---

[35] For the steps involved in setting up the local and central census-taking apparatus in 1891, see TNA, RG 29/9–16. It is a mistake to assume that there was a permanent Census Office, as is implied in M. Conk, 'Labor statistics in the American and English censuses: making some invidious comparisons', *Journal of Social History*, 16 (1982–3), pp. 83–102.

sought could be protracted and difficult. There was thus a constant tension between the GRO's desire to keep the household schedule as simple as possible, and the desire of bodies such as the Royal Statistical Society to ask questions which were of burning interest to them.

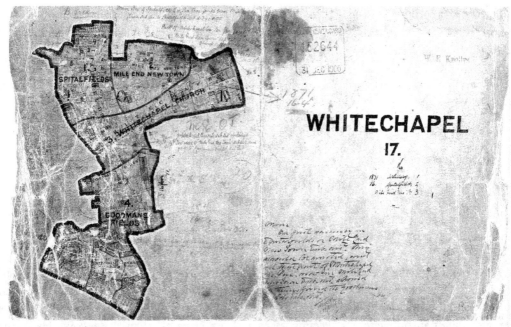

Figure 1.1 Registration district map of Whitechapel, 1891 (TNA, RG 18/215)

Nor should one imagine that the organisation of census-taking at the local level was an effortless process.[36] The local registrars had to advise the GRO on any changes to local administrative boundaries, which could be legion. They also had to forward to London a list of all institutions in their district, with the number of their inmates. If over a certain size, these were to be enumerated separately by the chief residing officer. The local registrars were also supposed to revise their plans of division. These documents, copies of which were held both locally and at the GRO, defined the enumeration districts into which each registration sub-district was divided for the purposes of census-taking. The 'plans', at least in the early years, were written descriptions of the districts rather than maps, which had been drawn up in 1841 on fairly rational principles. The registration districts were, at that period, meaningful administrative entities, being co-extensive with the new Poor Law unions of 1834. These were in turn sub-divided into districts for enumeration such that each should contain, in towns, no more than about 200 inhabited houses. The number depended, however, on the distance that the enumerators would have to travel; an enumeration district in the countryside contained fewer houses than in the town. Many registrars failed to change these plans from census to census and they became hopelessly out of date. The boundaries of numerous enumeration districts were not altered in line with local administrative

---

[36] Much of the following description of census-taking has been derived from the instruction books circulated to the registrars and enumerators prior to census day. See Appendix 7 for references to examples of these records.

changes, while shifts in the density of population caused ever wider variations in the numbers of households that they contained.[37] Some maps of districts survive at TNA in record series RG 18 (see Figure 1.1)

Once this basic groundwork had been laid, the local registrars selected an enumerator for each enumeration district. They could appoint anyone they liked, as long as they met the basic requirements:

> He must be a person of intelligence and activity; he must read and write well, and have some knowledge of arithmetic; he must not be infirm or of such weak health as may render him unable to undergo the requisite exertion; he should not be younger than 18 years of age or older than 65; he must be temperate, orderly and respectable, and be such a person as is likely to conduct himself with strict propriety, and to deserve the goodwill of the inhabitants of his district.

In Worcester in 1881, a 16-year-old farmer's son enumerated 1,924 people in a working-class part of the town but the mean age of enumerators appears to have been in the mid 40s.[38] From 1891 women could be enumerators, and Susan Lumas and her team of census indexers at TNA have spotted at least 34 in that year.[39]

In rural areas the enumerator might well have considerable local knowledge. In the case of Crosby Ravensworth in Westmorland in 1861, the enumerator was the local schoolmaster, John Sutherland, who had also officiated in 1841 and 1851. Sutherland's diary for the period shows him attending parish meetings, collecting tithes and church rates, filling out income tax forms and witnessing wills for neighbours, as well as collecting census returns. He also drew up his own private census of the parish in a printed book based on the form of the census returns. The latter had a column for remarks in which he noted in later years the subsequent marriages, deaths and migration of the people he had enumerated in the census. It is plain that Sutherland was thoroughly acquainted with the inhabitants of his parish but it is unlikely that such an intimate system of surveillance would have been so common in large cities.[40]

Enumerators were usually paid a fixed sum, and then so much for every 100 persons above 400 enumerated, plus so much for excess travelling. In 1871, for example, the enumerators were paid a fixed fee of one guinea; 2s 6d for every 100 persons in their district above the first 400 enumerated; 6d for every mile above the first five covered in delivering schedules; and 6d for every mile above

---

[37] A set of original plans of division for London districts in 1861 can be found in TNA, RG 9/4543. They contain the description of the enumeration districts, and the 'computed' numbers of houses and families therein. Presumably the computed were used to apportion the number and size of enumerators' books required.

[38] M. Drake and D. R. Mills, 'A note on census enumerators', *Local Population Studies Society Newsletter*, 29 (2001), pp. 3–9.

[39] S. Lumas, 'Women enumerators', *Local Population Studies Society Newsletter*, 14 (1994), pp. 3–5.

[40] Sutherland's diary and his 1861 census book are in the possession of his descendant, Mrs. Doris Jackson of Birk Nott, Heversham, Cumbria. Other returns, compiled by Sutherland in 1861 and 1871, can be found at the Cumbria Record Office, Kendal, among the Crosby Ravensworth parish records (Kendal, Cumbria Record Office, Crosby Ravensworth Parish Records, WPR/7/Misc). The author would like to thank Mr. Peter Park for drawing these records to his attention. See also B. Woolings, 'An Orsett census enumerator', *Local Population Studies*, 56 (1996), pp. 54–9.

the first five covered in collecting schedules. It was almost universally agreed that these rates of pay were insufficient in themselves to attract high-quality staff, or to encourage the greatest diligence.[41] The GRO pinned its hopes on attracting men of local standing who would undertake the work as a social duty. In the towns the registrars often appear to have depended on local government officers and schoolteachers, but in the countryside they probably fell back on a core of farmers and their kin.[42] The enumerators could employ an assistant out of their own pocket to deliver schedules and the like, although there is no direct evidence of how many did so.

Each enumerator was supplied by the registrar with a set of household schedules, an enumerator's book, and an instruction and memorandum book. In 1871, the latter contained columns for addresses, types of houses (private, public, shops, uninhabited, etc.), and the numbers of household schedules left and collected at each house, as well as a column for notes. There were also spaces for recording the numbers of people temporarily present or absent from the district. The enumerators used the book to order the houses, to mark down where houses were being built, or were uninhabited, and to keep a check on whether or not they had collected all the schedules distributed. These records do not appear to have been sent to the GRO, and consequently have not found their way into TNA.[43]

The enumerator left a household schedule with each householder. This gave instructions to the latter on how to enter the details required for each individual in the household on census night. This was usually in March or April in order to avoid the distortions in the data which would be caused by the seasonal movements of sections of the population during the summer. The information sought for each household, until 1901, was the address where its members lived, and for each person within it, name, marital status, relationship to the household head, age, sex, 'Rank, profession or occupation', parish and county of birth, and descriptions of medical disabilities.[44]

On the morning after census night the enumerator collected the schedules. If these were not completed properly he or she was supposed to ask for extra details on the doorstep, although there is considerable evidence that this was not done uniformly. If the householder was unable to fill in the schedule, perhaps because he or she was illiterate, the enumerator was to fill it in for them. The proportion of schedules that had to be filled out in this manner must have varied from district to district. In 1871, enumerators were asked to record the number of schedules that they filled in themselves on the page in their enumeration books given over to summary tables. In parts of Manchester the proportion so completed was 25 per cent; in Christ Church,

---

[41] E. Higgs, 'The struggle for the occupational census, 1841–1911', in *Government and Expertise: Specialists, Administrators and Professionals, 1860–1914*, ed. R. M. MacLeod (Cambridge, 1988), pp. 83–4. On occasion, the enumerators entered their own protests on the census returns, as in the case of the enumerator for All Hallows, Barking, London in 1851 (TNA, HO 107/1531, fo. 193).

[42] T. Arkell, 'Identity of census enumerators – Cornwall in 1851', *Local Population Studies*, 53 (1994), pp. 70–5; Drake and Mills, 'A note on census enumerators'.

[43] See Appendix 7 for references to examples of the memorandum books.

[44] See Appendix 7 for references to examples of the household schedules.

Spitalfields the proportion was 15 per cent; in Colyton in Devon it was 7 per cent; but in some Welsh-speaking parishes in Anglesey the majority were filled in by the enumerators.[45] Even within the same sub-district the proportion of returns completed by the enumerators could vary widely. In 1871, for example, in the six enumeration districts of Great Missenden in Buckinghamshire, the proportion of schedules filled out by the enumerators ranged from 5.3 to 64.7 per cent.[46] It is not possible to gauge the number of the schedules that had to be filled out for householders by their neighbours.

The enumerators then copied the household schedules into their enumerators' books, taking care to distinguish between houses and the differing households they contained.[47] In the process of doing so, some enumerators tended to standardise the information in the household schedules. They were also to fill in the tables at the front of the books giving the numbers of houses and persons on each page, and the numbers of persons temporarily present or absent. The books were supposed to be checked by the registrars and superintendent registrars before dispatch to the Census Office in London but this often appears not to have been done. The household schedules were sent to London at the same time.

In the Census Office the books were gone over again to sort out any problems or ambiguities in the data, reference no doubt being made to the household schedules. The clerks sometimes altered entries in the books and almost invariably corrected the enumerators' additions in the tables. Individual clerks then went through the books, abstracting particular headings of information for the published tables. One would deal with ages, another with birthplaces, and so on. In the process of doing so, they often ticked the items of information that they were dealing with to ensure that no entries were omitted. At the end of this process the household schedules appear to have been destroyed.[48]

Certain groups were enumerated separately for administrative convenience. As noted above, inmates of institutions of a certain size were recorded by the chief residing officer on special institutional schedules. Customs officers gave the masters of ships in port on census night, or who arrived in port within a stipulated period, a ship's schedule in which they were to record the members of the ship's crew and passengers. The Admiralty handled the dispatch of special enumeration books to every ship in the Royal Navy, while the War Office provided a headcount

---

[45] TNA, RG 10/505–11, Census Returns, Christ Church, Spitalfields; RG 10/2035–6, Census Returns, Colyton; RG 10/5742, Census Returns, Llanallgo and Llangwyllog, Anglesey. For Manchester, see P. Rushton, 'Anomalies as evidence in nineteenth-century censuses', *Local Historian*, 13 (1978–9), p. 483.

[46] M. Drake and D. R. Mills, 'The census enumerators: a Local Population Studies Society project', *Local Population Studies Society Newsletter*, 14 (1994), p. 2.

[47] There is at least one known case of an enumerator who sub-contracted this process to someone else, with the result that over a quarter of the houses in the district were omitted from the returns (S. Lumas, *Making Use of the Census* (London, 2002), p. 58).

[48] There appears to be no record of their subsequent retention, or of their transfer to TNA. They were certainly all destroyed by 1913. *Evidence and Index to the Second Report of the Royal Commission on Public Records, Vol. II, Pt. III* (PP 1914 XLVI [Cd.7456], Q 5570).

of soldiers serving abroad.[49] These officers or bodies sent the schedules or books that they collected directly to London, where they were amalgamated with the enumerators' books for the same locality for abstraction. In the case of shipping this could have bizarre effects on the published population tables for particular localities. The crew and passengers on a ship could be added to the population of a village simply because the ship was offshore on census night.[50]

It is important to recognise the comparatively short period of time which the GRO had to organise the taking of the census, and the relatively poor quality of some of the agents involved; illiterate householders, slap-dash enumerators and registrars who did not supervise the work properly. This explains, in part, why the GRO was so anxious to keep the census as simple as possible. Thus, the GRO fought bitterly, but unsuccessfully, to avoid having to ask for information on employment status that was sought by social scientists in 1891.[51] It also alerts one to the problematic nature of some of the data in the manuscript returns. The information in the enumerators' books was several stages removed from reality, and each stage could add its own accumulation of errors. Did householders and enumerators always understand what was asked of them? Did they have to make a guess as to the information to be supplied under certain headings? Did enumerators always understand what they were told by illiterate, and perhaps suspicious, householders? What errors or omissions were made by the enumerators in the process of copying the household schedules into their books? In general the work appears to have been done conscientiously but users must be aware of the failings of particular enumerators, local peculiarities and the problems associated with the interpretation of certain types of information.

The changing intellectual background to census-taking

An obvious question regarding this process, which is seldom asked, is to what purpose was this information to be put? The mid nineteenth century was certainly a period when the almost indiscriminate collection of statistics had become a mania, and the census can be seen as part of this movement to reveal the 'state of the nation'. The belief that certain laws of probability, which were discoverable by empirical research, underlay creation was a very powerful strand in the intellectual make-up of the period.[52] Thus, iron laws were said to underlie the workings of the free market economy that were seen as ensuring a fair distribution of resources. Opposition to the existing economic system must, it was believed, reflect ignorance or unreason. The collection of occupational data could serve, therefore, to reveal the true structure of the

[49] See Appendix 7 for references to examples of the institutional books, merchant ships' schedules, and Royal Navy ships' schedules.

[50] V. C. Burton, 'A floating population: vessel enumeration returns in censuses, 1851–1921', *Local Population Studies*, 38 (1987), pp. 36–43.

[51] K. Schürer, 'The 1891 census and local population studies', *Local Population Studies*, 47 (1991), pp. 24–6.

[52] For the development of statistics and of the theory of probability in this period, see I. Hacking, *The Emergence of Probability* (Cambridge, 1975); T. M. Porter, *The Rise of Statistical Thinking 1820–1900* (Princeton, N.J., 1986); I. Hacking, *The Taming of Chance* (Cambridge, 1990).

economy and so dispel radical discontent, which would lead in turn to the creation of sober citizens.[53]

The census also helped in the creation of this new citizenship. When combined with civil registration information on deaths, census data could be used to create statistics for deaths per 1,000, thus revealing unhealthy places and occupations which rational men and women could avoid. Such mortality rates were also used to inform local debates on public health in the new sanitary districts established under the 1848 Public Health Act. Life-tables compiled from this data were again intended to allow workers to insure their lives against ill health or death. Population totals for electoral divisions allowed the revision of electoral boundaries to ensure more equal representation. In this way census-taking was an extension of the project that had underlain the establishment of the GRO in the first place – the creation of liberal citizenship through the underpinning of property rights via the registration of births, marriages and deaths, and thus lines of descent. The motives for census-taking were thus far broader than the desire to foster 'biopower' for military purposes.[54]

However, it is also useful to see the mid-nineteenth-century censuses in terms of medical research. Given the sort of information gathered this might seem a surprising suggestion, but it is so only if one looks back at early Victorian medicine from the perspective of the present century. The central figure in the scientific elaboration of the mid-nineteenth-century censuses was William Farr, the GRO's redoubtable superintendent of statistics from 1838 until his retirement in 1880. Farr was a commissioner for the censuses of 1851, 1861 and 1871, and was said to have written the *Census Reports* of those years. He was certainly the main intellectual force within the Office. Farr came from a medical background and his most important work involved using the data obtained from the civil registration of deaths to plot the incidence and developmental laws of epidemic diseases. Farr was probably the greatest medical statistician of the century, and was president of the Royal Statistical Society in 1871 and 1872. His work was of great importance for the public health and sanitation movements of the period.[55] However, it should be noted that Farr was not the head of the GRO, and he was supremely fortunate in having a superior of great administrative skill in Major George Graham, who as registrar-general supported and contributed to his work.[56]

Farr's model for the nature and spread of disease was based initially on chemistry – the biological germ theory did not gain general acceptance in this country until the 1870s or later. He saw disease as being caused by the intake of various chemicals into the blood, initiating a process of chemical change that poisoned the system. Such chemicals could enter the body as dust particles, noxious fumes, suspended in water, and so on. But in common with other sanitarians

---

[53] For the background to the statistical movement of this period in Britain, see Cullen, *The Statistical Movement in Early Victorian Britain*.

[54] Higgs, *The Information State in England*, pp. 64–98.

[55] For an introduction to Farr's life and work, see J. M. Eyler, *Victorian Social Medicine: the Ideas and Methods of William Farr* (London, 1979).

[56] For Graham's role, see Higgs, *Life, Death and Statistics*, pp. 67–77.

of the age, he saw the primary source of such chemicals as being the concentration of human effluent in large cities, the result of the rapid urbanisation of the population. The more people in a given area, the higher, Farr reasoned, would be the level of mortality. This theory was one of the intellectual underpinnings of the movement to revolutionise the sanitary arrangements of the great cities.[57]

This was an additional reason why the GRO not only wanted to know the overall size of the population from the census but also the number of people in particular areas: hence the importance of knowing the population of defined administrative units, health being seen as in an inverse relationship to population density. This would also explain the interest shown in the census-taking process in the structure of households, age and marital status, which were seen as determinants of population growth, and in migration, the mechanism by which population was concentrated in the cities. Even the questions relating to occupations can be seen in this light. The census schedules made a specific point of asking householders not only to supply the occupations of the members of their households but also the materials upon which they worked. Farr appears to have believed that the material worked upon affected the character and life expectancy of workers, and he sought to use the data collected to construct occupational life-tables. These, in turn, were to be used to underpin the activities of working-class friendly societies. The medical paradigm certainly did not exhaust the reasons for taking the census but it explains many of the features of the process.[58]

In this light, it is interesting to examine the treatment of the data collected in the last column of the household schedule, that relating to medical disabilities. This column is usually ignored by historians but was plainly of great importance to the GRO. In the *1861 Census Report*, the largest section of the commentary, nearly a third of the whole report, was given over to an analysis of the contents of this column, despite the universal recognition that the information gathered on the blind and the deaf and dumb was highly unreliable and incomplete.[59] The only examples of follow-up surveys in the history of the nineteenth-century censuses relate to this material. Thus in 1861 the GRO found time to check the results of the returns of the blind and deaf and dumb by asking more detailed questions of those so afflicted in Herefordshire.[60] Between 1851 and 1891 the only major innovation introduced into the census schedule was the addition to this column of questions relating to the imbecility, idiocy or lunacy of household members; an enquiry that was hardly likely to produce very accurate data.

In the later nineteenth century the intellectual climate changed, and with it the type of material collected. Farr retired in 1880 and none of his nineteenth-century successors achieved his standing in the statistical community. With the gradual triumph of the germ theory of disease,

[57] Eyler, *Victorian Social Medicine*, pp. 97–108.

[58] E. Higgs, 'Disease, febrile poisons, and statistics: the census as a medical survey, 1841–1911', *Social History of Medicine*, 4 (1991), pp. 465–78.

[59] See, for example, *1861 Census Report* (PP 1863 LIII Pt. 1 [3221.], pp. 47–56).

[60] *1861 Census Report*, pp. 48–50. No returns from the survey appear to have survived. A similar exercise was carried out in 1881 (*1881 Census Report* (PP 1883 LXXX [c.3797.], pp. 68–9)).

improvements in sanitation, and the decline in the death rate and the rate of population growth, Farr's demographic and chemical paradigm for illness ceased to have the same relevance. In the late nineteenth century the rise of foreign economic competition during the Victorian Great Depression, eugenicist concern over the differential reproduction of the various classes in society, and a perceived heightening of class tensions stimulated greater interest in the economic and social structure of the nation. This applied not only to economists and sociologists, such as Charles Booth, but to government departments such as the Board of Trade and the Home Office,[61] and led to the demands for the broadening of the census questions that were voiced before the 1890 Treasury Committee on the Census.[62] These new preoccupations can be seen in a survey undertaken by the GRO in 1887 in which 'enumerators' obtained information on working-class conditions in selected districts of London. Men were asked their name and address, county of birth, marital condition, age, how long they and their family had been resident at their present home, the number of rooms occupied and weekly rent, time since last employment, cause of non-employment, means of subsistence when unemployed, and family contributions to income.[63]

In the 1891 census a question on whether a person was an employer, an employee or self-employed was introduced on the recommendation of the 1890 Treasury Committee. In the same year the number of rooms occupied by a household was to be given if the number was less than five. This was plainly linked to efforts to measure levels of overcrowding for the purposes of housing improvement, but could also be seen as a medical matter, since overcrowding and insanitary conditions were regarded as inextricably linked. A decade later the Home Office had a question added relating to whether or not a person was working at home, in order to allow an analysis of 'sweating' in various trades. Additional information was sought on the incidence of Welsh-speaking in Wales from 1891 onwards and of Manx on the Isle of Man from 1901.[64] Over the same period changes were made to the manner in which occupations were classified and abstracted in the published *Census Reports*.[65]

This examination of the history of the nineteenth-century censuses raises questions about the reliability of the information in the returns, and the comparability of the data between censuses. As the census-taking machinery was elaborated, and as the reasons for collecting the data changed, so did the instructions to householders and enumerators. An understanding of these changes is crucial to those wishing to use the censuses to compare the nation or specific communities over time. Parts II and III contain a more detailed discussion of these matters.

---

[61] Higgs, 'The struggle for the occupational census', pp. 78–82.

[62] *Report of the 1890 Treasury Committee on the Census* (PP 1890 LVIII [c.6071.]).

[63] *Conditions of the Working Classes. Tabulation of the Statement Made by Men Living in Certain Selected Districts of London in March 1887* (PP 1887 LXXI [c.5228]).

[64] Higgs, 'The struggle for the occupational census', p. 83. For other proposals for the 1901 census, see M. Woollard, 'The 1901 census: an introduction', *Local Population Studies*, 67 (2001), pp. 26–8.

[65] See ch. 13 for a discussion of occupational classification in the published *Census Reports*.

The archival history of the census returns

Just as the history of census-taking is not always what one might expect, so the subsequent physical history of the returns themselves is somewhat chequered.

As noted above, two types of record were created in the process of taking the first four censuses. First, there were the official returns on printed forms sent to John Rickman in London. These merely gave the number of people in the parish, the number of individuals or families in certain broad economic categories, the number of vital events in parish registers, and so on. The second type of records produced were the more detailed enumerations made by the local overseers of the poor in preparation for filling out their official returns. The latter were never intended to be sent to Rickman, and found their way into the local Poor Law records or the parish chest, and thence into local record offices and libraries.

Exactly what happened to the official returns after Rickman had finished with them is not certain. There is some evidence that Rickman retained them in his own possession.[66] By 1846, however, they were reported to have been deposited in the Tower. Suggestions that they should be transferred to the vaults of the House of Commons followed, but by 1862 they were in the new repository of the Public Record Office (PRO) at Chancery Lane.[67] Little attention appears to have been given to them so long as pressure on space at Chancery Lane was not serious. Towards the end of the century, however, the increasing accessions of modern departmental records began to make themselves felt there and it became necessary to review the material that had flooded into the PRO directly after its creation, much of which had been accepted without any attempt at proper archival selection.

In 1904 the then PRO's inspecting officers, led by Sir Henry Maxwell Lyte, and a Home Office representative reviewed the census returns for 1801–31. They recommended that these should be destroyed, since most of their contents had been reproduced verbatim in the published census reports.[68] The only real losses were probably the parish-level data on baptisms, burials and marriages, and the numbers of males aged 20 years and over in 100 named retail and handicraft occupations which were returned on 'Formula 2' of the official schedules for each parish in 1831. In the published report the registration data was only given in an aggregated form for hundreds, and that returned on Formula 2 for counties. On the other hand, given the uncertain archival history of the early census records before they came into the PRO, one cannot be certain that this material was even extant in 1904. The only centrally held records from the early censuses that were not destroyed were the clergymen's returns of 1831. These now form record series HO 71 at The National Archives in London (the successor to the PRO).[69]

[66] TNA, T 1/4753, Schedule of papers in the custody of the ex[ecut]ors of the late John Rickman.

[67] *Seventh Report of the Deputy Keeper of the Public Records* (London, 1846), p. 4; *Thirteenth Report of the Deputy Keeper of the Public Records* (London, 1852), pp. 2–3; *Twenty-fourth Report of the Deputy Keeper of the Public Records* (London, 1963), p. iv.

[68] TNA, PRO 17/1, Home Office destruction schedule, 31 May 1904.

[69] TNA, HO 71, 1831 Census, Clergymen's Returns.

It is quite erroneous to suggest, as some historians have done, that in 1904 the PRO destroyed nominal records similar to those of the post-1831 censuses, or even the household schedules of these later enumerations.[70] The former were never held centrally, and the latter were probably destroyed by the Census Office after they had been used to check the enumerators' books. Nor did the pre-1841 returns survive until 1931, as still others have claimed.[71]

Much of the archival history of the post-1831 returns is also extremely obscure. As early as 1845 the registrar-general was negotiating for the transfer of the 1841 returns to the PRO. These discussions proved abortive because the GRO would not undertake to box and list the documents. Similar negotiations were undertaken in 1852 with respect to the returns of 1841 and 1851. These appear to have related only to the enumerators' books and there is no direct evidence of any intention to transfer the household schedules, which had probably already been destroyed. Eventually, in 1854, the enumerators' books for the 1851 census were deposited in the PRO.[72] In 1859 the registrar-general and the PRO entered into an extremely obscure correspondence on the subject of the storage of census records. The registrar-general began by offering the PRO a further instalment of census returns (these may have been the returns of 1841). By the end of the year he was asking for the 1851 returns to be sent back to the GRO for consultation, in preparation for abstracting the data from the 1861 enumerators' books. By 1862 the PRO appears to have had the returns of 1801–41 in its safekeeping.[73]

The question of the PRO's receiving custody of the enumerators' books did not arise again until 1903. In that year the GRO offered the PRO the 1871 and 1881 returns in order to make room for the 1901 books. The PRO refused to take them unless the GRO also transferred the earlier enumerators' returns. In the following year the 1841 and 1861 returns were found in the roof of the Houses of Parliament in the custody of the Office of Works. The 1851 books could not be found and were presumed lost. At what point the 1841 returns had been removed from the safekeeping of the PRO is difficult to tell. The PRO again refused to take the later returns unless it received the earlier records as well and put the onus on the Office of Works to find storage space for them. By 1912 the 1851 enumerators' returns had been found and were transferred, along with the 1841 books, to the PRO. The 1841 returns were said to be 'somewhat disarranged'.[74] The later books were kept by the GRO for the purpose of

---

[70] R. Lawton, 'Introduction', in *The Census and Social Structure: an Interpretative Guide to Nineteenth Century Censuses for England and Wales*, ed. R. Lawton (London, 1978), p. 16.

[71] M. Drake, 'The census, 1801–1891', in *Nineteenth-Century Society: Essays in the Use of Quantitative Methods for the Study of Social Data*, ed. E. A. Wrigley (Cambridge, 1972), p. 31.

[72] *Seventh Report of the Deputy Keeper*, p. 4; *Eighth Report of the Deputy Keeper of the Public Records* (London, 1847), p. 2; *Fifteenth Report of the Deputy Keeper of the Public Records* (London, 1854), p. 19.

[73] TNA, PRO 1/23, George Graham to Sir F. Palgrave, 7 Feb. 1859; PRO 1/23, George Graham to Sir Francis Palgrave, 16 March 1857 (attached to correspondence of 7 Feb. 1859); PRO 1/23, George Graham to Sir Francis Palgrave, 20 July 1859; PRO 1/23, George Graham to Sir Francis Palgrave, 15 Dec. 1859; *Twenty-fourth Report of the Deputy Keeper*, p. iv.

[74] TNA, PRO 1/68, A. Mundy to PRO, 14 March 1903; PRO 1/68, S. R. Scargill-Bird to the registrar-general, 17 March 1903; PRO 1/69, A. Mundy to the deputy keeper of the public records, 19 Jan. 1904; PRO 1/69, S. R. Scargill-Bird to the registrar-general, 15 Apr. 1904; PRO 1/77, W. I. Jerred to the Treasury, 7 March 1912; PRO 1/77, R. A. Roberts to H. J. Comyns, 13 May 1912.

ascertaining the ages of claimants to old age pensions. It was not until 1962 that the 1861 returns came into the PRO. The rest of the nineteenth-century enumerators' books, however, had all been deposited with the PRO by 1974.[75]

Plainly the nineteenth-century census returns have not always been stored and administered in optimum archival conditions. It should not be surprising to discover that some of the earlier returns have been damaged, and even portions lost.

[75] *Fourth Annual Report of the Keeper of the Public Records* (London, 1963), p. 15; *Eighth Annual Report of the Keeper of the Public Records* (London, 1967), p. 19; *Eleventh Annual Report of the Keeper of the Public Records* (London, 1970), p. 19; *Thirteenth Annual Report of the Keeper of the Public Records* (London, 1972), p. 21; *Sixteenth Annual Report of the Keeper of the Public Records* (London, 1975), p. 16.

2 The structure of the enumerators' books

The aim of this chapter is to give a detailed physical description of the pre-1841 census returns, and the enumerators' books from 1841 onwards.[1] Much of the substance of the chapter can be found in the appendices at the end of the book. Such information is of importance from an archival point of view, and helps to put the information in the books into context. The chapter is best used, therefore, for reference purposes, as and when required. For the vast majority of those who wish to use the returns, however, this information will be of comparatively limited use and they would be advised to proceed to the following chapters.

The census returns of 1801–31

The official returns[2]

In 1801 two printed forms were sent by John Rickman to every parish in England and Wales. The first was the 'Form of Answers by the Overseers'. This was divided into nine boxes or sections. The first four were for the insertion of the name of the relevant county, hundred, city and town, and parish. The fifth related to houses in the parish, and was broken down into spaces for the number of inhabited houses, the number of families inhabiting them and the number of uninhabited houses. The next box was divided into two, for the number of males and females in the parish, and the seventh was for the total number of persons. The penultimate box was divided into three for the totals of persons chiefly employed in the three occupational categories outlined in Chapter 1 (i.e., agriculture; trade, manufactures or handicraft; and the number not occupied in the preceding classes). The last box was for the sum of the three occupational groups, supposed to be equal to the population of the parish shown in box number seven, although it is not clear how young children, or the very elderly, without jobs were to be treated.

The second form was the 'Form of Answers by the Clergyman', divided into columns for the insertion of data from the parish registers on the annual number of baptisms, burials and marriages. The columns for baptisms and burials had years in the margins starting in 1700, proceeding by decades until 1780, and then individual years up to 1800. The marriage column was marked off in individual years, starting in 1754 and going through to 1800. Both forms contained spaces for comments to be made on the information in the returns, and for attestations of its accuracy.

---

[1] See Appendix 7 for references to examples of the enumerators' books.

[2] Exemplars of most of the forms described here can be found attached to the schedules of the various pre-1841 Census Acts (see Appendix 1). Examples of some of the schedules can be found in Appendix 3.

The 1811 forms were somewhat similar, with the difference that the overseer's return was divided into boxes in which he was to supply, from left to right: the name and description of the parish; the number of inhabited houses; the number of families inhabiting them; the number of houses being built; the number otherwise uninhabited; the numbers of families (rather than persons) chiefly employed in the three economic categories; and, finally, the numbers of males, females and all persons. The overseer was asked to comment on the possible reasons for any change since the last census in the number of persons in the parish. Both overseers' and clergymen's returns were only marked off into the 10 years of the decade 1801–10.

The 1821 returns were almost identical to those of the previous census but an additional form was sent, on which the overseer was to give an account of the ages of the people in his parish. This was in two halves, for males and females, with each half divided into 13 columns headed under five, 5–10, 10–15, 15–20, 20–30, and then in units of 10, up to 100 and upwards. At the bottom of each column was a space for column totals.

In 1831 much more complicated questions were asked, and more complicated and numerous forms distributed. The form for the overseers was divided into a series of boxes, sub-divided in the following manner:

Main Heading	Sub-heading
1) Parish	
2) Number of inhabited houses	
3) Number of families occupying them	
4) Families chiefly employed:	1. in agriculture 2. in trade, manufactures and handicraft 3. in other than 1. and 2.
5) Number of persons	1. Males 2. Females 3. Total
6) Number of males 20 years and more	
7) Number of males employed in agriculture	1. Occupiers of land employing labourers 2. Occupiers of land not employing labourers 3. Agricultural labourers
8) Number of males in manufacturing or making manufacturing machinery	
9) Number of males in retailing or handicrafts	
10) Number of wholesale merchants, capitalists, bankers, professional persons and 'other educated men'	
11) Number of labourers employed by the preceding three classes	
12) Number of all other males 20 years old	

The form then provided spaces for the overseers to insert the following pieces of information:

1) the number of male servants under 20 years and 20 and over, and the number of female servants;
2) the occupations in which those in 8, above, were employed, and the proportion in 11) above employed in quarrying, mining, fisheries or public works;
3) reasons for the differences between 1831 and 1821;
4) general remarks.

The overseers were also supplied with 'Formula 2' on which were printed 100 of the most common occupations in the retail trades and handicrafts. The enumerator was supposed to add the numbers in his parish in each occupation to this form and use this to calculate the total number in the whole economic group. The list was to be appended to the rest of the schedule.

The clergy were given a form for the number of baptisms, burials and marriages in their parish that was similar to that of 1821. They were also supplied with a complicated table of 18 pages (one each for the years 1813–30) on which they were to indicate the ages of all those persons who appeared in their burial registers. Each page was divided into four columns that were further divided into columns for males and females. The columns had ages in years down one side and these were ruled across to create rows. The clergyman was to make slashes in the boxes formed to indicate the numbers of males or females of that age who were recorded as dying in the relevant year. Under the age of six years there was more than one row for each year. This was due to the higher rates of infant mortality expected. Space was also allowed for information on the 'Defective Registry of Ages', and the numbers in the burial grounds of 'Dissenters, Jews and others'. There was an additional form on which the clergy were asked to supply information about the numbers of illegitimate males and females born in 1830, the annual number of unregistered births, marriages and deaths, and general remarks.

The returns made by the clergymen in 1831 survive in TNA as record series HO 71.[3] The returns for each parish were sent to London under separate cover. The data they contained was aggregated by hundreds, and the results published for each county. The records themselves are collected into bundles by hundred and boxed by county.

The local listings[4]

As has already been mentioned, the Census Acts empowered the overseers of the poor and the clergy to ask all the questions necessary to make their returns. Some overseers took advantage of this clause to record information on named individuals and families that they then used to fill in the official returns (see Figure 2.1 for an example of a pre-1841 census listing). Some of these manuscript listings were considerable administrative achievements. That for Liverpool in 1801,

---

[3] 1831 Census, Clergymen's Returns (TNA, HO 71).

[4] Unless otherwise stated, the examples of local listings below are drawn from copies held in the archives of the Cambridge Group for the History of Population and Social Structure.

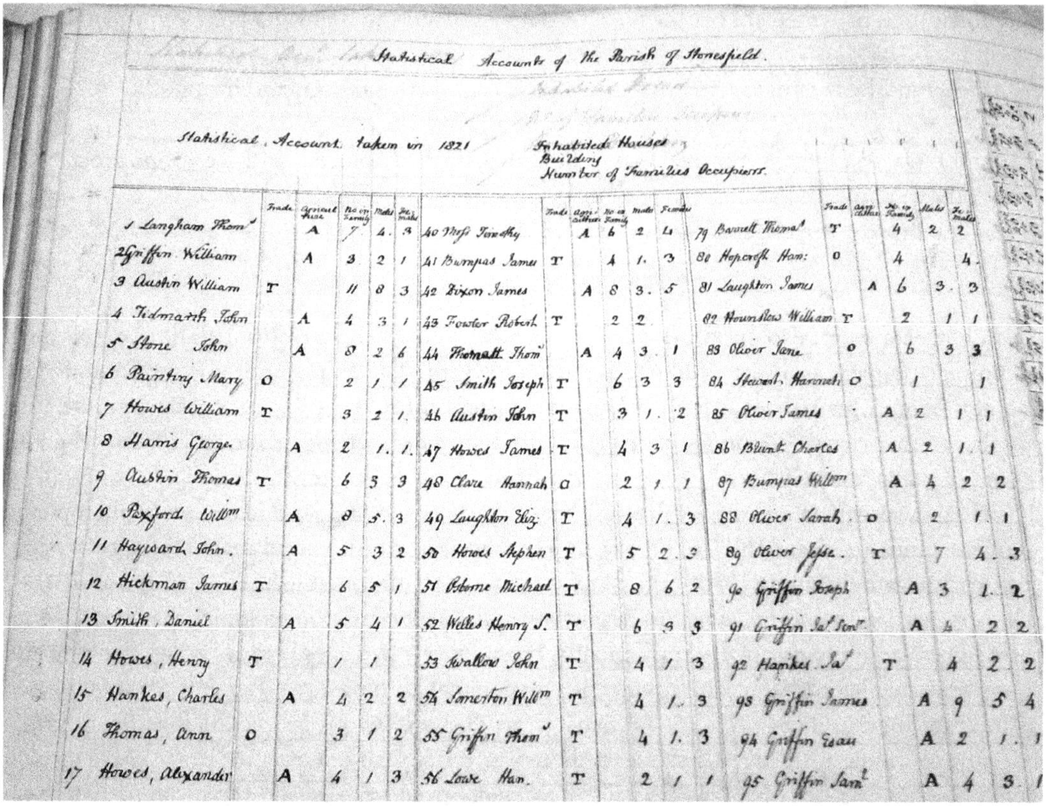

Statistical Accounts of the Parish of Stonesfield.

Statistical Account taken in 1821 — Inhabited Houses / Building / Number of Families Occupiers.

	Trade	Agriculture	No. in Family	Males	Females		Trade	Agriculture	No. in Family	Males	Females		Trade	Agriculture	No. in Family	Males	Females
1 Langham Thom^s		A	7	4.	3	40 Moss Timothy		A	6	2	4	79 Barrett Thomas	T		4	2	2
2 Griffin William		A	3	2	1	41 Bumpas James	T		4	1.	3	80 Hopcroft Han:	O		4		4.
3 Austin William	T		11	8	3	42 Dixon James		A	8	3.	5	81 Laughton James		A	6	3.	3
4 Tidmarsh John		A	4	3	1	43 Fowler Robert	T		2	2		82 Hounslow William	T		2	1	1
5 Stone John		A	8	2	6	44 Thornett Thom^s		A	4	3.	1	83 Oliver Jane	O		6	3	3
6 Painting Mary	O		2	1	1	45 Smith Joseph	T		6	3	3	84 Stewart, Hannah	O		1		1
7 Howes William	T		3	2	1.	46 Austin John	T		3	1.	2	85 Oliver James		A	2	1	1
8 Harris George		A	2	1.	1.	47 Howes James	T		4	3	1	86 Blunt Charles		A	2	1.	1
9 Austin Thomas	T		6	3	3	48 Clare Hannah	O		2	1	1	87 Bumpas Willm		A	4	2	2
10 Paxford Willm		A	8	5.	3	49 Laughton Eliz:	T		4	1.	3	88 Oliver Sarah	O		2	1.	1
11 Hayward John.		A	5	3	2	50 Howes Stephen	T		5	2.	3	89 Oliver Jesse.	T		7	4.	3
12 Hickman James	T		6	5	1	51 Osborne Michael	T		8	6	2	90 Griffin Joseph		A	3	1.	2
13 Smith, Daniel		A	5	4	1	52 Welles Henry S.	T		6	3	3	91 Griffin Ja^s Senr		A	4	2	2
14 Howes, Henry	T		1	1		53 Swallow John	T		4	1	3	92 Hankes Ja^s	T		4	2	2
15 Hankes, Charles		A	4	2	2	54 Somerton Willm	T		4	1.	3	93 Griffin James		A	9	5	4
16 Thomas, Ann	O		3	1	2	55 Griffin Thom^s	T		4	1.	3	94 Griffin Esau		A	2	1.	1
17 Howes, Alexander		A	4	1	3	56 Lowe Han.	T		2	1	1	95 Griffin Saml		A	4	3.	1

Figure 2.1 Statistical account of the parish of Stonesfield, Oxfordshire, 1821
(Oxfordshire Record Office, MSS. DD Par. Stonesfield 69)

for example, covers over 14,000 dwellings. Others must have been used locally for a considerable period of time. One example from Braintree in Essex appears to be the basis for the local 1821 census return but at the end it has a summary covering the period 1801–41.

The form of these local listings was usually based upon the official returns, especially in the case of the 1821 enumeration of ages, with the addition of the names of families or individuals. Information totally unconnected with the census, however, was sometimes collected. This included notes on bastardy cases in Smalley, Derbyshire, in 1801; whether people were baptised in Horton and Woodlands, Dorset, in 1821; the religious persuasion of parishioners in the Dorset parishes of Marnhull and Shaftesbury St James in the same year; and the types of houses in which families lived in Liverpool in 1801. In the 1821 listing for Hendon, the rent and numbers of both windows and dogs were recorded for each household.[5]

Plainly this sort of information, as well as the nominal data collected for compiling the official returns, would have been of use for local Poor Law and ecclesiastical purposes. This may explain

[5] Personal communication of Matthew Woollard, University of Essex, respecting Hendon. For information on the content of other returns, see Wall, Woollard and Moring, *Census Schedules and Listings, 1801–1831*.

why the local listings were preserved by the overseers of the poor and the clergy who produced them. Sometimes the link between census-taking and local administration can be seen from the documents themselves. In the case of Starston, Norfolk, a nominal listing for the 1801 census is attached to a document in the same hand giving the names of women and weekly allowances out of the poor rates. The last page of the listing for Horton in Dorset in 1821 not only gives the population total but also the number of male labourers, the level of money wages, the average poor rate per acre and the level of allowances for the aged and infirm. The 1801 nominal listing from Exton, Hampshire, appears at the end of a register of baptisms and burials compiled by the local rector, and indicates the earliest date at which family names appear in the register. The inclusion in the official returns of information relating to the Poor Law was suggested to the home secretary on more than one occasion.[6] The collection of information on windows and dogs in Hendon, both the objects of assessed taxes, points to the use of such documents in the assessment and collection of these imposts.

The intimate connection between early census-taking, Poor Law administration, taxation and the Established Church, may well have had some adverse effect on the willingness of certain sections of the population to co-operate in the decennial enumeration. This may explain why, later in the century, the GRO was so anxious to maintain the confidentiality of the information supplied, a tradition that has endured to the present day.

In some areas the process of local collection was expedited by the use of standard printed forms. An 1801 example from Midgley, Yorkshire, was printed at 'Jacobs Office, Halifax', and was based upon the official return with the addition of extra space for names. The three occupational groups in the official returns (those working in agriculture; in trade, manufactures and retailing; and in other work) were replaced, however, by farmers, traders and 'gentry'. Similar forms survive from Midgley in 1811, and for the Yorkshire parishes of Elland-cum-Greetland and Hipperholme-cum-Brighouse in 1801 and 1811. In Essex, printed forms based on the official returns, for dispatch to the magistrates of the division, have survived for Ardleigh and Horndon on the Hill in 1811 and 1821. These were printed in Chelmsford and bear the standard heading, 'The Population of the Parish of _____ in the County of Essex'.

As one might expect the most advanced examples of privately printed forms can be found in London. Some parishes in the City of London appear to have been using printed household schedules and enumeration books from 1801 onwards. St Nicholas Acons certainly had household schedules produced by the same printer for each of the first four censuses. There appears to have been no single London-wide format, however, although all show similarities to the aggregate returns that had to be sent to Rickman. Since the various forms were produced by different printers in the differing parishes they were almost certainly composed locally without any overall co-ordination. We cannot be sure, however, that every parish in the City used both printed household schedules and enumeration books for the

---

[6] TNA, HO 44/8, Item 119a, 19 July 1821, W. Henderson to Viscount Sidmouth; HO 44/20, Items 509–10, 29 July 1830, John Rickman to Thomas Venables.

whole period.[7] By 1831 printed household schedules were being used in Hammersmith in conjunction with a printed enumerator's book. Such forms may possibly have been the forerunners of the official household schedules and enumerators' books of 1841.

The census returns of 1841–1901

The overall structure of the records
The enumerators' books from 1841 onwards followed a set pattern, although their sizes varied according to the number of pages allowed for the insertion of information relating to houses, households and individuals. The overall structure of the books is summarised in Appendix 2.

The pagination of the enumerators' books
Although the enumerators' books were of a standard format for each census, they could contain differing numbers of pages for nominal information. Local registrars could presumably order different books to suit the size of the enumeration districts in the area under their control.

In 1841 there were four different-sized books:

> Book A of 20 nominal pages for less than 50 inhabited houses;
> Book B of 40 pages for 50–99 inhabited houses;
> Book C of 60 pages for 100–49 inhabited houses;
> Book D of 80 pages for 150 plus inhabited houses.

Each page contained 25 lines for entries. The 1851 books had a completely different format. The smallest books appear to have contained only 16 pages for nominal information, with only 20 lines to the page. There were at least six possible sizes of book, containing 16, 24, 36, 48, 60 and 72 pages. In 1861 the number of lines per page reverted to 25. The most commonly used books now contained 34 or 66 pages, but books containing 88 and 100 pages can also be found. In 1871 and 1881 the page of 25 lines was retained but a new range of books was printed, with the pagination increasing in multiples of eight. The smallest book contained 16 pages for nominal data, the next 24, and so on up to at least 80 pages. The 1891 and 1901 returns had a similar pagination but contained 31 lines per page.

The increasing number of different enumerators' books available over time, and the increasing number of lines per page, might reflect the increasingly wide differences between the populations of enumeration districts. As was noted in Chapter 1, many local registrars failed to revise the boundaries of enumeration districts to take account of changes in population densities. In very general terms, the more urban the area the larger the population of the

[7] London, Guildhall Library, Census Returns, MS. 3260/1–3, St Sepulchre; MS. 4306, St Nicholas Acon; MS. 6852, St Helen; MS. 7627, St Stephen and St Benet Sherehog; MS. 7697, St Catherine Cree; MS. 7753, St Anne's Blackfriars; MS. 8935, St Benet, Pauls's Wharf; MS. 10784, All Hallows Lombard Street.

enumeration district, and the larger the book used. In rural areas, with a greater distance between houses, the population of enumeration districts was, on average, smaller. It must be noted, however, that there is no consistent or infallible relationship between the size of an enumeration district and the size of the book used. Many enumerators did not fill their enumerators' books and the empty pages were removed. In some cases the returns were too large for the first book used, and pages from a second, or indeed a whole new book, were tacked on to the end.

Preliminary tables

The enumerators' books contained tables in which the enumerators were expected to summarise the contents of their books, or to provide information to place their returns in context. These always included a table giving the number of persons, houses and (from 1851 onwards) households recorded on each page, which information would be used by the Census Office to produce preliminary calculations of the size of the population. These calculations were published as interim reports while the main task of digesting the census data was undertaken. The enumerators do not appear to have filled in these tables very accurately since their totals frequently had to be corrected.

The other tables usually provided information on why people were not at home, or were temporarily present. The tables for 1841, however, appear to have represented a more concerted effort to ask subsidiary questions, along the lines of earlier enumerations. This partly reflected the absence of special arrangements to deal with certain groups of people which were introduced thereafter. After 1881 these tables were replaced by others showing the number of persons, houses and households in the differing administrative areas within the enumeration district. Over time the tables became less of a supplement to the contents of the books, and more of a summary. (See Appendix 6 for information sought in the various tables.)

The structure of the nominal pages

The pages for nominal information, which made up the bulk of the enumerators' books, were of a standard format divided into columns for the relevant information. The headings of the columns showed the type of information to be supplied in each. The page was then divided horizontally by lines, each line being for the information on a particular individual. At the bottom of the page were boxes for the total number of houses, males and females in the relevant columns. The books contained a set of instructions and an example of how to fill in the information required. (Examples of these pages, with a summary of the column headings, can be found in Appendix 3.) The instructions for filling in the information are discussed in detail in succeeding chapters.

The Welsh returns and special arrangements for Jewish immigrants

Special arrangements had to be made for those parts of Wales and Monmouthshire in which English was not understood. A Welsh translation of the household schedule was available from 1841 onwards. The enumerators' books, however, were always to be filled out in English. From 1871 onwards the enumerators were asked to distinguish each case where a Welsh schedule had

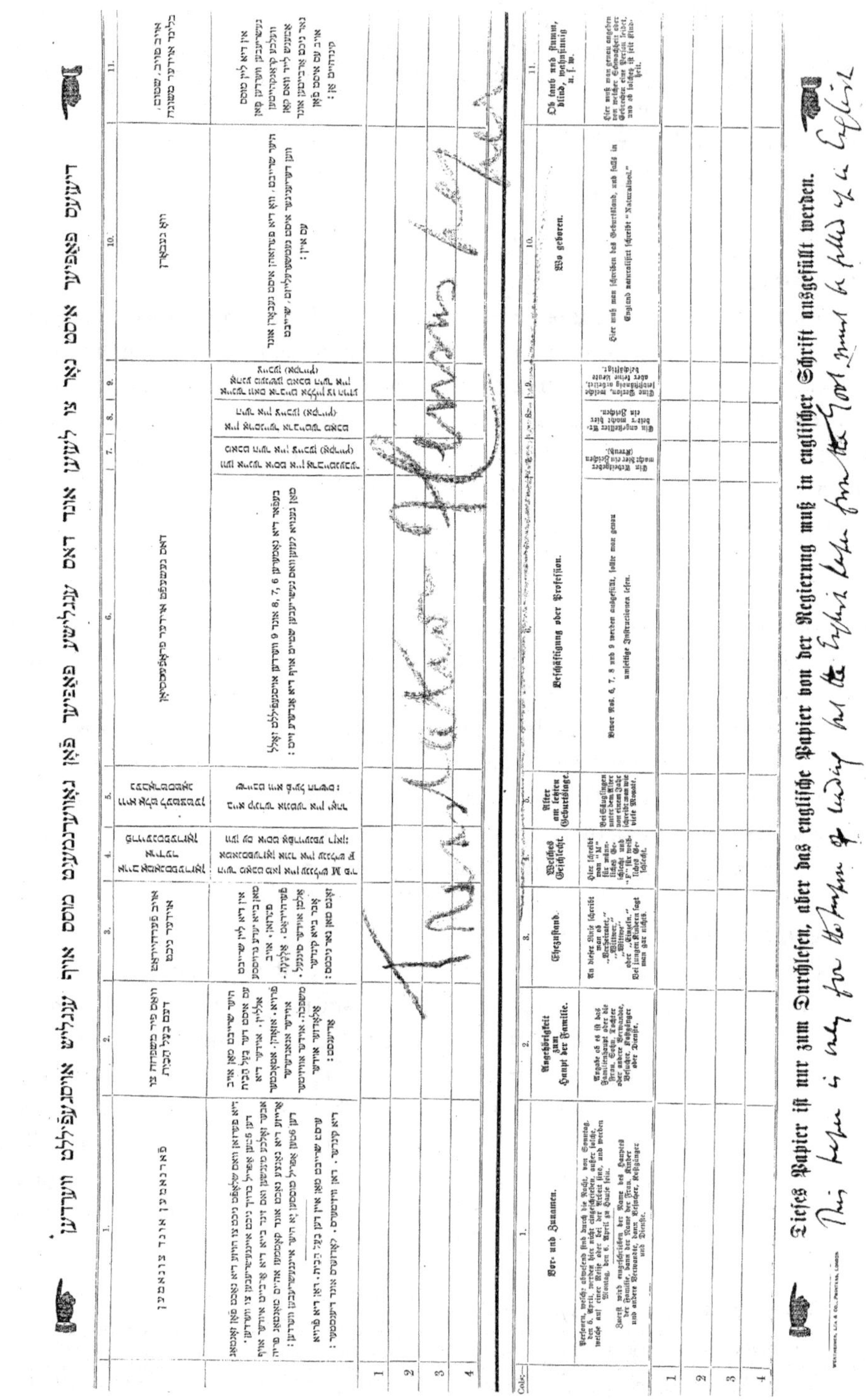

Figure 2.2 A mock-up of the household schedule in Yiddish and German.

been used by writing 'W' in the first column of the book, immediately under the number of the schedule.

From 1841 to 1881 the normal enumerators' books were used in Wales and Monmouthshire. In 1891, however, a special question on Welsh-speaking was introduced which applied solely to this area. There were now two special household schedules for Wales and Monmouth, in English and Welsh, which contained an extra column for 'Language spoken'. People were to write 'English' if they only spoke English, 'Welsh' if they only spoke Welsh, and 'Both' if they spoke English and Welsh. There was also a separate enumerator's book, in English, for Wales and Monmouthshire that contained this extra column. Similar arrangements were made in 1901, although children under three years of age were to be excluded from the returns relating to language.[8]

A mock-up of the household schedule in Yiddish and German was produced for the information of the Jewish population of East London in 1891 and 1901.[9] In 1891 the Board of Guardians for the Relief of the Jewish Poor drew up a circular, also in Yiddish and German, to accompany the mock-up, and paid for it to be typeset. A similar document was issued in 1901, and the Chief Rabbi undertook to encourage his co-religionists to fill up the schedule properly (see Figure 2.2).[10] Returns were to be made on the normal English household schedules with the mock-up serving as a crib. How far this was successful can be judged by the quality of the returns for the East End in 1901, analysed in Chapter 12.

The returns for the Islands in the British Seas

The Islands in the British Seas were the Channel Islands and the Isle of Man. They came under the GRO along with England and Wales for the purposes of census-taking. The lieutenant-governors of the islands appointed a superintendent to oversee the process of census-taking for a parish or island. That person in turn appointed enumerators for the enumeration districts.

The enumerators' books were very similar to those used in England and Wales.[11] The main difference was that the geographical data sought at the front of each book and at the top of each

---

[8] Examples of the household schedules issued in Wales can be found in various TNA series: 1841, no copy appears to have survived; 1851, HO 45/3579; 1861, RG 27/3, Item 4; 1871, RG 27/4, Item 10; 1881, RG 27/5, Item 10; 1891, RG 27/6, Item 68; 1901, RG 19/11. Examples of the 1891 and 1901 English-language household schedules with an extra column for language spoken in Wales can be found in TNA, RG 27/6, Item 68 and RG 19/11 respectively. An example of the 1891 enumerator's book with the extra column can be found in TNA, RG 27/6, Item 73. An example of the 1871 instruction to the enumerators regarding the marking of Welsh schedules with a 'W' can be found attached to TNA, RG 10/5628, fo. 2, p. ii. The author would like to thank Dr. W. T. R. Pryce for bringing this reference to his attention. Similar instructions for 1881 and 1891 can be found in TNA, RG 27/5, Item 35 and RG 27/6, Item 39.

[9] For 1891, see TNA, RG 27/6, Item 63; for 1901, see TNA, RG 19/11.

[10] TNA, RG 19/11, Schedules: preparation of forms for occupiers and institutions in English and Welsh; schedule for vessels; correspondence regarding translation and supply of schedules in German and Yiddish; reference to and specimen of enumeration book for public institutions (AA): letter of the secretary of the Board of Guardians for the Relief of the Jewish Poor, 7 Jan. 1901; letter of the Chief Rabbi, 18 Dec. 1900.

[11] Examples of these books can be found in the census series open at TNA. For 1891, see RG 27/6, Item 75. The 1901 household schedule can be found in TNA, RG 19/23.

page was much simpler. In 1851 the enumerators were to supply the name of the island, the parish and the relevant town or village (see Chapter 3 for the respective headings in England and Wales). In 1841 householders only had to indicate whether or not the members of their households were born on the island of residence, as opposed to the county of residence in the case of England and Wales. In 1901, however, a separate household schedule and enumerator's book was produced for the Isle of Man. This had an extra column for information to be supplied on those who spoke the Manx language.

Annotations and alterations

The enumerators' books were regarded by the GRO as merely the raw material from which the Census Office produced the tabular returns in the published *Census Reports*. The books were checked both locally and in London to ensure that they contained no obvious errors. The census clerks then went through each book, taking one head of information at a time, abstracting the data on tally sheets (see Chapter 13). In this process the books were altered and annotated by the local registrars and the census clerks. On the pages of the original books these marks are in coloured inks, crayon, or pencil, and can easily be differentiated from the enumerators' returns. It is, however, much more difficult to differentiate such additions from the original entries on monochrome microfilm.

The marks fall into four main categories: factual corrections; additional information; marks to highlight information; and ticks used to mark each piece of information to ensure that none was overlooked. Factual corrections are quite easily detected. Sometimes households were enumerated in the wrong parish, or even in the wrong registration district, and this would be noted. On other occasions enumerators placed ages in the wrong sex column, or placed a town in the wrong county in the birthplace column. These were often noted and corrected. As already remarked, the addition in column totals, and in the summary table of the numbers of persons, houses and households on each page, frequently had to be corrected. Insertion of information often took place in the column for occupations. The Census Office abstracted occupations under certain standard headings using occupational dictionaries specifically designed for the purpose. Thus, all weavers, spinners, piecers and other operatives in the cotton industry were placed under the heading 'Cotton Manufacture' in the published reports. Sometimes these standard headings, or their numbered codes, were written in beside the actual term used by the enumerator. In this way 'Carpenter' was added to 'Packing case maker', 'Die maker' to 'Brass stamp cutter', and so on. Highlighting, in the form of coloured crayon, is often found in the case of the birthplaces of those born outside the county being enumerated. The clerks had to produce tables showing the counties of birth of migrants in each county. The procedure adopted was first to highlight the birthplaces of such persons in the books and then to tabulate the data. As the clerks were abstracting the data from the enumerators' books they often ticked each piece of information to ensure that they did not miss any. Sometimes birthplaces were ticked off in the column for medical infirmities and this can cause some confusion. It is generally safe to assume that information in the latter column was given in writing.

3 The geographical structure of the returns

Census information was collected within a geographical framework. The purpose of the census was not simply to record the number and characteristics of the population but to give such information for administratively significant areas. The enumerators' books themselves are the returns from a particular area, which in turn was part of what had usually been an administrative entity in 1841 when the original plans of division had been drawn up. The nineteenth century was, however, a period of rapid change in administrative boundaries, and a single enumeration district could come in time to contain parts of several bureaucratic entities. These had to be recorded within the body of the enumerators' books. Subsequently the books themselves were arranged physically in the topographical order in which their populations were recorded in the published *Census Reports*. This was based on a breakdown into counties, and within these into hundreds, or registration districts, and then into parishes, and so on.[1] This physical arrangement has been carried over into the reference system used at TNA for ordering the census records. For a glossary of the administrative areas mentioned in the returns see Appendix 4.

The enumeration district

The enumerators' districts were sub-divisions of the registrars' sub-districts. These in turn were parts of the superintendent registrars' districts set up for the purpose of the civil registration of births, marriages and deaths. These enumeration districts had originally been established in 1841, and descriptions of them were retained by registrars in their plans of division. The enumeration districts were, as far as possible, to be made up of meaningful entities, such as parishes and townships, or parts thereof.[2]

The enumeration districts were also supposed to be of a standard size. It was assumed in 1871, for example, that if the town districts contained 200 houses, and if rural districts were so arranged that an enumerator would not be required to travel more than 15 miles, the number of houses being less than 200, the districts would not be too large. Where there were great changes in population, registrars were advised to sub-divide or amalgamate the enumeration districts in order to prevent any becoming either too large or too small. Since administrative boundaries

---

[1] For a breakdown of the various areas shown in the *Census Reports*, see Office of Population Censuses and Surveys and the General Register Office, Edinburgh, *Guide to Census Reports, Great Britain 1801–1966*, pp. 270–3.

[2] TNA, RG 27/1, p. 19.

were also changing, the areas covered by enumeration districts could soon become meaningless in administrative terms.[3]

Before 1891 the emphasis had been on retaining the boundaries of the previous censuses, in order, no doubt, to facilitate comparability. Many registrars failed to revise the boundaries of districts, and considerable distortions resulted. This was especially serious where enumeration districts were originally made up of parishes with detached parts, that is, where a certain portion of the parish was geographically separate and surrounded by the land of another parish. In time these anomalies might be removed by transferring the detached part to the parish in which it lay, but it might still be included in the enumeration district covering the original parent parish. In 1857 a start was made on bringing the whole country within the normal systems of local administration with the passing of the Extra-Parochial Places Act (20 Vict., c. 19). This decreed that places named as extra-parochial in the *1851 Census Reports* were to be deemed parishes for the purposes of Poor Law administration, and were to appoint overseers of the poor. The process was accelerated by the Divided Parishes Acts, especially that of 1882 (45 & 46 Vict., c. 58), which stated that detached parts should be incorporated into the parish surrounding them. In this piecemeal manner, administrative and political arrangements in England were gradually standardised and unified. In 1891, registrars were positively encouraged to alter the areas of the enumeration districts to take account of these changes. Many registrars appear to have altered their boundaries as a result, but not sufficiently to remove all anomalies.[4]

According to an internal GRO memorandum produced in preparation for the 1911 census,[5] the populations of the 1901 enumeration districts were distributed according to Table 3.1.

Table 3.1 Distribution of the population of the 1901 enumeration districts

Districts with populations in the range of (persons)	Number
1–500	10,539
501–1,000	10,770
1,001–1,500	11,521
1,501–2,000	2,910
2,001–2,500	493
2,501–3,000	112
3,001–3,401+	23

Source: TNA, RG 19/45, p. 18.

This was despite the fact that in 1901 the GRO had instructed registrars that enumeration districts should not contain more than 1,500 persons.[6] Similarly, enumeration districts could

[3] TNA, RG 27/4, Item 2, pp. 13–14.
[4] TNA, RG 27/6, Item 6, pp. 11–18.
[5] TNA, RG 19/45, p. 18.
[6] TNA, RG 19/45, p. 19.

contain parts of two or more administrative counties, civil parishes, urban and rural districts, and so on. In the registration district of Chester in 1901, 262 out of 814 enumeration districts contained two or more parts of various administrative divisions.[7]

It is very difficult to give general guidance on the extent to which enumeration districts changed over time. In practice each locality varied according to individual circumstances, such as changes in population, the conscientiousness of local officers, and so on. In rural areas with stable populations the districts might stay the same throughout the period, but this can hardly have been the case on the outskirts of rapidly expanding towns. One might well expect there to be a marked disjuncture between 1881 and 1891 because of the instructions to the registrars noted above.

A registrar's district would thus comprise a number of enumeration districts. Each of these would have a number to distinguish it from the others. In 1841 each enumeration district was generally numbered 1, 2, 3, and so on, within each registrar's district. The numbering in 1851 was much more complicated. In some registrars' districts the enumerators' districts were numbered as in 1841. In others, however, one finds runs of numbers such as 1A, 1B, 1C, 2, 3, 4, 5A, 5B, and so on. These might subsequently be renumbered so that 1A became 1, 1B became 2, and so on. From 1861 onwards the straight-through numbering system, 1 to *x*, tended to reassert itself, although sub-numbering persisted in some districts. The numbering systems used, of course, abound in local idiosyncrasies.

The front page, or front cover, of the enumerators' books was always used to describe the geography of the enumeration district. In 1841 this page carried three types of information. The first section related to the ancient administrative areas in which the enumeration district fell: the county; the parliamentary division; the hundred, wapentake, soke or liberty; the parish; the township; the city, borough, town or county corporate; the parliamentary city or borough; and the municipal unit. Not all of this information was given, of course, since some of these entities were mutually exclusive. The second section gave the names of the superintendent registrar's district and the registrar's district, and the number of the enumeration district. The page was completed by the third section, a description (usually fairly brief) of the enumeration district. The information in the second and third sections was supplied by the registrar, that in the first section was supplied later by the clerks at the Census Office.[8]

In 1851 the front page of the enumerator's book was headed by six boxes in which the enumerator inserted information supplied by the registrar on the areas within which the district fell: the county and parliamentary division; the parliamentary city or borough; the municipality; the superintendent registrar's district; the registrar's district; and the number of the enumeration district. There then followed a much larger space for the description of the district. This was often given in terms of the streets and numbers of houses in towns, and of administrative areas

---

[7] TNA, RG 19/45, p. 15.
[8] TNA, RG 27/1, pp. 43, 48.

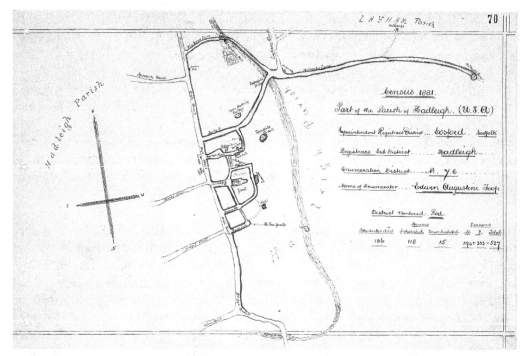

Figure 3.1 Enumerator's map of part of the parish of Hadleigh, 1881 (TNA, RG 11/1834, fo. 70)

covered in the countryside. In 1861 the information required was much simpler, being the names of the superintendent registrar's division and the registrar's sub-division, and the number and description of the enumeration district. This was also the standard practice in 1871 and 1881.

In 1891 and 1901 the same information was given on the front page but the description of the enumeration district was now broken down into a delineation of its boundary, and a separate description of its contents. In 1901 the dividing line between rural districts was usually to be the centre of well-defined roads, while in a town the districts were to be described as being bounded on the north by the centre of such and such a street, on the east by the centre of another named road, and so on. The statement of contents was supposed to give an exhaustive list of all the streets, roads, groups of houses and detached parts.

It is important not to confuse this description of the streets or houses in the enumeration district with the order in which these appear in the nominal returns in the body of the book. The latter was left completely up to the enumerator, who was not necessarily constrained by a description that might have been set down decades before by a now deceased registrar. The strangely aberrant forms of the description of enumeration districts that can be found in the books are an indication of how comparatively little control was exercised over the local officers. There are, for example, cases where maps of the district have been supplied, or where the description includes details of the local geology and wage rates.[9] (See, for example, Figure 3.1.)

[9] TNA, HO 107/1967, fo. 203; HO 107/1971, fo. 61; RG 10/112, fo. 19.

Internal geographical references

As has been noted above, an enumerator's book could contain parts of several administrative units. The 1841 enumerators do not appear to have been given any clear instructions as to how to differentiate the returns for these entities. From 1851 onwards, however, the enumerators were instructed that the returns for particular parishes, townships, hamlets, wards, villages, etc., were not to be confounded.[10] The whole of one parish, for example, had to be entered before the entries for any part of another parish were begun. At the end of the entries for such administrative areas the enumerator had to write across the page 'End of the parish (etc.) of ———'. The rest of the page was to be left blank, with the returns for the next administrative area starting on the next page.

Given the complexities of local administrative boundaries, it was inevitable that enumerators and registrars would not always correctly identify administrative areas. Such lapses were sometimes spotted by registrars or census clerks who inspected the books, and an attempt made to correct the entries.

In order to provide an easy means of reference to the geographical entities covered in the various parts of the books, each page had space at the top for information on the administrative areas covered therein. As the century drew to a close the number of such entities generally increased because of various administrative reforms. In consequence the information to be entered at the top of each page also became more complex and extensive. From 1851 onwards the enumerators were also required to show the number of schedules issued, and the number of houses and persons, in each administrative area in a summary table at the beginning of the book. (See Appendix 5 for the page headings for geographical data, and Appendix 6 for information on the tables in the various enumerators' books.)

When extracting information from the census enumerators' books it is essential to note the enumeration unit to which it relates. Data relating to the number of people in a particular civil parish may, for example, give a different headcount to that for an enumeration district with the same name.

The overall topographical arrangement of the records

The references given to the census returns are dependent upon the order in which they have been boxed. This is based, in turn, upon the order of places in the population tables in the printed parliamentary reports. The records were so arranged in order that the latter could act as finding-aids to them.

From 1851 onwards the published reports were arranged by registration divisions, which were made up of registration counties. The latter were broken down into superintendent registrars'

---

[10] TNA, HO 45/3579.

districts, and these into registrars' sub-districts.[11] The returns have been boxed, numbered and subsequently filmed in this order. The published reports were then arranged according to the places, parishes, townships, and so on, within sub-districts. The arrangement of the records at this level, however, does not necessarily correspond exactly to the geographical order shown in the published reports.

The returns for 1841, as is so often the case, were treated in a very different manner. The information was collected on the basis of superintendent registrars' districts, registrars' sub-districts and enumerators' districts. The enumerators' books were, however, subsequently rearranged into ancient counties (in alphabetical order), and then into hundreds, wapentakes, sokes and liberties, and within these into parishes. The returns from enumeration districts in particular hundreds, wapentakes, etc., were collected together and inserted into folders. This was done so that the published information derived from the returns could be arranged by the ancient administrative divisions of the country, as in the pre-1841 *Census Reports*. This explains why, at the front of each enumerator's book, the contents were described in terms of the ancient territorial divisions of the country, as well as the registration divisions. To complicate matters further, at some point certain counties in the 1841 returns were rearranged yet again. In the case of Lincolnshire and Kent, the records were re-sorted to place the parishes in alphabetical order. The arrangement of the records for Lancashire is even more complicated. The records were numbered and filmed in this complex order. Their arrangement does not, therefore, duplicate that found in the published population tables for 1841.

---

[11] For a list of the registration districts, 1851–1901, see Lumas, *Making Use of the Census*, pp. 84–106.

4 Special returns

The administration of the census from 1841 onwards was based on the assumption that people lived in relatively stable households or families. The first stage in the process of data capture was the distribution of 'household schedules' to each occupier, in which he or she was to record the details of the members of his or her household on census night. But considerable numbers of people were not in 'normal' households on census night and special arrangements had to be made for their enumeration. These included the inmates of institutions, the crews of vessels afloat, and the Army. Special arrangements also had to be made for the enumeration of itinerants and night workers.

Inmates of institutions

According to the 1840 Census Act the 'master or keeper ... of every public or charitable institution which shall be determined upon by the said [census] commissioners, shall act as the enumerator of the inmates thereof'. In order to produce a list of such entities, superintendent registrars were obliged to send a return of these institutions (defined as every gaol, prison, penitentiary, house of correction, hulk or prison ship, workhouse, almshouse, hospital, infirmary, asylum, madhouse, public school, endowed school, college, barrack and 'other public or charitable institution') in their districts to the GRO.[1] The census commissioners then decided which institutions would be enumerated by their head officers. The superintendent registrar was provided with a list of these, which was passed down to the normal enumerators for information. The former also received special institutional enumerators' books which they forwarded to the heads of the institutions.[2] The latter enumerated the inmates of their institutions and passed their books on to the Census Office in London. Institutions not subject to these special arrangements were treated as if they were households by the normal enumerators. It is difficult to say on exactly what criteria institutions were selected for special treatment in 1841. The number of inmates does not appear to be a consistent guide, although very large and important institutions would usually be treated separately. Nor were particular types of institutions treated in a consistent manner. Some small asylums, for example, were returned in special institutional books, while others appear as households among the normal returns.

This plainly caused problems for the Census Office. Although the 1851 procedures respecting institutions were almost the same as in 1841, the superintendent registrars were now asked to

[1] TNA, RG 27/1, pp. 21–2.
[2] TNA, RG 27/1, pp. 77–8. See Appendix 7 for references to examples of the institutional books.

return the number of inmates they contained at the beginning of the year. Institutions that had more than 200 inmates were now automatically to be treated as special cases to be returned in institutional books, although some smaller institutions were also to be enumerated in the same manner. The figure of 200 was retained for the censuses of 1861–81. In 1891, however, the critical number of inmates was reduced to 100. Since the census was taken several months after the superintendent registrars made their surveys of institutions, some exceeding the critical size on census night were treated as normal households while others containing fewer than that number were enumerated in the special institutional books.[3]

Although the household returns and the institutional books were forwarded to the Census Office separately, they had to be brought together to enable the calculation of population totals for each locality. The institutional books are usually associated with the areas in which they stood. In 1841 they can most often be found at the end of the household returns for the place concerned, or at the end of the returns for the hundred in which they lay. In later years they can be found at the end of the returns for the relevant place, or for the registration district. The returns have also been microfilmed in this order.

The format of the institutional books was similar to that of the household returns. The main differences were:

1) the geographical information carried at the head of every page of the household returns only appeared on the first page of the institutional returns;
2) the columns for information on addresses and housing were omitted;
3) the column for relation to head of household was replaced by one for 'position in the institution' in 1851, and by another for 'relation to head of family or position in the institution' thereafter;
4) the preliminary tables only gave information on the number of males and females per page, and the total number of officers, members of officers' families and inmates;
5) there was no division of the population into houses or households.

From 1851 onwards the information on the residents of the institution had to be entered in a set order. First came the master or head of the institution, and then his or her spouse, children, other relatives and servants. Then came the officers, their families and servants, visitors, and so on. The inmates were the last to be enumerated.

The quality of information in the institutional returns varied according to the conscientiousness of the officers, and the type of inmates being enumerated. Very young children at boarding school might not know their place of birth, while elderly people in workhouses might not be seen as having any occupations. The returns relating to occupations are generally rather poor. It

---

[3] *1851 Census Report: Population Tables, I* (PP 1852–3 LXXXV [1631.], p. xii); *1861 Census Report*, p. 1; *1871 Census Report* (PP 1873 LXXI Pt. II [872–I.]), Appendix B: mode of taking the census, p. 169; TNA, RG 27/5, Item 17; TNA, RG 27/6, Item 6, p. 16.

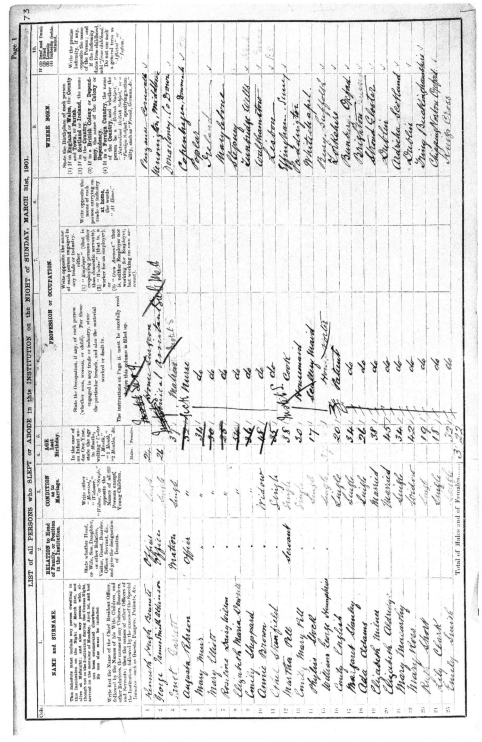

Figure 4.1 Female lock hospital for the treatment of VD, 1901 (TNA, RG 13/12, fo. 73, p. 1)

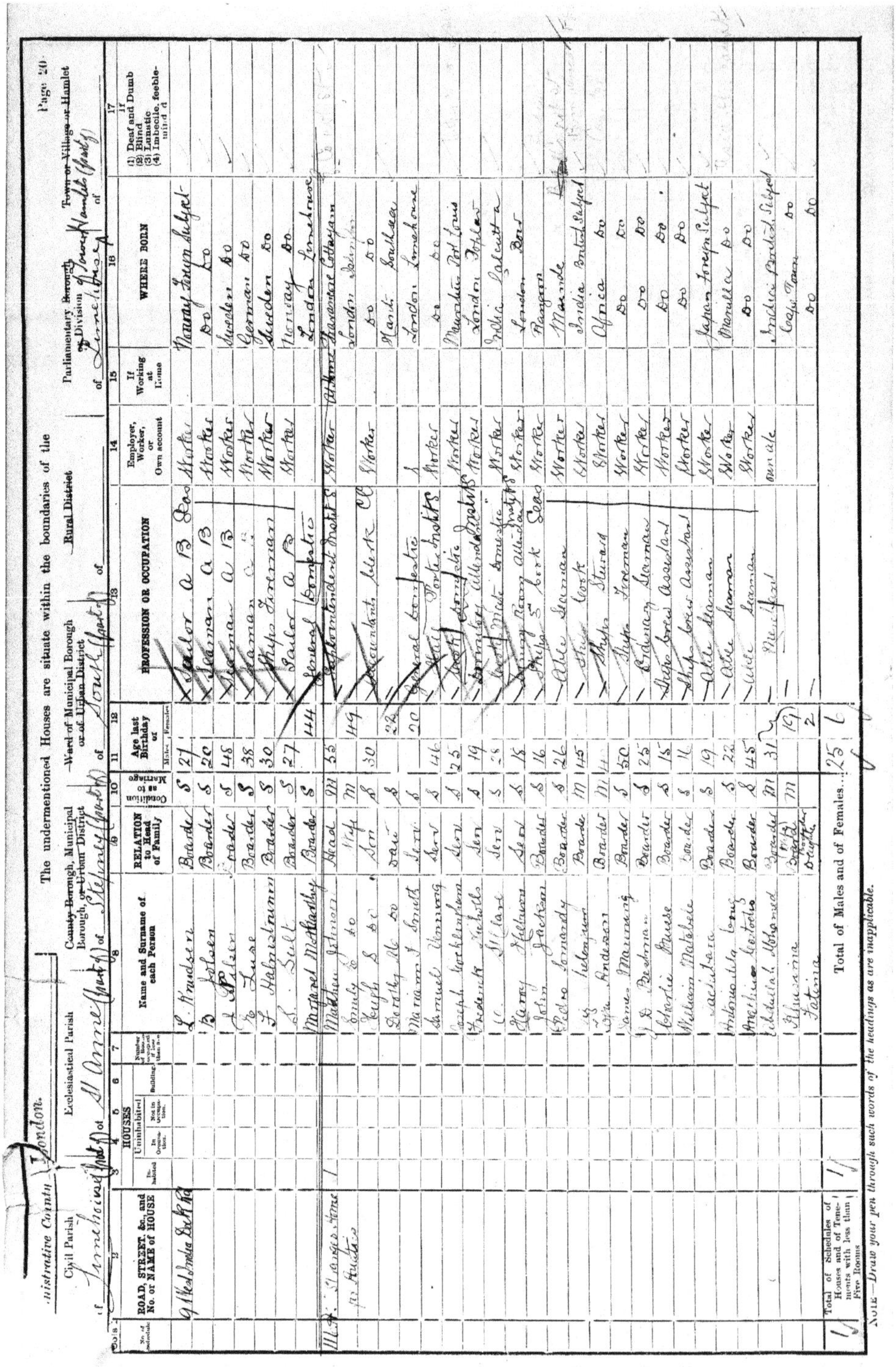
The undermentioned Houses are situate within the boundaries of the

Page 20

Administrative County: London. Civil Parish: Limehouse (part of). Ecclesiastical Parish: St Anne (part of). Borough, or Urban District: Stepney (part of). Ward of Municipal Borough or of Urban District: South (part of). Parliamentary Division: Tower Hamlets (part of). Town or Village or Hamlet: Limehouse.

No. of Schedule	Road, Street, &c., and No. or Name of House	Name and Surname of each Person	Relation to Head of Family	Condition as to Marriage	Age (Males)	Age (Females)	Profession or Occupation	Employer, Worker, or Own account	If Working at Home	Where Born
	9 Whe...ela Bch Rd	L. Knudsen	Boarder	S	27		Sailor A B Sea	Worker		Norway Foreign Subject
		B. Johlsen	Boarder	S	20		Seaman A B	Worker		Do Do
		... Olsen	Boarder	S	48		Seaman A B	Worker		Sweden Do
		E. Luse	Boarder	S	38		Seaman	Worker		German Do
		J. Halmstromm	Boarder	S	30		Ships Foreman	Worker		Sweden Do
		S. Sult	Boarder	S	27		Sailor A B	Worker		Norway Do
		Margaret McHardy	Boarder	S		44	General Domestic	Worker		London Limehouse
114	Strangers Home for Asiatics	Mathew Johnson	Head	M	55		Superintendent Institution	Worker	At Home	[illegible]
		Emily do do	Wife	M		49				London [illegible]
		Hugh do do	Son	S	30		Accountant's clerk	Worker		Hants Southsea
		Dorothy do do	Daur	S		22				London Limehouse
		Marian J. Smith	Serv	S		20	General domestic			
		Samuel [illegible]	Serv	S	46		Porter Institution	Worker		Mauritius Port Louis
		Joseph [illegible]	Serv	S	25		Porter Institution	Worker		London Poplar
		Frederick Nicholls	Serv	S	19		Attendant Institution	Worker		India Calcutta
		C. St Clare	Serv	S	28		Male domestic Institution	Worker		do do
		Harry [illegible]	Servt	S	18		Dining room attendant	Worker		London Bow
		John Jackson	Boarder	S	16		Ships 5th cook Sea	Worker		Rangoon
		Pedro Lonardy	Boarder	S	26		Able Seaman	Worker		Manila
		[illegible]	Boarder	M	45		Ships cook	Worker		India British Subject
		Ojo Anderson	Boarder	M	41		Ships Steward	Worker		Africa Do
		James Manning	Boarder	S	50		Ships Foreman	Worker		Do Do
		J. E. Beckman	Boarder	S	25		Ordinary Seaman	Worker		Do Do
		Charlie Prusse	Boarder	S	15		Ships [illegible] Assistant	Worker		Do Do
		William Matebele	Boarder	S	16		Ships [illegible] Assistant	Worker		Do Do
		[illegible]	Boarder	S	19		Able Seaman	Worker		Japan Foreign Subject
		Antonio Vila Louis	Boarder	S	22		Able Seaman	Worker		Manilla Do
		[illegible]	Boarder	S	45		Able Seaman	Worker		Do Do
		Abdullah Mohamed	Boarder	M	31		Mendicant	Own acc		India British Subject
		[illegible]	Boarder (Wife)	M		19				Cape Town
		Fatima	Daughter			2				Do
1	Total of Schedules of Houses and of Tenements with less than Five Rooms	1	Total of Males and of Females		25	6				

NOTE.—Draw your pen through such words of the headings as are inapplicable.

Figure 4.2 Strangers' Home for Asiatics, Limehouse, 1901 (TNA, RG 13/322, fo. 119, p. 20) is almost impossible to reconstruct the possible relationships between inmates within institutions since only their status in the institution is usually given. In 1861 it is even difficult to identify inmates by name since only initials needed to be returned. On the other hand, one might assume that the information relating to medical disabilities would be more reliable in workhouses and hospitals. For examples of the inmates of institutions returned in special institutional schedules, and in households in the census enumerators' returns, see Figures 4.1 and 4.2.

The enumeration of the Army

Soldiers in barracks in England and Wales were always enumerated in the same manner as the inmates of other institutions. Small barracks were treated as private households to be enumerated by the ordinary enumerator. Barracks large enough to be treated separately were returned in institutional books, marked 'B' for barracks in 1851 and 1861, and possibly in other years, by the resident barrack or quarter master. The position of barrack returns in the records is similar to that of other institutions. Members of the British Army stationed abroad were never fully enumerated. Instead the military authorities provided the Census Office with information as to the numbers of officers, other ranks, wives and children, either by place or by regiment.[4] Nominal information on this considerable body of men and women was not collected as part of the census until 1911.[5]

The enumeration of the Royal Navy

The enumeration of the Senior Service was more comprehensive than that of the Army.[6] Members of the Royal Navy ashore in England and Wales on census night were always recorded in the usual household and institutional returns. From 1861 onwards the commanding officers of Royal Naval vessels, both in home waters and abroad, were furnished with special naval schedules in which they were to record the names and relevant details of the officers and crew.[7] In 1841 and 1851 some attempt appears to have been made to gather information regarding the members of the Royal Navy on board ship. In 1841 only a headcount was probably attempted but in 1851 special schedules appear to have been issued to the commanding officers of vessels in British ports.[8] Given the lack of detailed instructions or surviving ships' schedules, it is difficult to be dogmatic on the subject.

[4] TNA, RG 27/1, pp. 139–40; *1851 Census Report: Population Tables, I*, p. xvii; *1861 Census Report*, pp. 3–4; TNA, RG 27/4, Items 41 and 42; TNA, RG 27/5, Items 37 and 38; TNA, RG 27/6, Items 20 and 21; TNA, RG 19/19.

[5] For other records relating to the members of the nineteenth-century British Army in TNA, see the Information Leaflet series on The National Archives website <http://www.catalogue.nationalarchives.gov.uk/researchguidesindex.asp> (30 Sept. 2004).

[6] For other records relating to the members of the nineteenth-century Royal Navy in TNA, see the Information Leaflet series on The National Archives website <http://www.catalogue.nationalarchives.gov.uk/researchguidesindex.asp> (30 Sept. 2004).

[7] See Appendix 7 for references to examples of the Royal Navy ships' schedules.

[8] TNA, RG 27/1, pp. 140–1; *1851 Census Report: Population Tables, I*, p. xvii; *1851 Census Report: Tables of the Population and Houses* (PP 1851 XLIII [1399.], p. iv).

The naval schedules of 1861–81 contained columns for name and surname, rank or rating ('quality' in 1861), condition, age and birthplace. These returns related to passengers as well as to servicemen. They also contained three tables giving an abstract of the numbers returned on each page of the book; the number of officers, men, boys and marines on board and on shore; and the number of passengers and other persons on board on census night but not borne on the books of the ship. The schedules of 1891 and 1901 contained columns for name and surname, relation to vessel (member of the crew, etc.), condition as to marriage, age last birthday, profession or occupation, whether employer, employee or self-employed (for passengers only), birthplace and medical disabilities. There were schedules containing differing numbers of pages for vessels of differing sizes.

If nominal returns were made for naval vessels in 1841 and 1851, they do not appear to have survived. In 1861 the returns for such vessels in both home and foreign waters can be found at the end of the record series, alongside those for the merchant marine. They do not appear to be in any particular order. Thereafter only the returns of naval vessels at sea or in foreign waters were placed at the end of the record series. The schedules for those in British ports can usually be found at the end of the household returns for the registration district in which the port lay.

The enumeration of the merchant marine

Any attempt to describe the enumeration of the merchant marine in the nineteenth-century censuses must, of necessity, be a very complex business. The main reason for this is that the enumeration of the merchant marine, unlike almost every other aspect of the census, was not done on one day but was spread over a period of time. This period varied from census to census. Nor were all merchant vessels, or those on board them, treated in the same manner. These complexities confused the officers responsible for enumeration, who sometimes failed to follow their instructions properly, thus compounding the problem.[9] The very vagueness of some of these instructions, and the loss of some of the returns, makes a comprehensive description of the process even more difficult. The following should be regarded as a rough outline of the enumeration of the merchant navy rather than as an exhaustive account.[10]

Throughout the period, the crew and passengers of merchant vessels, of whatever nationality, who were on shore on census night were treated as other land dwellers and enumerated in the household returns. It could be argued that such people were not normal residents since they were in transit, but this is a rather narrow, legalistic point of view. The individuals who made up the floating population of ships' crews and passengers may not have been normally resident in

[9] For an example of the problems caused, see M. Woollard, "'Shooting the nets': a note on the reliability of the 1881 census enumerators' books', *Local Population Studies*, 59 (1997), pp. 54–7.

[10] For other records relating to the members of the nineteenth-century merchant marine in TNA, see the Information Leaflet series on The National Archives website <http://www.catalogue.nationalarchives.gov.uk/researchguidesindex.asp> (30 Sept. 2004).

specific ports but the presence of such people was a typical feature of many coastal towns. To exclude this group from any analysis would give a hopelessly distorted picture of the population, society and economy of Liverpool, Southampton and the East End of London. The enumeration of the crews and passengers of merchant ships who were on board on census night is far more complex, and is best treated on a census-by-census basis.

In 1841 no attempt appears to have been made to make a complete enumeration of the crew and passengers of merchant ships. Instead, the GRO asked the General Register and Record Office of Seamen to provide the number of seamen's names on its register on 6 June 1841, after deducting those reported dead. Only a global figure for the total number of merchant seamen was given in the *1841 Census Report*.[11] This caused problems for the registrars of births, marriages and deaths in ports. The populations of their districts were calculated on the basis of the population on shore. Those registered as dying in the districts, however, were drawn from this population plus those on board ship in harbour. Consequently, calculations of deaths per 1,000 population, the most important nineteenth-century sanitary statistic, were hopelessly inflated. This was extremely serious given the Victorian concern over the health of ports.[12]

From 1851 onwards some attempt was made to capture the population of vessels in harbour. Indeed, the GRO's net was spread even wider to include vessels in certain categories which arrived in port within a certain period of time after census night. The sea-going population to be enumerated in 1851 comprised three groups:

1) those who slept on board vessels in harbour on 30 March 1851 (census night);
2) those on that night who were at sea in vessels engaged in the home trade (all vessels trading or sailing within the limits of the coasts of the United Kingdom, Jersey, Guernsey, Sark, Alderney, the Isle of Man, and of Europe from the Elbe to Brest);
3) those who were absent from the United Kingdom in ships normally sailing to and from other foreign parts.

The third group was not supposed to be enumerated fully, a headcount being undertaken via the General Register of Seamen. The first and second groups were to be enumerated by the customs officers.[13]

The ships in harbour on census night were sub-divided into two groups:

1) ships of foreign nations;
2) British ships in the home or foreign trade.

---

[11] TNA, RG 27/1, p. 142; *1841 Census Report: Abstract of the Answers and Returns*, p. 297.

[12] This was especially true with regard to the spread of venereal disease (see, for example, P. McHugh, *Prostitution and Victorian Social Reform* (London, 1980)).

[13] See Appendix 7 for references to examples of the merchant ships' schedules, and the instructions to customs officers.

In the case of foreign vessels, the name and nation of the vessel, and the number and sex of persons on board, were returned by the customs officers, distinguishing foreign from British subjects. For the purpose of enumerating persons aboard British vessels in the home trade (but apparently not in the foreign trade), a special ship's schedule was produced for recording the names and details of the crew and passengers.[14] On 15 March 1851 the customs officers gave a ship's schedule to the master of every British ship in port. They also gave one to the master of every British ship that arrived at the port unprovided with a schedule from that day until census day, 30 March. Early on the morning of 31 March, the customs officers collected the returns filled in by the masters of the ships in port on that day. From the surviving accounts it is not clear if this included British vessels engaged in foreign trade as well as those in the home trade. Ships engaged in the home trade which were at sea on census night were supplied, either before their departure or on their return, with ships' schedules, which were collected as the vessels arrived in British ports from 31 March to the last day of April. On the last day of April the ships' schedules collected were sent directly to the Census Office in London.

This process was plainly very complex. The intention was to restrict a nominal enumeration to the crew and passengers of British vessels engaged in the home trade, either in port on census night or arriving within a month. It is not clear if British vessels engaged in foreign trade were so enumerated, although the wording of the schedules would indicate not. The apparent destruction of most of the ships' schedules for this census makes it difficult to settle the question. For all other vessels only a headcount was officially attempted.

The 1851 ship's schedule was, with minor changes, used throughout the nineteenth century, the only major additions being extra columns to bring the information sought into line with the household schedules. On the front of the schedule the master of the ship was to indicate the port to which the ship belonged; its name; its registration number and date of registration; its tonnage; whether it was employed in the home trade, conveying passengers or fishing; the name of the master; and the number of his master's certificate. He was also to record the date and port at which he received the schedule, the position of the ship at midnight on 30 March 1851, and the port at which he delivered the schedule. Inside, the master was to indicate the names of the passengers and crew; the number of the master's or mate's certificate; the number of the register ticket; if people were members of the crew ('C'), passengers ('P') or visitors ('V'); their condition as to marriage; their sex ('M' or 'F'); their age last birthday; their rank, profession or occupation; their birthplace; and the usual medical disabilities. In later censuses a box was also provided in which the master inserted the number of persons from the vessel on shore on census night. In 1901 their names and full census details had to be given. Information on whether the vessel was powered by steam or sail was sought from 1891 onwards.

The administrative arrangements for the enumeration of the merchant marine in 1861 can be traced with much greater certainty. A ship's schedule similar to that of 1851, and known as

---

[14] *1851 Census Report: Population Tables, I*, p. xvii.

'Form A', was given by the customs officers to the master of every British foreign-going, home-trade and coasting ship or vessel in port on 25 March, or which arrived between that day and census day, 7 April. These were to be collected on 8 April. On the arrival in port of any British home-trade or coasting vessel between that day and 7 May, the master was to be asked if he had handed in his census return at any UK port. If not he was requested to fill in a ship's schedule and to hand it to the customs officer. Another schedule, known as 'Form B', was used by the customs officers to record the number of persons who slept on board ships of foreign nations or British colonies on census night, distinguishing between foreigners and British subjects, and by sex.[15] This was done by the enumerators who went on board such ships on 8 April.

These instructions should have meant that only British ships in the coasting or home trade which arrived in port within a certain period, or British ships in the foreign trade which were in port on census night, should have been issued with ships' schedules. British foreign-going ships in foreign waters before 8 April should not have been given schedules, and only a headcount should have been taken of those on foreign vessels in port on census night. An examination of the schedules, however, reveals British ships which were in the Baltic and Mediterranean on census night. These were apparently foreign-going vessels which were mistakenly given schedules by the customs officers.

The arrangements in 1871 were slightly different. In that year only ships' schedules, Form A of 1861, were used. These were to be delivered to all British and foreign vessels which arrived in port from 25 March until census day on 2 April. These were collected in port on 3 April. Further forms were only to be handed to British vessels in the coasting and home trade which arrived in port from that day until 2 May. Thus, foreign vessels in port on census day were fully enumerated for the first time. This process was repeated in 1881, the respective periods being 26 March to 3 April, and 4 April to 3 May.

The system of enumeration changed once more in 1891. Ships' schedules were to be left on board all vessels, whether British, foreign or colonial, which were in port on 30 March, or which arrived up until 5 April, census day. Such schedules were also to be given to every British vessel and every foreign vessel 'employed in the coasting trade of the United Kingdom' arriving between 6 April and 30 June. This meant that the situation had been greatly simplified. All vessels in port on census day were now fully enumerated, as were all British vessels, and foreign vessels engaged in the UK coasting trade, which arrived in port in the period up to the end of June.

The instructions for 1901 were similar to those of the previous decade, the two periods now running from 23 to 31 March, and from 1 April to 30 June. The simplicity of the 1891 arrangements was compromised, however, by the following instruction to the customs officers:

---

[15] TNA, RG 27/3, Item 41.

In the cases of vessels absent from the United Kingdom on the night of the 31st of March, and on the 1st of April, but arriving before the 30th of June, Masters of Vessels may be informed that no particulars of passengers need be entered upon the shipping schedules, and that, if the vessel is foreign-going beyond the 'Home Trade' limits, particulars respecting members of the crew under an Agreement to be delivered up in the United Kingdom need not be entered upon the shipping schedule.

The position of the schedules within the census records can be summarised quite quickly. No schedules appear to have been issued in 1841. Shipping schedules were issued in 1851 but very few appear to have survived. The 1861 schedules can be found at the end of the household returns with those for the Royal Navy. In 1871, 1881, 1891 and 1901 the shipping returns are usually at the end of the household returns for the place or port to which the ships were nearest on census night, or with those for the place or port at which they delivered their schedules. The schedules for Royal Navy vessels at sea or in foreign ports during the census period are usually found at the end of the record series as a whole, although the returns may not be complete.

Fishing vessels

Alas, further complications were introduced into the enumeration of the population at sea by the special arrangements that were made for the enumeration of fishing vessels.[16] As with other shipping, no attempt was made to enumerate fishing vessels in 1841. The surviving accounts of the 1851 census are not detailed enough to reconstruct the position in that year. The 1851 ship's schedule, however, asked the master to state if his ship was employed in the home trade, conveying passengers, or fishing. Fishing vessels may, therefore, have been treated in the same manner as other vessels.

In 1861 fishing vessels were to be given ships' schedules if they were in port on 4 April, or arrived between then and census day, 7 April. But whereas all British coasting and home-trade vessels arriving up until 7 May were also to be given a schedule, only fishing vessels arriving up until 20 April were to be so treated. Fishing vessels were handled in much the same way in 1871 and 1881, except that in the period before census night they were now treated in a similar manner to other vessels. While other British vessels arriving in port after census night were given ships' schedules from 3 April to 2 May in 1871, and from 4 April to 3 May in 1881, fishing vessels only received them up until 14 and 15 April respectively. In 1891 and 1901, however, British fishing vessels, and 'every fishing boat of foreign nationality which brings fish regularly to ports of the UK', were to be treated in the same manner as other vessels. This simplification of procedures corresponds to that for the enumeration of other vessels in this period.

The distribution among the household returns of the ships' schedules for fishing vessels is similar to that for other shipping.

---

[16] The schedules used for fishing vessels were the same as those used for other merchant ships. See Appendix 7 for references to examples of the merchant navy schedules, and the instructions to customs officers.

Vessels engaged in inland navigation

In order to complete a description of the enumeration of the floating population in the nineteenth century, it only remains to consider the population of vessels engaged in inland navigation. Such vessels that came into the areas of ports and harbours under the jurisdiction of the customs officers were treated by them in the same way as fishing vessels. The only exception to this was in 1851, when the customs officers merely forwarded to London the vessel's name, description and port where returned, as well as the number of males and females on board.[17]

The population of such vessels on canals and inland navigable waters was treated in a rather different manner. No attempt appears to have been made to make a nominal enumeration of these vessels in 1841 and 1851. Enumerators were merely asked to calculate the numbers of males and females on such vessels and to insert this figure in one of their preliminary tables. In 1841 application was also made to the canal companies to provide an estimate of the number of such people.[18]

From 1861 onwards some attempt was made to enumerate this floating population, and a calculation of the number of such persons was no longer supplied by the enumerators. The arrangements for 1861 were extremely *ad hoc*. The registrar was to enumerate vessels within his sub-district 'according to the circumstances of each case'. He was advised to find where such vessels might be moored from the owners or managers of wharves, or the canal companies, and then to employ a 'trustworthy person' to visit them on census morning to obtain the necessary nominal information using the standard ship's schedule of that year.[19] These returns can now be found at the end of the household returns for the enumeration district, or registration sub-district, in which the vessel lay on census night.

From 1871 onwards it became the responsibility of the enumerators to enumerate such vessels.[20] They handed the person in charge of the vessel a ship's schedule, and collected it when completed. The information that it contained was then entered into their enumerators' books at the end of the household entries. From 1881 this applied not only to vessels which had been given schedules prior to census day but also to barges and the like which appeared in the enumeration district on that day.

Itinerants and travellers

Institutions and water-borne vessels created special problems for census-takers but they could be easily traced and treated as if they were households. People travelling, especially those 'on the

[17] *1851 Census Report: Population Tables, I*, p. xvii.

[18] TNA, RG 27/1, pp. 81–2.

[19] TNA, RG 27/3, Item 12.

[20] See Appendix 7 for references to examples of the instruction books circulated to the registrars and enumerators prior to census day.

tramp', were a potentially greater problem because they were much less easy to track down. They slipped through the census net because they were not resident as part of a household on census night. In the nineteenth century many people moved about the country looking for work according to the seasons or the social calendar, or were employed in circuses and fairs, or as drovers.[21] The censuses of this period were usually taken in March or early April, in order to avoid the movements of population associated with the agricultural harvest. In many areas, however, there may have been itinerants sleeping rough at census time.

In 1841 no special arrangements appear to have been made to include the itinerant population in the nominal returns. This was a serious omission since the census of that year was taken in June when the movement of itinerants during the summer was already under way. The enumerators were instructed to insert in one of their summary tables the number of persons sleeping in barns, sheds, tents or in the open air, 'or who from any other cause, although within the District, have not been enumerated as inmates of any dwelling-house'.[22] In order to get some idea of the numbers travelling at night by railway, canal and coach, enquiries were made with the railway and canal companies, and with 'Mr Horne of the Golden Cross, Charing Cross', a famous coaching inn.[23] There is at least one entry for railway passengers but these appear to have been people on a train waiting in Southampton railway station, who were enumerated along with the railway employees at work.[24]

In 1851 those sleeping in barns, sheds, tents and in the open air were treated as in the previous census. The enumerators were instructed that persons travelling by railway or coach were to be returned at the house or hotel at which they stopped, or took up their residence, on the morning after census night, although the wording to this effect was not very clear on the household schedules.[25] This became the standard instruction to enumerators and householders for the rest of the century. In 1861 the number of those in barns, sheds, tents and in the open air was no longer explicitly given in one of the preliminary tables. On the other hand, as full particulars as possible of such people were now to be provided in the main body of the returns. This information was to be given at the end of the household schedules under a heading 'List of persons not in houses'.[26] From 1871 onwards particulars regarding such persons were to be entered in their proper place in the roads, lanes or outhouses in which they slept. Such barns, sheds, tents, and so on were not, however, to be reckoned as houses.[27] For examples of people enumerated in caravans or sleeping in the open air, see Figures 4.3 and 4.4.

---

[21] See R. Samuel, 'Comers and goers', in *The Victorian City: Images and Realities, Vol. I*, ed. H. J. Dyos and M. Wolff (London, 1976), pp. 123–60.

[22] TNA, RG 27/1, p. 46.

[23] TNA, RG 27/1, pp. 81–2.

[24] TNA, HO 107/417, bk. 7, fo. 9.

[25] TNA, HO 45/3579.

[26] TNA, RG 27/3, Item 17, p. i.

[27] See Appendix 7 for references to examples of the enumerators' books.

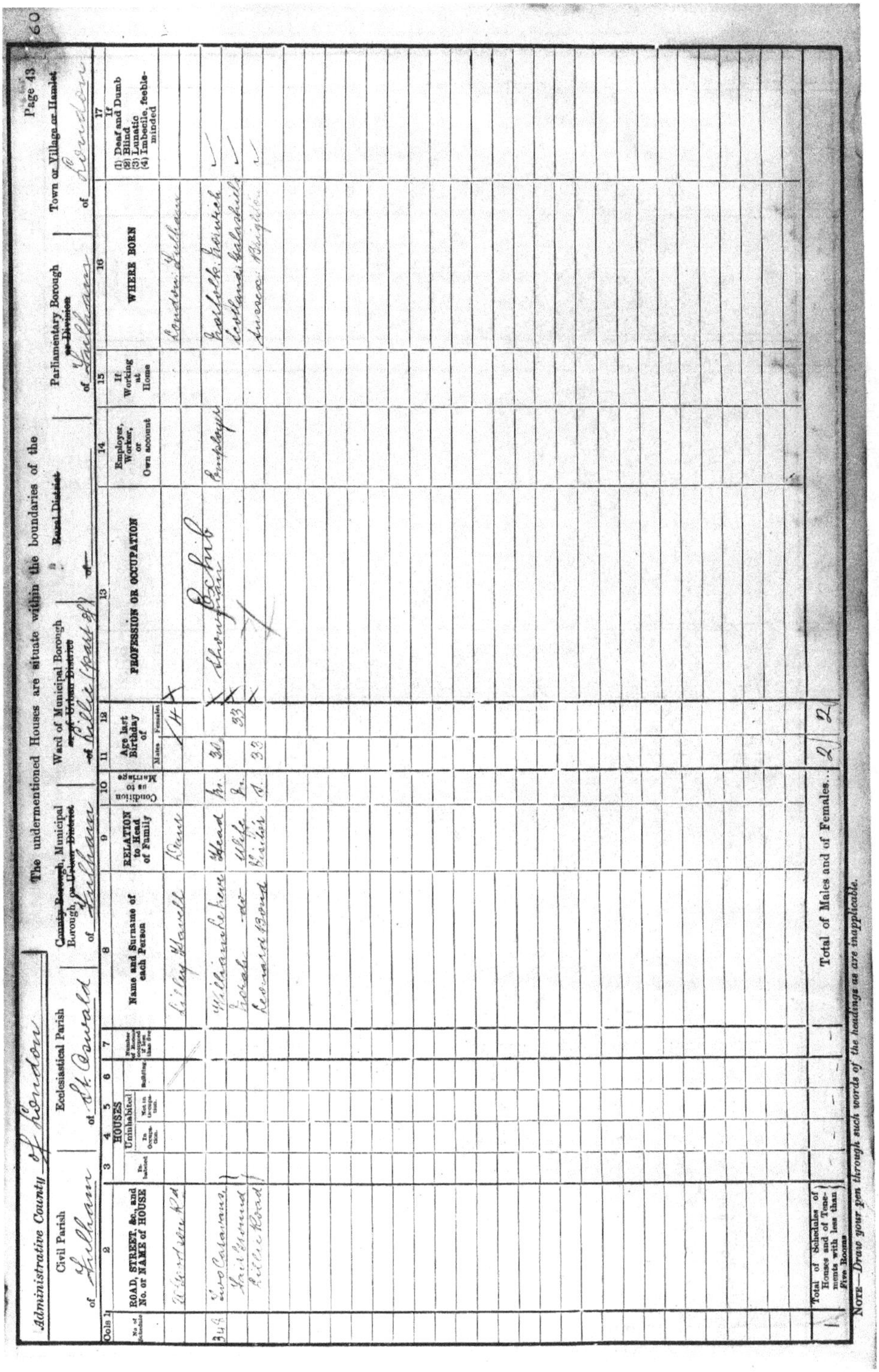

Administrative County of London — The undermentioned Houses are situate within the boundaries of the — Page 43

Civil Parish	Ecclesiastical Parish	County Borough, Municipal Borough, or Urban District	Ward of Municipal Borough or of Urban District	Rural District	Parliamentary Borough or Division	Town or Village or Hamlet
of Fulham	of St Oswald	of Fulham	of Lillie (part of)	—	of Fulham	of London

No. of Schedule	Road, Street, &c., and No. or Name of House	Name and Surname of each Person	Relation to Head of Family	Condition as to Marriage	Age last Birthday of Males	Age last Birthday of Females	Profession or Occupation	Employer, Worker, or Own account	If Working at Home	Where Born	If (1) Deaf and Dumb (2) Blind (3) Lunatic (4) Imbecile, feeble-minded
	[illegible] Rd	Lilley Howell	[illegible]			14				London Fulham	
348	Two Caravans, Fair Ground, Lillie Road	William Scherer	Head	M	30		Showman	Employer		Norfolk Norwich	
		Sarah do	Wife	M		33				Scotland Galashiels	
		Leonard Bond	Visitor	S	33					Sussex Brighton	
Total of Schedules of Houses and of Tenements with less than Five Rooms: 1		Total of Males and of Females			2	2					

NOTE—Draw your pen through such words of the headings as are inapplicable.

Figure 4.3 Caravan dwellers in Fulham, 1901 (TNA, RG 13/61, fo. 60, p. 43)

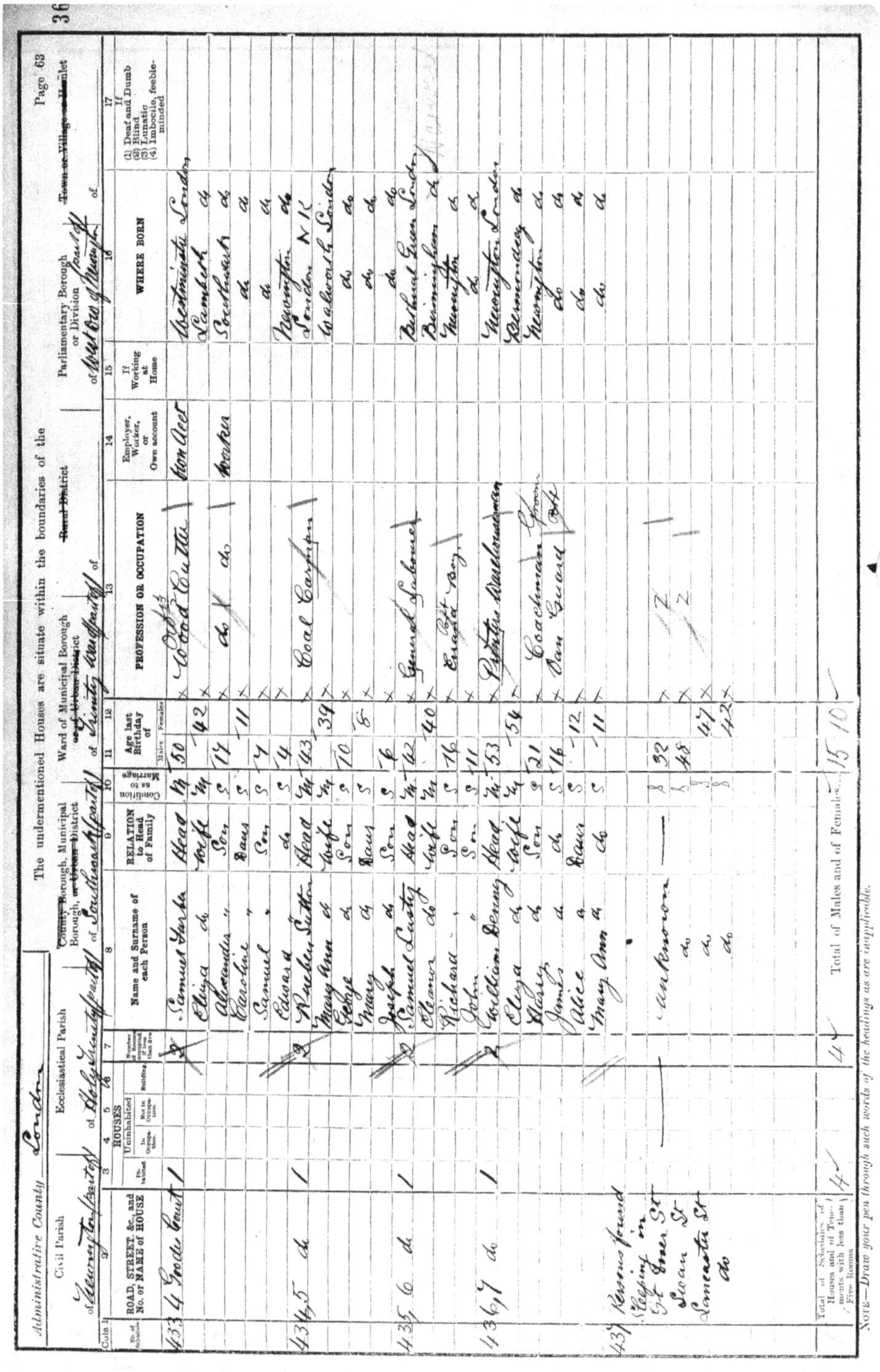

Administrative County London — The undermentioned Houses are situate within the boundaries of the — Page 63 — 36

Civil Parish of Newington (part of) | Ecclesiastical Parish of Holy Trinity (part of) | County Borough, Municipal Borough, or Urban District of Southwark (part of) | Ward of Municipal Borough or of Urban District of Trinity Ward (part of) | Rural District of | Parliamentary Borough or Division of West Div of Newington (part of) | Town or Village or Hamlet of

No. of Schedule	ROAD, STREET, &c., and No. or NAME of HOUSE	HOUSES Inhabited	Number of Rooms occupied if less than five	Name and Surname of each Person	RELATION to Head of Family	Condition as to Marriage	Age last Birthday of Males	Age last Birthday of Females	PROFESSION OR OCCUPATION	Employer, Worker, or Own account	If Working at Home	WHERE BORN	If (1) Deaf and Dumb (2) Blind (3) Lunatic (4) Imbecile, feeble-minded
433	4 Goodes Court	1	2	Samuel Sarker	Head	M	50		Wood Cutter	Own Acct		Westminster London	
				Eliza do	Wife	M		42				Lambeth do	
				Alexander "	Son	S	17		do do	Worker		Southwark do	
				Caroline "	Daur	S		11				do do	
				Samuel "	Son	S	7					do do	
				Edward "	do	S	4					Newington do	
434	5 do	1	2	Reuben Sutton	Head	M	43		Coal Carman			London N K	
				Mary Ann do	Wife	M		39				Walworth London	
				George do	Son	S	10					do do	
				Mary do	Daur	S		8				do do	
				Joseph do	Son	S	6					do do	
435	6 do	1	2	Samuel Lasty	Head	M	42		General Labourer			Bethnal Green London	
				Eleanor do	Wife	M		40				Birmingham do	
				Richard "	Son	S	16		Errand Boy			Newington do	
				John "	Son	S	11					do do	
436	7 do	1	2	William Denny	Head	M	53		Printers Warehouseman			Newington London	
				Eliza do	Wife	M		54				Bermondsey do	
				Harry do	Son	S	21		Coachman Groom			Newington do	
				James do	do	S	16		Van Guard			do do	
				Alice do	Daur	S		12				do do	
				Mary Ann do	do	S		11				do do	
437	Persons found Sleeping in Gt Dover St			Unknown	—		32						
	Swan St			do			48						
	Lancaster St			do				47					
	do			do				42					
Total of Schedules of Houses and of Tenements with less than Five Rooms		4	4	Total of Males and of Females			15	10					

NOTE—Draw your pen through such words of the headings as are inapplicable.

Figure 4.4 Sleeping rough in Southwark, 1901 (TNA, RG 13/372, fo. 36, p. 63)

Night workers

The census was based upon the principle that the householder should record the people who slept in his or her house on census night. In 1841, however, no special arrangements appear to have been made for those away from home on night shifts. In theory they should not have been included in the census, although householders may have done so in many cases. The enumerators, however, were asked to estimate in their tables the numbers of such people down pits and mines.[28] From 1851 onwards night workers were to be enumerated in their homes if they returned there the next day.[29]

[28] TNA, RG 27/1, p. 46.
[29] See Appendix 7 for references to examples of the instruction books circulated to the registrars and enumerators prior to census day.

PART II

THE INTERPRETATION OF CENSUS DATA

5 Information relating to houses

The information in the census returns relating to housing is important for several reasons. For the historian of housing the ratio of people to houses, the amount of unoccupied property, and the number of families in tenements with under five rooms are important indications of the state of the housing market, and of the degree of overcrowding. Medical historians interested in the impact of the latter on the spread of diseases also need to use this material. For the social and economic historian the layout of streets, their social composition and the extent to which differing social classes lived next to each other are all significant matters.

Unfortunately, the data relating to housing in the census can be extremely difficult to interpret, especially in heavily built-up areas. What exactly constituted a 'house', what made one 'uninhabited', and what was a 'room', were never adequately defined in the period. Nor were addresses necessarily stable entities. Some of these problems will be outlined here in general terms. The practice of different enumerators and local conventions could differ widely, however, and these need to be considered individually in any local study.

Information relating to 'houses' in the census returns

At first sight the information relating to houses appears fairly unambiguous. (The descriptions given here should be used in conjunction with the examples of pages from the enumerators' books shown in Appendix 3.) In 1841 the 'Place' column contained the names of houses, streets or places, but not necessarily the numbers of houses. The column headed 'Houses' was divided into two columns; for uninhabited houses or those being built, and for inhabited houses. The beginning of an inhabited house was marked by the enumerator with a number '1' in the latter column, adjacent to the name of the first person in the house. The end of the house was to be marked by double oblique strokes (//) inserted after the name of the last person in the house, on the line dividing the houses and names columns. An uninhabited house, or one being built, was to be recorded by placing '1 U' or '1 B' respectively in the relevant division of the houses column, by the names of the people in the inhabited house nearest to which it stood.

In 1851 the enumerator was expected to record the name of the street, place or road, and the name or number of the house in the second column of the schedule. Under the last name in any house he was to draw a line across the page from left to right as far as the fifth column. Where there was an uninhabited house to be recorded, or one being built, this was done by writing in the address column, on the line under the last name in the last inhabited house, 'one house uninhabited', 'three houses building', and so on. A line was then drawn under this in the same manner as for inhabited houses.

In 1861 the address column was similar to that of the previous census. The houses column of 1841 was, however, reintroduced. The beginning of an inhabited house was marked by the enumerator with a number '1' in the relevant column, adjacent to the name of the first person in the house. The end of the house was to be marked by double oblique strokes (//) inserted after the name of the last person in the house, on the line dividing the houses and names columns. An uninhabited house, or one being built, was to be recorded by placing '1 U' or '1 B' respectively in the relevant division of the houses column, immediately below the name of the last person in the adjacent inhabited house. The entries for the next house were to start immediately underneath. The addresses of such houses were also to be inserted. This layout was to be repeated in 1871, 1881 and 1891, although the double oblique strokes now ran in the opposite direction (\\). In the latter year, however, a new column was added for the number of rooms occupied by each family in the house, if under five. This number was to be supplied next to the name of the head of the household. In 1901 the houses column was broken down into four divisions: inhabited houses; uninhabited houses which were usually in occupation; uninhabited houses which were not usually in occupation; and those which were being built. The enumerator was now only expected to place a number '1' in the relevant column. The question as to the number of rooms inhabited was repeated. In all the censuses the enumerators were expected to total the numbers of each type of house on the page, and to give this information at the foot of each house column.

These apparent certainties begin to dissolve, however, as one explores the meaning of the terms used.

The definition of a house

In a rural setting, or the middle-class suburbs of large towns, the identification of a house or cottage might be fairly simple. But in the 'rookeries' of the great cities, where older buildings had been sub-divided and rooms partitioned to squeeze in the ever-increasing urban population, there were insuperable problems. Buildings frequently clustered behind and, in part, on top of others, two front doors might serve the same block, and one flat sometimes went over the top or through into part of a neighbouring building. Much the same could be said of cellar dwellings which existed in some mid-century towns.[1] There were also constant problems with outbuildings which might, or might not, be occupied, with or without the knowledge of their owners. The 1841 instructions to the enumerators were not particularly helpful: 'By "House" is meant *Dwelling-House*; and every building in which any person habitually sleeps must be considered as a

---

[1] The census officials were themselves uncertain as to whether or not these should be treated as separate habitations (TNA, RG 9/3010, fo. 51).

dwelling-house.'[2] But what of buildings which provided temporary shelter for a person on census night, and how did one define a 'building'?[3]

From 1851 onwards the house was defined as the space between the external and party walls of a building.[4] This was as much a legal as a physical description since a party wall was one between two buildings or pieces of land intended for distinct occupation, in the use of which each of the occupiers had a partial right. The definition depended in part, therefore, on finding an 'occupier'. In the maze of dark back-alleys and courts in London and the industrial cities it might have been difficult for enumerators to make such an identification. This definition of the house created anomalies in the late nineteenth century, with the erection of model or industrial dwellings for the working classes, the precursors of modern high-rise blocks. Each block was officially treated as a single but sub-divided house, although each flat was a self-contained dwelling unit. In Scotland, where such buildings had been common from a much earlier date, the definition of a house had long since included that of a dwelling with a door opening directly on to a common stair. To complicate matters still further some enumerators, following common sense but not their instructions, chose to regard every such flat as a separate house.[5]

The introduction in 1891 of the question on the number of rooms occupied by each household appears to have made the situation worse. This entity was termed a 'tenement' by the GRO. Many enumerators appear to have assumed that a tenement and a house were the same thing, and the house became the space occupied by a single household.[6] The household in turn was a difficult entity to define (see Chapter 6).

What was included and excluded from the definition of a house varied from census to census.[7] In 1841, buildings such as churches or warehouses, 'which were never used or intended to be used as dwelling-houses', were not to be counted as houses. On the other hand the enumerator was given the rather garbled instruction that,

> In the case of a house having a stable or outhouse belonging to it, in or over which some person of the household sleeps, the enumerator must take care that such person is neither inserted as an inmate of such other detached building in which he sleeps, which must be entered as a separate dwelling house.

---

[2] 1841 and 1851 Census Returns (TNA, HO 107).

[3] For some of the problems associated with interpreting the 1841 definition of the 'house', see E. Higgs, 'The definition of the "house" in the census of 1841', *The Local Historian*, 19 (1989), pp. 56–7.

[4] See Appendix 7 for references to examples of the instruction books circulated to the registrars and enumerators prior to census day.

[5] *1891 Preliminary Census Report* (PP 1891 XCIV [c.6422.], p. vi); *1890 Report of the Treasury Committee on the Census* (QQ 1734–6); TNA, RG 19/45, fo. 49.

[6] *1891 Census Report* (PP 1893–4 CVI [c.7222.], p. 20); Schürer, 'The 1891 census and local population studies', p. 23.

[7] See Appendix 7 for references to examples of the enumerators' books and instruction books circulated to the registrars and enumerators prior to census day.

This could be taken to mean that a stable slept in by a groom was to be counted as a separate house. In 1861, the enumerators were told to ignore the 'out-offices attached to a mansion' and the outbuildings of farms. But a stable or coach-house, if a detached building containing dwelling rooms, was to be regarded as an inhabited house. This applied presumably even if the 'dwelling room' was a mattress in the corner of the stable on which a young groom slept. In 1901 it was pointed out that blacksmiths' forges, workshops and stables, without sleeping accommodation, should not be treated as houses.

The carelessness of the enumerators when filling out their books also creates difficulties. Occasionally long lines or double slashes defining a house have been accidentally omitted, while short lines and single slashes defining a household might be drawn in error as long lines and double slashes. These errors can often be spotted by changes of address, or by consulting the totals for the numbers of houses at the bottom of each page. But even this may fail where the address information is minimal or confused.

The census authorities were fully aware of all these problems and admitted privately that in urban areas the numbers of houses shown in the enumerators' books and reproduced in the *Census Reports* were 'misleading and often valueless'. They also felt that, in the absence of any indication of the size of houses, it was dangerous to use the changing numbers of houses from census to census as part of an index of overcrowding.[8] If census material is to be used to study urban housing conditions, it must, therefore, be treated with great caution. If addresses, rate books, maps and street directories exist, these should be consulted to identify possible problems of mis-enumeration. In many cases, however, this will not be possible. In such circumstances, the double oblique stroke and the '1' in the inhabited houses column, or the long line in 1851, may have to be accepted as indicating the existence of a new house. It should be recognised, though, that such 'houses' may not necessarily be particularly meaningful entities in urban areas.

The only exceptions which seem useful to allow are the following:[9]

1) Where the '1' or the long line is placed in the middle of a nuclear family (as indicated in the 'relationship to head of family' column and by a similar surname), and where the entry for the 'head' of this family is not preceded by a '1' or a long line, the marks may be assumed to be misplaced and suitable adjustments may be made to correspond with the sense. If this is not done, members of the same family will appear to be living in the same household but in different houses, which is plainly nonsensical.

2) Long lines and double strokes are occasionally omitted at the bottom of pages. Where it is suspected that this has occurred, reference should be made to the total of inhabited houses at the foot of the next page and, where this total can only be correct if the first

---

[8] TNA, RG 27/45, fo. 50; *1901 Census Report* (PP 1904 CVIII [Cd.2174.], p. 37).

[9] These are based on M. Anderson, 'Standard tabulation procedures for the census enumerators' books 1851–1891', in Wrigley, *Nineteenth-Century Society*, pp. 139–40.

household on the page did indeed occupy a separate house, this may be taken as a substitute indicator, and a new house counted.

3) It may occasionally happen that a long line or double strokes are followed (from 1851) by the term 'lodger'. This should normally be taken to indicate a house where the head was absent so that the lodger should be taken as a 'head equivalent'. This conclusion should always be verified against the total at the foot of the page, and against the address when given.

4) Some enumerators occasionally fail to include the entry '1' in the inhabited house column in cases where they indicate a new house by a double stroke, and by a new and different address in the address column. In such cases it should be assumed that the '1' has been omitted. Unfortunately, enumerators frequently omitted addresses and so they cannot be used as a general indicator.

The definition of uninhabited houses and those being built

The ratio of empty houses, or those being built, to occupied houses in the census books and reports has been used to give an indication of 'spare capacity' in the housing market.[10] There are problems, however, in accepting such calculations uncritically. These stem from the definition of a 'house', the use of the term 'uninhabited' and the fact that the census was a snapshot of the housing market on one particular day every 10 years.

The census 'house' was defined, at least from 1851 onwards, in terms of the space of a building between party walls. Except in 1841, the house was not specifically defined as a 'dwelling house' in which people lived. It could presumably be interpreted as a lock-up office, shop or warehouse. An 'uninhabited house' might, therefore, be a building which was never inhabited, as opposed to one which was temporarily vacant. In the course of the nineteenth century such buildings became more common, especially in the commercial centres of towns. An increasing ratio of uninhabited to inhabited houses does not necessarily mean increased 'spare capacity' in the market for human habitations. Many uninhabited dwelling houses might not be available in the housing market because they were only empty on census night while families were away visiting. These problems led the census authorities in 1901 to make a distinction between uninhabited houses in occupation for business or other purposes and those not in occupation for any purpose, although they admitted that the distinction appeared to have been lost on enumerators and householders. Any calculations of the ratios of empty to inhabited houses must, therefore, be treated with caution.

Much the same could be said about houses being built. A declining ratio of houses being built to those completed on census night has little meaning unless one can assume that the time needed

---

[10] B. R. Bristow, 'Population and housing in nineteenth-century urban Lancashire: a framework for investigation', *Local Population Studies*, 34 (1985), pp. 12–26. Bristow is plainly aware of the problems of using the census data relating to housing.

to complete houses remained constant throughout the nineteenth century. If builders could put up houses more quickly because of changing techniques, then on any one day there would need to be fewer houses in the process of being built to maintain the building/built ratio over the whole year. The speed of building might also vary, of course, from region to region. Nor does the number of houses being built on one day in every 10th year necessarily indicate the state of the construction industry over long periods. The figures in any census year might indicate quite temporary conditions. In 1891, for example, it was believed that the low number of houses being built was due to the severe and prolonged frost in the early months of the year.[11] All such calculations need to be treated with extreme caution, and with due regard to changing local conditions, temporary aberrations and changes in building techniques. They also depend upon the assumption that the 'house' itself is a meaningful entity.

Addresses in the census

The addresses of houses are of fundamental importance for historians tracing individuals, or those attempting to reconstruct residential patterns and mobility rates. The nineteenth century was, however, a period of rapid urban expansion, and of a revolution in postal services. These had a profound effect on the system of addresses used nationally, and create problems for modern researchers. The enumerators were given very clear instructions with regard to the provision of address data. In 1841 it was only necessary for the enumerator to give the name, if any, of the house, or the name of the street, part of the town, village or hamlet in which it stood. From 1851 onwards, though, they were specifically instructed to give the number of the house as well.[12]

This depended, however, on the existence of proper addresses in the first place. The rapid expansion of towns and the sub-division of houses in the early nineteenth century had left addresses in chaos. The Town Improvement Clauses Act of 1847 provided that local authorities should from time to time renumber houses and buildings, and this requirement was incorporated into the 1875 Public Health Act. Street numbering systems, therefore, did not become formalised in towns until the 1850s at the earliest. Liverpool, for example, renumbered on a uniform basis in 1856, with the painting and affixing of 40,538 new numbers.[13] But even as late as the 1881 census, the GRO was still haranguing the chairmen of urban sanitary authorities on the need for standard numbering systems.[14] Street numbering was often shambolic well into the Victorian period.

This was especially serious in slum districts with courts leading off main streets, cellar dwellings and sub-divided houses. An additional problem might be the 'loss' of numbers in a street due to

---

[11] *1901 Census Report*, p. 36.
[12] See Appendix 7 for references to examples of the enumerators' books.
[13] R. Lawton, 'Census data for urban areas', in Lawton, *The Census and Social Structure*, p. 129.
[14] TNA, RG 27/5, Item 39.

the demolition of houses for a railway station or public works. Similarly, on the outskirts of nineteenth-century towns, at times of urban expansion, new houses were constantly being added to the ends of streets. An address found in a document post-dating the census by only a few years might not have existed at the time of the decennial enumeration. The opposite problem can be found when whole areas of cities were swept away for major works, such as slum clearances. One should also remember that not all the houses in a street would necessarily be in the same enumeration district. The middle of streets often formed the boundaries of such units, and it is not unusual to find the odd-numbered houses in one enumeration district and the even in another.

The introduction of the straight-through numbering of streets could cause its own problems. In the nineteenth century, house building was usually in the hands of small speculative builders. Easy access to loans, and the convention of sub-contracting in the building trades, meant that such builders needed neither direct employees nor much capital of their own. Houses tended to be put up in small numbers by adding a run of perhaps five or six to the end of an existing street.[15] Each of these speculations could be given a separate name, Such-and-Such Terrace, Such-and-Such Place, and so on; each block having its own numbers starting from '1'. Streets could be sub-divided into a series of such runs of numbers. In time these streets might be renumbered, so that the addresses ran consecutively throughout their length. This process was going on in London in the 1860s and 1870s. Addresses may not, therefore, be stable over time.

In the countryside the names of outlying farms or prominent residences would probably be stated, but difficulties begin to arise when trying to identify the houses along main streets of villages, or in the populous and unnumbered streets of small towns. In country districts there might rarely have been a street number to give, and a considerable collection of dwellings might take the name of the principal house in the area.

The majority of addresses can, of course, be found in the returns with a little effort, and street indexes exist in many record offices for this purpose. In some urban areas, however, one may need to have recourse to contemporary maps, rate books and commercial and postal directories to locate families and houses. This assumes, of course, that houses were put down in the returns in the order in which they appeared on the ground. In rural areas it may be necessary to go through a whole parish to find a particular family.[16]

The census and studies of residential proximity

An interesting use to which the census books have been put has been the study of class segregation in cities, as, for example, in John Foster's *Class Struggle and the Industrial Revolution*.[17] This is done

---

[15] H. J. Dyos, *Victorian Suburb: a Study of the Growth of Camberwell* (Leicester, 1977), pp. 122–37.

[16] See *Local Communities in the Victorian Census Enumerators' Books*, ed. D. R. Mills and K. Schürer (Oxford, 1996), section 6, which talks about the problems of house repopulation.

[17] J. Foster, *Class Struggle and the Industrial Revolution: Early Industrial Capitalism in Three English Towns* (London, 1974), pp. 125–31.

by comparing the social status of people who lived next to each other. What proportion of the middle classes lived next to members of the working classes, and how did this figure change over time? In most cases the proximity of households can be checked by comparing addresses, but in areas where house numbers are not given, such studies depend upon the enumerators' having entered houses in their books in the order in which they appeared in the streets.

It should be noted, however, that the enumerators were never explicitly instructed to enter the household returns in any particular order. From the point of view of the census authorities it was important that the houses in a particular administrative area should be grouped together for abstraction but for most purposes it did not really matter in what arrangement the houses appeared within these areas. In practice, geographical ordering was only implicit in the instructions given to the enumerators. The examples of how to fill out their books always showed the houses enumerated as they appeared in the streets. At the same time they were instructed that uninhabited houses, and those being built, should appear in the order in which they were to be found in the street.[18] This, of course, enforced a similar arrangement upon the inhabited houses.

Nor were enumerators explicitly instructed to follow a route based on the description of the district on the front of their books. They were instructed to work out their own routes, and were not constrained by wording which might have been set down 20 or 30 years before. Nor does the order of the returns in the books necessarily reflect the way in which the enumerators collected them. They could collect the returns in any manner which suited them and rearrange them at home for entering in their books. One should not confuse the process of collecting the household schedules and that of copying them into their enumerators' books.

The vast majority of returns do indeed follow streets and might even reflect the way in which the enumerators collected the schedules, but there are examples where this does not hold true. In Ramsgate in 1851 the houses in one enumeration district are all in order within streets but the latter are not arranged topographically. The enumerator presumably bundled his schedules under street headings and wrote these into his book at random. In the harbour area of the town at the same date, one enumerator listed all the inns first, taking them out of the order in which they appeared in the streets.[19] There may even be cases, where there were no uninhabited houses, or those being built, to constrict their freedom of action, in which enumerators placed houses in no topographical order at all. In the case of Winthorpe in 1881, for example, Mills and Pearce have noted that the household schedules appear to have been inserted in an order which ensured that as many as possible of the households fitted on a page, rather than straddling two.[20]

---

[18] See Appendix 7 for references to examples of the instruction books circulated to the registrars and enumerators prior to census day.

[19] R. S. Holmes, 'Identifying nineteenth-century properties', *AREA*, 6 (1974), pp. 276–7.

[20] D. R. Mills and C. Pearce, *People and Places in the Victorian Censuses: a Review and Bibliography of Publications Based Substantially on the Manuscript Census Enumerators' Books, 1841–1911* (Cambridge, 1989), p. 4.

Where address data are given, these problems can easily be spotted. In cases where this is vague or confused, one can compare the position of named inns and public houses in the census returns and on maps to check consistency, or consult local trade directories. If this is not possible, and this is often the case in small townships lacking full street numbering, the returns should be used for spatial analysis with considerable caution. It is always advisable to study the conventions employed by individual enumerators before embarking on such exercises.[21]

Even when houses are arranged in a topographical sequence one must not assume that households which appear immediately adjacent to each other in the enumerators' books are 'next-door neighbours'. In country areas there might be large distances between houses. In the towns the social composition of the residents of street frontages might be very different from that of the courts behind. In the enumerators' books the last house in the street frontage and the first in the court might appear adjacent to each other but on the ground they would be separated by an alleyway marking a spatial and social boundary. In such cases the consultation of contemporary maps is again of great importance. Valuation Office maps in the record series IR 121–35 at TNA are particularly valuable (see Figure 12.1, below p. 151).

The number of rooms in tenements and overcrowding

The interpretation of information sought in 1891 and 1901 on the number of rooms inhabited by a family is extremely important for those interested in the history of housing and overcrowding but is also extremely problematic. The householder was responsible for providing this information in 1891 but this became the enumerator's job in 1901.[22] The place on the schedule in which the return had to be made was not very conspicuous and was limited to families occupying less than five rooms. This led to incomplete returns and undoubtedly to omissions, particularly in the case of flats and maisonettes.[23]

Nor did the Census Acts or the instructions to the householders or enumerators ever define a 'room'. Should sculleries, pantries, washrooms, landings, lobbies, closets, shops, offices and stores be included or not? In the case of caretakers in warehouses, offices and banks, should the number of rooms be restricted to the number of rooms in which the person or family resided?[24] This was compounded by the difficulty of defining a 'family' or 'household'. Such problems were never resolved in this period. There might also have been cases where householders, especially those sub-letting, were reluctant to give information which might have led to disagreeable proceedings against them for overcrowding.[25] Even as late as the 1981 census, a post-enumeration

---

[21] It is not clear from Foster's work cited above (n. 17) whether or not he has fully taken all these matters into consideration (Foster, *Class Struggle and the Industrial Revolution*, pp. 263–4).

[22] See the household schedules for 1891 and 1901: TNA, RG 27/6, Item 68 and RG 19/11 respectively.

[23] TNA, RG 19/45, fo. 28a.

[24] TNA, RG 19/45, fo. 28b.

[25] C. Charlton, '"Bag in hand, and with a provision of papers for an emergency" – an impression of the 1891 census from the pages of some contemporary newspapers', *Local Population Studies*, 47 (1991), pp. 83, 86.

survey revealed that in the case of 28.6 per cent of households the number of rooms inhabited had been given incorrectly. One might expect an equivalent, or even higher, level of mis-enumeration in nineteenth-century censuses.[26] Presumably these problems would have been consistent over time, and the comparison of large areas from census to census is probably justified. Schürer, for example, points to the extremely high levels of overcrowding revealed by the returns in the coal mining districts of the North East.[27] But the figures should be used with great caution when comparing individual or small numbers of households in time and space.

[26] F. Whitehead, 'The GRO use of social surveys', *Population Trends*, 48 (1987), pp. 46–7.

[27] Schürer, 'The 1891 census and local population studies', pp. 22–4.

6 Information relating to households

Introduction

In the manuscript censuses, the people found within a house, however that was defined, could be further divided into 'families' or 'households'. In many areas, especially in the countryside, one might expect to find one socially meaningful group of people per house. In cities, however, more than one biological family or socially linked group of individuals could occupy a house. For social and economic historians, and historical demographers, the household, or family, in the census returns is of considerable importance. The study of household structure gives an insight into the workings of the nineteenth-century family, an institution of unrivalled importance in the reproduction of the population and of social mores.

It should be noted, however, that the household in the census is an administrative artefact. It does not correspond to the biological family, or to the sum total of relationships between kin and other members of society. The household in census terms was defined as those people present in a house on census night which a householder placed on his or her household schedule. Those absent from home for any length of time should not have appeared on this return, although the temptation to enter members of the household normally resident might have been strong. Sons and daughters who had grown up and left home should not have appeared in a household, nor, of course, would those yet to be born. Lastly, the rigorous demarcation of the population into households in the census may lead one to overlook the importance of relationships between households (especially between women), the role of kin living nearby and the support given by friends and workmates. The temptation to see Victorian society as constructed solely from the building blocks of census families should be resisted.

This has led historical demographers to refer to the census households as 'co-residing groups' rather than as families. In this chapter the term 'household' is used in this specific sense to designate the grouping of individuals by administrative convention in the process of census-taking. This entity, however, had considerable social meaning, especially since relationship to head was always couched in terms of the relationship to the head of 'the family'.[1]

A more immediate problem is how to define the boundaries of such households. Essentially, how did the enumerators recognise a 'householder' to whom they should give a household schedule? Nineteenth-century households tended to be far more complex entities than those of

---

[1] See Appendix 7 for references to examples of the household schedules.

today, with more living-in relatives, lodgers and servants. This represented the existence of the institution of domestic servitude and the lack of housing, especially in the rapidly expanding cities. Should these people be included in the 'household'? Are the census households groups of people who interacted in a socially meaningful manner? These are extremely complicated issues, and one should not be surprised that they caused confusion at the time.

The household on the page

Leaving aside, for the moment, the definition of a census 'household', it is usually quite easy to spot those groups of people so designated on the pages of the manuscript books.[2]

In 1841 the beginning of the first 'family' coincided logically with the beginning of the house but its end was signified by a single oblique stroke on the dividing line between the houses and names columns. The next 'family' then began, ending with a single stroke unless it happened to be the last household in the house. The end of a house was marked, of course, with a double stroke. In 1851 the end of the 'family' was marked by a line across the page, similar to that indicating the end of a house, but only running across part of the second column, as well as the third and fourth. The line for the end of the house ran completely across the first four columns. In addition the beginning of a new household was marked by a new schedule number in the column provided for that purpose. The conventions in the following censuses were a mixture of those of 1841 and 1851. From 1861 onwards oblique strokes were used in the same manner as 1841 but the beginning of each household was also marked by a new schedule number. In 1841 and 1861 the oblique stroke sloped from left to right but this was reversed from 1871 onwards. The 'short line' was only used in 1851.

The definition of the household

The census household comprised those persons whom an 'occupier' put down on his or her household schedule. But how was the enumerator to identify such a person, and how were they in turn expected to define the members of their 'family'?[3] In law the occupier had to 'retain his quality of master, reserving to himself the general control and dominion over the whole house. If he does, the inmate is a mere lodger'.[4] The position of master ultimately depended on who had control over the outer door. The treatment of lodging houses could be highly problematic.[5] But was the lodger part of the occupier's household? Such distinction would anyway have been difficult to draw in overcrowded cities.

---

[2] See the examples in Appendix 3.

[3] See Appendix 7 for references to examples of the household schedules and enumerators' books.

[4] J. Marle in *Tom v. Luckett* (1847).

[5] J. Wiles in *Smith v. Lancaster* (1869). For lodging houses, see B. Trinder, *The Market Town Lodging House in Victorian England* (Leicester, 2002).

The 1841 instructions on this matter were really quite minimal. The enumerator 'must cause a householder's schedule paper to be left at every house in his district for the occupier, and where a floor or room is let separately, a separate paper for each occupier of every such floor or room'. The definition of the household depended, therefore, on the position of the occupier as the person who paid rent. It is not clear, however, how someone sub-letting from the occupier was treated, although they should presumably have been dealt with as part of the occupier's 'family'. Given the absence of a column for relationship to the head of the household in 1841, it is difficult to reconstruct the treatment of lodgers.

In 1851 the enumerator was instructed to leave a separate schedule with each occupier, 'understanding by "occupier" either the resident owner or any person who pays rent, whether (as a tenant) for the whole of a house or (as a lodger) for any distinct floor or apartment.' The intention here was plainly to define the household in terms of the occupation of a distinct space within a house. But what about those cases in which lodgers did not occupy a 'distinct floor or apartment', sharing part of the house with their landlords, or those from whom they sub-let? The examples of how to fill in the schedules given to the householders and enumerators did not help to answer this question. These did not show anyone whose relationship to the head of the household was lodger or boarder, the households being made up of people related by kinship and marriage, servants and apprentices.

The 1851 definition of the occupier was repeated in 1861 but an attempt was made to introduce a distinction between the differing types of lodger noted above. The enumerators were now instructed that the following were among the cases in which one household schedule should be left:

> for a family consisting of a man, his wife, and children;
> of parents, children, servants and visitors;
> for a family consisting of parents and children, *with boarders at the same table*, and the servants of the family, if any;
> for a *lodger alone*, or *two or more lodgers boarding together*.[6]

Similar wording was used in 1871 and 1881.

These instructions, with the new definition of a family in terms of commensality, were plainly designed to define the household as those persons in exclusive occupation of a room or rooms within a house. One would have expected, however, that a lodger given a household schedule of his or her own would have been treated as the head of a household in the relationship to head column but this was not in fact the case. In the examples supplied to the householders a boarder was shown as part of the household of the main occupier of a house. But in the enumerator's example, while a solitary 'lodger' was treated as a separate household (i.e., was marked off from the rest of the occupants of the house by a single oblique stroke), he or she was still described as a 'lodger' in the column for relationship to the head of the household. In one respect the

---

[6] Author's italics.

solitary lodger was regarded as a separate household and in another as part of a different co-residing group. This plainly caused confusion among householders and enumerators, and subsequently among historians.

The definition of the 'occupier' in terms of the payment of rent could also cause confusion where accommodation came with the job. In the City of London, for example, it is not uncommon to find the first enumerated person in a household living in a bank described as 'messenger' rather than 'head'. Presumably his family lived on the premises rent-free in a caretaker role, the 'occupier' being the banker who employed him. The messenger could not be described as a lodger or boarder since he did not live in the same building as the occupier.

In 1891 an attempt was made to eliminate some of these ambiguities. The definition of the occupier supplied to the enumerator dropped the term 'lodger' altogether: 'As a general rule, the term "occupier" is to be understood to apply *to the resident owner, or to a person who pays rent whether for the whole of a house, or for a tenement consisting of one or more rooms.*'[7]

Similarly, the enumerator was instructed that a household schedule should be left with 'the occupier of a tenement living alone, or for two or more lodgers living together in one tenement'. This appears to have been an attempt to raise the household status of lodgers not boarding with the families from whom they sub-let. The effect was spoilt, however, by the example given to the enumerator. Here the lodger who formed a separate household in 1881, but was still a 'lodger' in relationship to the household head, had now become a 'head' in his own right. On the other hand, two other persons described as 'lodgers' in their relationship to the head of the family had appeared as part of another household. There was no indication as to how these differed from a 'boarder' in another household.

The situation was finally clarified in 1901 when the enumerators were instructed to leave a household schedule, among others:

a) for the head of a family occupying the whole or part of a house. NOTE – A *'family'* is held to include a man, and his wife and children (if any), also any relatives, visitors, servants, and *persons boarding with the family, and residing together under one roof;*

b) for a lodger (with or without family) separately occupying a room or rooms, *and not boarding with any family in the house.*

In the examples supplied to householders and enumerators, the term 'lodger' had disappeared. Every household was made up of a head, his relatives and servants. One household contained a 'boarder'. The lodger boarding alone, or with other lodgers, had finally achieved full household status.[8] This might mean that declining household size in the census might merely reflect a redefinition of what counted as such an entity.

---

[7] Author's italics.

[8] For a study of a local market for lodgings, and the problems of defining 'lodgers' in the census, see J. Emerson, 'The lodging market in a Victorian City: Exeter', *Southern History*, 9 (1987), pp. 103–13.

Definitions of the household used in census studies

The nineteenth-century census authorities plainly had a clear picture of what they thought a household ought to look like. It was made up of a husband and wife, their relations by birth or marriage, servants and apprentices. The family had exclusive possession of a house or apartment which they owned or rented from a landlord. Experience showed, of course, that this ideal was often not achieved in the working-class areas of towns and cities, where individuals and families sub-let from other households. An attempt was made to distinguish between the boarder who shared a common table with the household of which he or she was a member, and the lodger or group of lodgers who ate separately and constituted a separate household. But the attachment to the Victorian ideal of the family was strong enough to ensure that the latter remained 'lodgers' in relationship to the head of the 'family' until at least 1891.

Anyone who has compared the work of differing enumerators is conscious that they interpreted these instructions differently. Some turned every lodger into a separate household, others always combined them with other households, while still others followed their own idiosyncratic conventions. The census authorities were themselves aware of these problems and believed that many lodgers who were treated as members of other households by the enumerators lived in quite separate social groups.[9] Similar problems arose with regard to those persons described as 'visitors'. When did a distant relative or friend staying with a family cease to be on a visit and become a boarder or lodger? In cases where short stays in houses belonging to others were institutionalised, as in seaside resorts, a large proportion of the population might fall into this ambiguous category.

These considerations should remind users of the census returns that they are only 'snap shots' of households on one night every 10 years. They do not necessarily reveal the 'normal' patterns of family life in individual cases. In 1851, for example, the members of Charles Dickens's household could be found scattered in three places. Charles Dickens was a 'visitor', along with two of his brothers, at a house in Bloomsbury, while his wife was a 'lodger', in the company of her sister, at a lodging house in Great Malvern. The rest of the author's household were recorded at the family home in Devonshire Terrace, Marylebone.[10] The household arrangements found in the census returns might best be conceived in terms of frozen frames of cinefilm rather than as static structures.

Faced with these problems historians have attempted to establish conventions for defining the household, or 'co-residing group', in the census. According to one set of conventions, in all nineteenth-century censuses from 1851 onwards the household should be defined as comprising all the names listed in an enumerator's book from one entry 'head' in the 'relation to head of family' column to the last name preceding the next entry 'head'. In the case of the 1841 census returns, where there is no information on the relationship to the head of the family, one has to take all those persons falling between the conventional strokes marking the beginning and end

---

[9] *1891 Preliminary Census Report*, p. v.
[10] Lumas, *Making Use of the Census*, p. 59.

of households as the co-residing group. But given the problems associated with the use of these marks, such 'co-residing groups' should be treated with great caution.

One important exception which has normally been made to this rule are occasional cases where other terms are used instead of, and as a practical equivalent to, 'head'. In some of these cases the head was absent from home on census night but the enumerator recorded relationships by reference to him or her, with the result that the first entry for the household in the relationship to head column is 'wife', 'servant', 'wife, head absent', and so on. In other cases the head was at home but was identified by some term other than 'head'. Widows, for example, are occasionally recorded as 'widow' rather than as head. In such instances historians have applied the following rules. Where in 1851 a long or short line, and in other censuses a single or oblique stroke or a '1', is followed by an entry which suggests that the person first named is a head equivalent, or a head under another title, a new household has been counted. This exception has not been applied, however, in cases where this entry could reasonably refer to a relationship to the head of the previous household. In particular the term 'lodger' is never taken as a possible head equivalent, and historians have entered all lodgers as part of the previous household. The only exception to this is where 'lodger' follows the usual markers for a new house, and this is verified by the total number of houses at the bottom of the page or by a new house address.

A second exception to the general rule relating to households stated above is where two successive individuals are both listed as 'head', or head equivalent, but no line or oblique stroke is drawn between them and there is no other indication of a new 'census family' (both, for example, have the same schedule number). Both are included in the same co-residing group, it being assumed that they share the headship.[11]

Given the evident confusion on the part of enumerators and householders, these general conventions are reasonable. It should be remembered, however, that these conventions do not remove the deficiencies in the data; they only allow one to treat them in the same manner. Many of the lodgers in the censuses from 1861 onwards, who under these conventions are treated as members of other households, were quite correctly shown by the enumerators as making up separate social entities. By indicating (with short lines or single strokes) that lodgers formed separate households, while retaining the former designation in the relation to head column, enumerators were being consistent within the rules set down. The instructions given also changed over time and reinforced the separate household status of lodgers boarding on their own or with other lodgers. By defining the household in terms of the people grouped under the term 'head' the above conventions may tend to enlarge the average size of the household in the period 1861–81 in comparison with other censuses.

It is unfortunate, but perhaps understandable, that historians established such conventions on the basis of the study of only two censuses (those of 1851 and 1861), and in apparent ignorance

---

[11] Anderson, 'Standard tabulation procedures for the census enumerators' books 1851–1891', pp. 136–7.

of some of the instructions given to the householders and enumerators. It should also be noted that the classic historical studies of Victorian household structure are based on the manuscript enumerators' books for 1851.[12] Since these were compiled before the full elaboration of the concept of commensality in the mid-Victorian censuses, this may well affect the extent to which the findings of such studies can be compared with those based on later returns.

Such problems are not overcome by using an alternative set of conventions in which one simply ignores boarders, lodgers and visitors when analysing census data.[13] Since changing census instructions would tend to alter the characteristics of people who fell into such categories, one would not be excluding the same population at each census. A person or family who would be described as 'lodgers' in one census might be raised to the status of separate households at the next. This procedure may certainly improve consistency within the returns of one census but would not necessarily do the same between differing censuses.

In most cases, and especially in rural areas, there are few difficulties as to what constitutes a census household. In cities, where there are problems with sub-letting and the proliferation of boarders and lodgers, the standard conventions noted above provide a rough and ready means of coping with the data. The larger the number of enumerators' books covered, the greater the likelihood that the distortions introduced by such conventions will be evened out and comparisons between differing census populations facilitated. In comparing the work of individual enumerators, however, one must always be conscious of their individual idiosyncrasies. Some of these difficulties may be overcome by noting the schedule numbers in the enumerators' returns. Each household schedule filled out was given a different number which from 1851 onwards ran consecutively in the first column of the enumerators' books (see the examples in Appendix 3). These can be used to reconstruct how individual enumerators interpreted their instructions. In cases where there are a large number of lodgers or visitors in the population the results of any study which uses the above conventions should be treated with caution. This is especially true of comparisons across censuses for which the instructions regarding households differed.

---

[12] M. Anderson, *Family Structure in Nineteenth Century Lancashire* (London, 1971); A. Armstrong, *Stability and Change in an English Country Town: a Social Study of York 1801–51* (London, 1974).

[13] This appears to be the convention implicit in P. Laslett and R. Wall, *The Household and Family in Past Time* (London, 1974), pp. 26–7, 34–6, 86–8; and in J. Knodel, 'An exercise on household composition for use in courses in historical demography', *Local Population Studies*, 23 (1979), pp. 10–23.

7 Information relating to individuals

Although the falsification of census returns was a criminal offence, it is plain that the information collected on individuals was not always completely accurate. Certain types of information, such as name, are usually reliable but others (age for example) are only a rough guide to nineteenth-century reality. This was not usually the result of deliberate evasion but reflects the general ignorance of the precise information required, and prevailing levels of literacy. In an age when form-filling and document-keeping by the masses was unknown, many people did not know their precise date or place of birth, and merely hazarded a guess. Although modern researchers may be able to compare at one point in time the information supplied by householders at different censuses, such *aides-mémoire* were not available to the Victorians themselves. In many cases the household schedules had to be filled out by the enumerators or neighbours, and these may have misunderstood accents, or made hasty and unwarranted assumptions. Illiterate householders and untrained enumerators may also have been confused as to the type of information required. In some cases unconventional marital relationships, socially unacceptable physical and mental disabilities, or shameful occupations, may have been ignored or glossed over.

Although census data *en masse* give a reliable approximation to the features of nineteenth-century society, one should not expect that all the data on individuals are strictly accurate, or consistent over time. This is undoubtedly more of a problem for those tracing individuals than for other students of the period, and can sometimes be overcome by tracing the former through more than one census. Those who deal in aggregate data can often take solace in the fact that any discrepancies are usually within reasonable bounds, and may cancel each other out. The information relating to occupations is perhaps the most difficult to interpret, and the data in this column are considered separately in Chapter 8.

Names

Names are probably the least problematic element of the information relating to individuals in the census. In 1841 only the forename was to be given, but in 1851 the enumerator was instructed that the initial of the second Christian name 'may be inserted'. From 1891 onwards the instruction was that this initial 'must be inserted'. If a name was not known, 'n.k.' was to be substituted. For several persons in succession with the same surname, 'do', for 'ditto', was to be used for every surname but the first.[1]

---

[1] See Appendix 7 for references to examples of the enumerators' books.

Differences between names do appear from census to census but are usually not very frequent. They may reflect copying errors made by the enumerator, inverting forename and surname, using one too many 'dittos', leaving out letters, and so on. Equally they may reflect the differing ways in which enumerators heard and interpreted names when interrogating illiterate householders on their doorstep. In this way 'Ann Apling' becomes 'Ann Aplin', 'Ellinor Daniels' becomes 'Ellen Daniel', 'Richard Meirieth' becomes 'Richard Meredith', and so on.[2] One can usually establish that these are one and the same person by the coincidence of other personal details and those of other members of the household.

Cases can occasionally be found where there are confusing differences between the head's surname and that of his or her family: William Simpson has Sarah Lee as his wife, although his children are called Simpson; Henry Steel has Hannah Hall as his wife but his son is called William Hall.[3] A variety of explanations can be put forward for such anomalies but these may have more to do with ambiguities in the relationship to head column than with the names of the individuals concerned.

Relationship to head of family

The information in the relationship to head column is sometimes more difficult to interpret. This reflects nineteenth-century usages that were different from our own, and confusion as to the exact status of individuals in the household. Fortunately, such problems are usually restricted to a discrete number of terms, and can often be spotted with a little care.

In 1841 there was no relationship column in the census schedules. Enumerators were merely told to 'Set down one after the other those who have the same surname, beginning with the heads of the family, and put no others between them'.[4] Certain conventions have been established by social historians in order to assign relationships to the members of 1841 households.[5] These are very rough and ready rules, and great caution should be used in any attempt to compare differing populations from the 1841 census, or to compare these results with later censuses. It is assumed that the first listed person is the head. To allocate persons of the same surname, the following rules are applied:

1) the first listed woman within 15 years of the head's age is assumed to be his wife. Other women, provided that (from consideration of their ages) they are born when the head and wife (where applicable) were aged not below 15 and not over 50, are assumed to be daughters. Any other women are treated as relatives;

---

[2] See also B. Woollings, 'An Orsett census enumerator', *Local Population Studies*, 56 (1996), pp. 57–8.

[3] P. M. Tillot, 'Sources of inaccuracy in the 1851 and 1861 censuses', in Wrigley, *Nineteenth-Century Society*, p. 106.

[4] 1841 and 1851 Census Returns (TNA, HO 107).

[5] W. A. Armstrong, 'Social structure from the early census returns', in *An Introduction to English Historical Demography*, ed. E. A. Wrigley (London, 1966), pp. 229–30.

2) other males bearing the same name are regarded as sons, provided that they too were born when the head and wife were aged not less than 15 and not more than 50. Other males are regarded as relatives.

These conventions become more difficult to apply, of course, where the first person in a household is a woman. Further rules cover the allocation of those not bearing the head's surname. Domestic servants are taken as being all those so described in the occupation column, unless they have the same name as the head (in which case they are taken to be children or relatives), or unless the head of the household is also by occupation described as a servant (whereupon they are regarded as lodgers). All those not covered by the above rules are placed in a residual category of lodgers.

In 1851 a relationship column was introduced into the household schedule. This carried the instruction, 'State whether wife, son, daughter or other relative, visitor or servant'. In 1861 'boarder, etc.' was added to the list, as was 'head' in 1871. The instruction remained the same for the rest of the century, except for the suppression of the 'etc.' after boarder in 1881. At various times certain abbreviations were suggested: 'daur.' for daughter, 'serv.' for servant, 'F.-in-Law' and 'M.-in-Law' for father-in-law and mother-in-law respectively, and so on.[6]

It should be noted that the headship of a household was a social position and did not necessarily reflect biological descent. Thus, in one household an aged widow may be described as head but in another case a son or daughter who has taken over running the affairs of the group might be so designated. Occasionally two men or women sharing a set of rooms might both be put down as joint heads. Sometimes the usual head of the household was absent and this was denoted by the first person in the household being described as a wife, son, servant or some other term.

Nineteenth-century usages for kin relationships were sometimes different from those of today. Relationships by marriage appear to cause particular problems. A brother-in-law or son-in-law could be described as a 'brother' or 'son', while a 'daughter-in-law' might mean a stepdaughter. Similarly, the offspring of married children resident in the household were sometimes called 'son' or 'daughter' rather than grandchild; the relationship has 'slipped', referring to their parents rather than to the head-grandparent. Sometimes the presence of an unmarried daughter of child-bearing age in the household raises the suspicion that the infant 'sons' and 'daughters' of elderly parents might be illegitimate grandchildren.[7] The term 'nurse child' is also ambiguous since it could cover a child sleeping in a house for one night, or a case of adoption.

The confusion between lodger and boarder, and the ambiguities relating to visitors, have already been noted (Chapter 6). Such designations probably have to be accepted at face value but relationship data from enumeration districts with large numbers of boarders, lodgers and visitors, as in the case of coastal resorts, should be treated with caution. On occasion the term 'lodger' could be used in an inexplicable manner. In 1841, for example, Abraham and Ruth Prior appear

[6] See Appendix 7 for references to examples of the enumerators' books.
[7] Woollings, 'An Orsett census enumerator', p. 58.

in the census returns with Abraham at the head of the household. In 1851, however, Ruth is described as head, with Abraham relegated to the end of the household's return as 'lodger'. In 1861 Abraham and Ruth reappear as man and wife, with Abraham as the household head. One wonders what Victorian domestic drama was being played out here![8]

The term 'servant' can cause confusion, especially since it could also appear in the occupational column. Service in the nineteenth century was a legal relationship between master and servant rather than a defined set of tasks. The term 'civil servant' still preserves some of this original meaning. Apprentices, shop workers, domestic servants and living-in agricultural labourers could all be regarded as servants. Since it was the nature of the social relationship that was important, the distinction between a paid employee and the poor country cousin who did housework in return for her keep must have been a fine one. Similarly, the extent to which the relationship 'servant' and the occupational designation 'housekeeper' were used to conceal unconventional, or complicated, marital relationships is difficult to quantify. People with domestic service occupations were also not necessarily servants in the households in which they lived; they could be lodgers and kin who were unemployed, or who went out to work in other houses during the day. The interpretation of occupational data on domestic servants is examined in more detail in the next chapter.

On occasion the meaning of the term 'relationship' could be hopelessly misconstrued, as in the case of the farm labourer living in a shed at the bottom of a farmer's garden who described his relationship to the head of the family as 'friendly'.[9]

Marital status

The 1841 census did not ask for information on marital status but this became a standard feature from 1851 onwards.[10] In that year the householder was instructed to 'Write "Married", "Widower", or "Unmarried", against the names of all Persons except Young Children' in the column headed 'Condition'. The examples supplied to the enumerators showed the use of the abbreviations 'Mar.', 'Widr.' and 'U.' for such marital conditions. In 1861 'Un.' was indicated as the abbreviation for unmarried, while 'W.' for widow was also introduced. In 1871 'Unm.' was substituted for 'Un.'. At the following census the abbreviations were as before, although the column heading now became 'Condition as to marriage'. In 1891 the term 'Single', abbreviated to 'S', was substituted for that of 'Unmarried', and 'Mar.' became 'M'. The abbreviation for 'Widow' now became 'Wid.'.

The information supplied in this column is usually self-explanatory but there may be some cases of doubtful enumeration. According to the 1881 *Census Report* the number of wives in the

---

[8] TNA, HO 107/786, bk. 5, fos. 6–7; TNA, HO 107/1829, fo. 64; TNA, RG 9/1255, fo. 43. The author would like to thank Mrs. Carrie Eldgridge for this information relating to her ancestors.

[9] TNA, RG 9/1783, fo. 35, p. 22.

[10] See Appendix 7 for references to examples of the enumerators' books.

population exceeded the number of husbands by 61,064.[11] The number of 'married' women under the age of 20 years whose husbands were absent is especially high. This might reflect the absence of spouses in the armed forces or merchant marine, or cases where young women were living at home until they and their husbands could afford to set up a home. On the other hand, were such women only engaged? In the not uncommon case of mature married women who are also described as heads of households, is one to assume that their husbands were away from home, that they would have been described as heads even if their husbands had been at home, or that they were separated? Did some women, Roman Catholics perhaps, still regard themselves as married to husbands who were dead? On the other hand, might some separated couples have enumerated themselves as 'Widow' or 'Widower' to hide feelings of shame?

These and similar questions must remain in the realms of speculation, and each case must be considered on its merits. However, it is suggestive that recent work by Garrett, Reid, Schürer and Szreter on anonymised data from the census of 1911 indicates that in that year high levels of married women living without a spouse are associated with high levels of female employment. Thus, in the cotton town of Bolton in 1911 no fewer than one married woman in 12 was living in a household without her spouse. Such women may possibly have been separated from their husbands, and yet able to support themselves and their families on their own wages.[12]

Age recording

The recording of ages is without doubt one of the most problematic features of the manuscript census returns. The instructions regarding age reporting given in 1841 were rather confusing. The householder was told to:

> Write in figures the age of every person, opposite to their names, in one of the columns headed 'Age of Males' or 'Age of Females' according to their sex. For persons aged 15 years and upwards it is sufficient to state within what period of five years their age is, writing down the *lowest* number of that period: thus, for persons aged 15 and under 20, write 15– for 20 and under 25, write 20– for 25 and under 30 write 25– for 30 and under 35 write 30–, and so on up to the greatest age; but the *exact age* may be stated if the person prefers it. For persons under 15, write the number of years; for infants under one year the number of months.[13]

The enumerators were instructed to treat the ages reported in a slightly different manner. The age of every person under 15 was to be given exactly as stated. Those aged 15 or above were to have their ages expressed to the lowest term of five years within which their age fell. Those aged 20 to 24 years, for example, were to be recorded as 20. If no more could be ascertained respecting the age of a person than that they were a child or an adult, the enumerator was to write 'under

[11] *1881 Census Report*, p. 23.

[12] E. Garrett, A. Reid, K. Schürer and S. Szreter, *Changing Family Size in England and Wales: Place, Class and Demography 1891–1911* (Cambridge, 2001), p. 66.

[13] TNA, RG 27/1, p. 58.

20' or 'above 20' according to the circumstances. The ages given were, therefore, only very approximate, and there must have been ample room for confusion.

In 1851 householders were given no general instructions regarding age reporting, although the appropriate column in the household schedule was headed 'Age [last birthday]'. The householder was instructed, however, that for infants under one year, he or she should 'state the Age in *Months*, writing *"Under 1 Month"*, *"1 Month"*, *"2 Months"*, etc.'. The enumerator was instructed to enter 'the number of *years* simply' in the ages column, except in those cases where the age was expressed in months, when 'Mo.' had to be written after the figures. The instructions in subsequent censuses followed this general form.[14] From 1851, therefore, the instructions to the householders and enumerators were fairly clear and straightforward, although one cannot be certain to what extent individuals read these instructions carefully, or could read them at all.

Despite these instructions, the ages reported in the census must be regarded as only rough approximations of fact. In a period before systematic record-keeping many people had only an approximate idea of their date of birth, and in some cases there may have been temptations to give incorrect information. In very general terms one can say that the majority of ages stated will be consistent from census to census. A person aged 40 in the census of 1851 will appear as 50 in 1861. In a sizeable minority of cases, however, there will not be 10 years between the two ages recorded. Most discrepancies will be in the order of one or two years but larger differences are by no means uncommon. The censuses were taken on differing dates each year (see Appendix 1) but the differences were too small to have caused the discrepancies observed. In some cases, of course, such discrepancies will be 'self-righting'; those who describe themselves as 30 at one census and 36 at the next, might describe themselves, 10 years later, as 50.

In the case of Preston, Anderson has calculated that, while 53 per cent of a sample of people reported consistently between the censuses of 1851 and 1861, only four per cent of the ages were 'wrong' by more than two years.[15] Similarly, Tillott found that in the parishes of Hathersage (Derbyshire) and Braithwell (Yorkshire), consistency rates of 61 per cent and 68 per cent respectively were recorded between censuses. On the other hand, five per cent were inconsistent by more than two years.[16] In the case of Colyton in Devon in the four censuses between 1851 and 1881, all households headed by someone with a surname beginning with A or D were traced by the author.[17] Out of 55 observations of the ages of men between censuses, none was more than two years discrepant. In the case of the 57 observations for women, four per cent were more than two years out. Members of the Cambridge Group for the History of Population and Social Structure have studied the age recording of all the inhabitants of Colyton between 1851 and 1861. In the case of males, they discovered that only 51.5 per cent recorded themselves as 10

[14] TNA, HO 45/3579.

[15] M. Anderson, 'The study of family structure', in Wrigley, *Nineteenth-Century Society*, p. 75.

[16] Tillott, 'Sources of inaccuracy', p. 108.

[17] 1851, TNA, HO 107/1862; 1861, TNA, RG 9/1373; 1871, TNA, RG 10/2035–2036; 1881, RG 11/2129.

years older in 1861, but only 6.9 per cent were discrepant by more than two years. In the case of women the equivalent figures were 52.4 per cent and 9.5 per cent.[18]

A similar analysis was undertaken by the author for the parish of Llangefni in Anglesey, where all households headed by someone with a surname beginning with A, D or M were traced over the period 1851–81.[19] Of the 39 observations of the ages of men between two censuses, 10 per cent were discrepant by more than two years. In the case of women, out of 44 observations, only 55 per cent showed a gap of exactly 10 years, and 12 per cent showed discrepancies of more than two years. On the other hand, as a result of an exhaustive cross-checking of census ages with other sources in six Kentish parishes in the censuses of 1851–81, Perkyns has concluded that, of her checkable population, 75.3 per cent of ages were correct and 93.8 per cent had no error greater than one year.[20] The standard of age reporting plainly varied from place to place.

Many age discrepancies may merely reflect clerical error as enumerators filling up their books confused '3' and '8', or multiples of '10'.[21] The inconsistencies in the data also probably reflected the ignorance of many people respecting their exact age, leading them to make a guess. When doing so there appears to have been a tendency for people to round their ages to multiples of 10 and five, to 30, 40, 50, 60, etc., and to a lesser extent to 35, 45, 55, etc. This was at the expense of contiguous years, although there is evidence that there was a greater tendency to round ages down rather than up (it has been suggested that this tendency set in after the age of 20 years).[22] It has also been reported in one study that there appears to be a rather high coincidence between the ages of husband and wife, which may indicate that married couples guessed at an age together.[23] It is important, therefore, to select age bands or cohorts with care when aggregating age data.

Similarly, there appears to be a general tendency to think in terms of age next birthday rather than age last birthday, especially in the case of children. Children of seven years five months became eight, because they were 'in their eighth year'. This is especially serious in the case of children aged under one year, and the numbers recorded as in their first year of life are therefore underestimated. This may be partly explained by the fact that this was how ages often had to be stated for insurance purposes. Alternatively, there may have been a desire not to 'waste' some months of the age, a tendency which may well have been present up to the age of 15 years. The

---

[18] The author would like to thank Jean Robin of the Cambridge Group for supplying him with the results of her research in this area (published as J. Robin, *From Childhood to Middle Age: Cohort Analysis in Colyton, 1851–1891* (Cambridge, 1995)).

[19] 1851, TNA, HO 107/2520; 1861, TNA, RG 9/4362; 1871, TNA, RG 10/5742; 1881, TNA, RG 11/5586.

[20] A. Perkyns, 'Age checkability and accuracy in the censuses of six Kentish parishes 1851–1881', *Local Population Studies*, 50 (1993), p. 33 (reprinted in Mills and Schürer, *Local Communities in the Victorian Census Enumerators' Books*).

[21] Perkyns, 'Age checkability', p. 37.

[22] *1881 Census Report*, p. 17. Further discussion of this tendency to 'age heaping', and statistical measures of it, can be found in the introduction to K. Schürer and D. R. Mills, 'Population and demography', in Mills and Schürer, *Local Communities in the Victorian Census Enumerators' Books*, pp. 74–7.

[23] W. T. R. Pryce, 'The census as a major source for the study of Flintshire society in the nineteenth century', *Journal of the Flintshire Historical Society*, 25 (1973–4), p. 127.

under-enumeration of children under one may also reflect an erroneous impression on the part of some parents that new-born children who had not been christened or named need not be included in the census.[24] The GRO itself calculated that, as late as 1911, the enumeration of children aged less than two years was some 68 per cent short of the number of births recorded between April 1909 and April 1911.[25]

There may have been pressures to falsify some ages. It has been suggested that there was a tendency to raise the age of children in their early teens since, under the Factory Acts, children were not allowed to work until they were 13 years old. Working families may have put down incorrect ages in order to get round restrictions on the employment of their children.[26] It is also suggested that a number of girls aged 10 to 13 increased their ages in order to get into domestic service, but that this tendency rapidly declined after the age of 19.[27] There may, for example, also have been an incentive for young domestic servants to exaggerate their ages in order to gain higher wages.[28] Some of the very elderly may have exaggerated their ages. There may have been a tendency for working-class men and women in their fifties to describe themselves as over 60, as those over that age, if still able-bodied, were entitled to outdoor relief on the Poor Law. If they were inmates of workhouses they also had a number of privileges, such as a better diet. There certainly appears to be an under-enumeration of men and women aged 55 to 59. The figures for the very elderly, especially those over 85, appear to have been grossly inflated.[29]

On the other hand, the *1851 Census Report* suggested that some women depressed their ages after their twenties because that was the age at which women in England usually got married, 'either because they are quite unconscious of the silent lapse of time,– or because their imaginations linger over the hours of that age,– or because they choose, foolishly, to represent themselves as younger than they really were, at the scandalous risk of bringing the statements of the whole of their countrywomen into discredit'.[30] Whether or not this reflected crude sexism, or practical experience, is difficult to determine. However, there does appear to be an over-enumeration of women aged 20–29 in the Victorian censuses, based on comparing the ages given in the censuses and relevant life-tables.[31]

There appears to be a propensity for the wealthier classes to record their ages more consistently but little work has been done on the subject. Class-specific influences were plainly complex. While working-class men in their late fifties may have exaggerated their age, members of the

---

[24] *1881 Census Report*, p. 18; *1891 Census Report*, p. 28; *1901 Census Report*, p. 51; W. A. Armstrong, 'The census enumerators' books: a commentary', in Lawton, *The Census and Social Structure*, p. 35.

[25] Garrett, Reid, Schürer and Szreter, *Changing Family Size in England and Wales*, p. 68. See also R. Lee and D. Lam, 'Age distribution adjustments for English censuses, 1821–1931', *Population Studies*, 37 (1983), pp. 445–64.

[26] For the opposition to the Factory Acts, see, for example, U. R. Q. Henriques, *The Early Factory Acts and their Enforcement* (London, 1971), pp. 12–15.

[27] *1881 Census Report*, p. 17; *1891 Census Report*, p. 28; *1901 Census Report*, p. 67.

[28] *1901 Census Report*, p. 51.

[29] Lee and Lam, 'Age distribution adjustments for English censuses'.

[30] *1851 Census Report: Population Tables, II* (PP 1852–3 LXXXVIII Pt. 1 [1691-I.], pp. xxiv–xxv).

[31] Lee and Lam, 'Age distribution adjustments for English censuses'.

middle classes may have reduced theirs to ward off the threat of retirement.[32] It has also been proposed that small, rural parishes may have better age recording than urban areas with a more mobile population. In such rural areas the closeness of the community may have made the mis-statement of ages more difficult, although this is hardly born out in the case of Llangefni mentioned above.[33]

The *Census Reports* after 1881 comment on the decreasing tendency of young girls to exaggerate their ages. The age reporting among the very young and the elderly is also said to have improved, but this was apparently not the case with regard to the tendency for women to record themselves as in their early twenties. This improvement may reflect the spread of compulsory education in the period after the 1870 Education Act.[34]

These observations raise the question of how far people believed that the census was confidential. Since enumerators were often local government officers, school attendance officers or teachers, it would not be unusual if some working-class households were cautious about giving what might be regarded as awkward information. Servants may have lied to their employers if they were claiming to be older than they really were.[35] Many of these patterns noted in the age data are of an aggregate nature – they are what can be observed in the published age tables after balancing out many opposing tendencies. There is no guarantee, of course, that these patterns will be manifested in every population, and certainly not in the case of every individual. Those wishing to undertake record linkage also need to treat the ages given in the census as approximations, and should look at a range of years for the births in registration records. But if a man or woman is said to be 50 in the 1851 census, one can be reasonably sure that they were born in the period 1799–1803.

Sex

The recording of the sex of the population was intimately bound up with age recording. This may reflect the desire of the officers of the GRO to use the data for the construction of separate life-tables for men and women. The practice creates some minor problems for the interpretation of the data supplied.

In 1841 there was no separate column for sex on the householders' returns. Instead there were two columns for age, one for males and one for females. This layout was repeated in the

---

[32] D. Thomson, 'Age reporting by the elderly and the nineteenth century census', *Local Population Studies*, 25 (1980), p. 21 (reprinted in Mills and Schürer, *Local Communities in the Victorian Census Enumerators' Books*).

[33] Thomson, 'Age reporting by the elderly', p. 23.

[34] *1901 Census Report*, pp. 51–8.

[35] *1881 Census Report*, p. 18; *1891 Census Report*, p. 28. On the general problems of obtaining information from working-class households in cities, see the testimony of Charles James White, a census enumerator in Mile End in 1881, before the 1890 Treasury Committee on the Census (*1890 Report of the Treasury Committee on the Census* (QQ 1850–9)).

enumerators' returns. From 1851 onwards the household schedules contained a column for sex in which 'F' for female and 'M' for male were to be inserted. There was then a separate age column. The enumerators' books, however, retained the double age column. The enumerators had to combine two pieces of information, on sex and age, from the household schedules when filling in their returns.[36] Occasionally the enumerators made a slip and inserted the age in the wrong column. These problems can usually be detected by subsequent emendations made by the census clerks, or by checking the name column. The *1891 Census Report* noted that these slips were not random. Each enumerator had a tendency to make errors in the same column. The majority making errors tended to put the ages of males in the column for women.[37] This probably reflects the manner in which enumerators worked from left to right when filling in their books. The number of cases involved, however, is very small.

Birthplace data

The information relating to birthplaces in the census is of considerable importance to all students of nineteenth-century society but is essential for the historian of population migration, and to those making record linkages with parish registers. Despite its importance, comparatively little work has been done on the accuracy of this information, especially since there is little against which to check it. This is somewhat disturbing since what research has been done indicates that the census is not always a perfect source.

The quality of the birthplace data in the 1841 census is far from satisfactory. The household schedule contained two columns for this information headed 'Whether born in the same county' and 'Whether born in Scotland, Ireland, or Foreign Parts'. Householders were instructed to write 'yes' or 'no' in the first column. In the second column they were to write 'Scotland', 'Ireland' or 'Foreigner'. The latter designation only referred to those born outside the UK who were not British subjects. Those born abroad who were British subjects were to be entered in the first column with the word 'no'. The number of British subjects born outside the UK but resident there in 1841 cannot, therefore, be calculated. The enumerators were instructed to abbreviate these entries when copying them into their enumeration books, using 'Y', 'N', 'S', 'I' and 'F' respectively.[38]

In 1851 more informative answers were required. In the case of those born in England, householders were to indicate first the county, and then the town or parish of birth. This order was to be followed in all subsequent Victorian censuses. In the case of those born in Scotland, Ireland, the British Colonies, the East Indies or Foreign Parts, the country of birth was to be stated. The term 'British Subject' was to be added to the latter where appropriate. Interestingly,

---

[36] See Appendix 7 for references to examples of the household schedules and enumerators' books.

[37] *1891 Census Report*, p. 25.

[38] Some care needs to be given in distinguishing 'I' and 'S' which can often be confusing in Victorians hands. See Appendix 7 for references to examples of the household schedules and enumerators' books.

Wales was not mentioned in the instructions on this matter until 1891, when the principality was treated in the same manner as England. Presumably the Welsh had simply been overlooked, and this may affect the form of some entries. Some other minor changes were introduced in the course of the century. In 1861 a distinction was to be made between 'British Subject' and 'Naturalised British Subject'. In 1871 those born in Scotland, Ireland, the British Colonies or the East Indies were to state the country or colony of birth; and those born in Foreign Parts the particular state or country. The 1901 census broke the population down into four groups in the following manner:

State the Birthplace of each person
1   If in England and Wales, the County and Town, or Parish.
2   If in Scotland or Ireland, the name of the County.
3   If in a British Colony or Dependency, the name of the Colony or Dependency.
4   If in a Foreign Country, the name of the Country, and whether the person be a 'British Subject', a 'Naturalised British Subject', or a 'Foreign Subject' specifying nationality such as 'French', 'German', &c.

The increased specificity of the returns relating to those born abroad may reflect both increasing concern over the loyalty of foreign nationals in any approaching European war and the growing popular animosity towards Jewish immigrants that led to the restrictions placed on immigration in the 1905 Aliens Act.[39]

One may have doubts as to the extent to which householders understood the instructions with regard to those born outside the UK but those relating to people born in England, Scotland and Ireland appear fairly straightforward. It may be something of a surprise, therefore, to discover that the chief clerk of the GRO in 1910 claimed that:

the Birthplace Tables were probably the most inaccurate of any of the Census Tables but feared they could not be dispensed with as some people seemed to attach considerable importance to the figures. Not only did a great many people not know in which county they were born but a place which was now a town might easily have been a small village at the time of the birth of persons aged 20 years and upwards who were enumerated in other towns.[40]

The chief clerk may have been exaggerating the deficiencies of the returns but they must certainly not be regarded as 100 per cent accurate.

In the case of mid-nineteenth-century Preston, Anderson has shown that, of the 475 persons he traced in two successive censuses, a minimum of 14 per cent had a discrepancy in birthplace between the two years. Some of these were not of great importance but in half of the cases migrants into Preston became non-migrants and vice versa.[41] If one looks at the samples from

---

[39] B. Gainer, *The Alien Invasion: the Origins of the Aliens Act of 1905* (London, 1972).
[40] TNA, RG 19/48B, p. 69.
[41] Anderson, 'The study of family structure', p. 75.

Colyton and Llangefni mentioned in a previous section, similar problems arise. In the former case, out of 112 observations across censuses, there were 10 discrepancies. In the case of Llangefni there were 23 discrepancies out of 83 observations. Similar work on the birthplaces of household heads in Colyton in 1851 undertaken by the Cambridge Group revealed that 15.7 per cent of male heads changed their place of birth, at one or more censuses, between 1851 and 1881.[42] The equivalent figure for female heads was six per cent. More reassuringly, a comparison of census birthplaces with baptism records in six Kentish parishes by Perkyns for the censuses of 1851–81 revealed an error level of only four per cent. However, her work indicated variations between adjacent areas, with one of her parishes having error rates twice that of another. Presumably the abilities and conscientiousness of enumerators were crucial here. She also pointed to problems with particular groups of household members, especially servants, lodgers and visitors.[43] A study by Razzell indicated that levels of discrepancies may have been higher in urban than in rural areas. In Bethnal Green, between 1851 and 1861, 75 double entries out of 440 traced showed such discrepancies – a rate of 17 per cent.[44]

As Anderson points out, many of these discrepancies are minor and easily explained. Variations in the spelling of place-names were common, especially in Wales and Cornwall. Enumerators unfamiliar with the local accent, or with the pronunciation of a place-name, might note the latter phonetically, as they heard it on the doorstep. Some birthplaces, for example, lack the first letter because of a dropped 'h'. Long Welsh place-names can cause particular problems if they were truncated. A birthplace given as 'Llanfair', for example, might refer to Llanfair Dyffryn Clwyd or Llanfair Talhaearn; 'Llanrhaeadr' could be intended for Llanrhaeadr-yng-Nghinmeirch or Llanrhaeadr-ym-Mochnant. One must also be careful not to read 'N.K.' (not known) for 'U.K.'. Sometimes the change reflects greater or lesser specificity; 'Colyton' in one census becomes the tithing of 'Colyford' within the parish of Colyton in the next.[45] But in a minority of cases the parish of birth changes. In Colyton and Llangefni these changes mostly reflected the substitution of the name of neighbouring parishes for the original place of birth, and were invariably within the same county. Sloppy clerical work by enumerators, especially when using 'dittos', may account for many apparent birthplace changes.[46] Those undertaking record linkage might be advised, therefore, to check the birthplaces of their population in more than one census before going to local parish records.

Occasionally the grasp of British geography shown by householders and enumerators was not strong. Entries such as 'Kendal, Lancashire' and 'Penrith, Lancashire', and the placing of Birmingham freely in a number of Midland counties, testify to these problems. However, as has

---

[42] Information supplied by Jean Robin of the Cambridge Group for the History of Population and Social Structure.

[43] A. Perkyns, 'Birthplace accuracy in the censuses of six Kentish parishes 1851–81', *Local Population Studies*, 47 (1991), pp. 44–5 (reprinted in Mills and Schürer, *Local Communities in the Victorian Census Enumerators' Books*).

[44] P. E. Razzell, 'The evaluation of baptism as a form of birth registration through cross-matching census and parish register data: a study in methodology', *Population Studies*, 26 (1972), p. 123.

[45] In the case of the Cambridge Group's calculations, the substitution of Colyton and Colyford has not been counted as a change of birthplace.

[46] Perkyns, 'Birthplace accuracy', p. 46.

been noted before, the nineteenth century was a period of great reorganisation in local government, and some changes in the county of birth may reflect boundary changes.

There was also a tendency to record the place of residence, or the earliest one which could be remembered, as the place of birth. The latter may, of course, have changed their names in the intervening years. In institutions such as workhouses there appears to be a propensity on the part of some returning officers to give the location of the institution as the place of birth. In the case of extremely ill people in hospitals, or of the senile elderly in workhouses, such practices are understandable. On the other hand, Wrigley has calculated that in 1851 between 135 and 150 individuals in Colyton were inaccurately claiming Colyton birth, at a time when the total of those stated as being born outside the parish was only 1,032. He has also noted the tendency of recent migrants to change their place of birth to Colyton.[47] This pattern may possibly have had something to do with the workings of the Poor Law. In order to obtain poor relief in one's place of residence it was necessary to prove 'settlement' in the parish. One did so through a combination of claiming birth there, or through living in the parish for a set period. Although the latter gave the poor the right not to be 'removed' to their place of birth, claiming one's place of residence as one's birthplace may have been seen as extra insurance.[48] This tends to reduce the overall level of migration shown in the census, and should be borne in mind by historians when discussing population movements in this period.

It must also be remembered that the census only indicates the place of birth and the place of residence on census night. It does not indicate all movements between these dates. A person recorded as having been born in their place of residence may have travelled round the world between the date of their birth and census night. Such movements can sometimes be detected by the birthplaces of children. It is essential to understand that the census data merely provide a picture of the final results of migration and not a full record of the migration itself.

The exact status of those born abroad is sometimes difficult to determine. It was generally believed in the GRO that people did not understand the instructions relating to naturalisation.[49] The number of foreigners by both birth and nationality may be inflated by the omission of 'British Subject' or 'Naturalised British Subject'. On the other hand, it was suggested that some foreigners, especially refugees, may have falsified their returns by claiming British birth or nationality in order to avoid further persecution. There are instances of individuals who added 'Naturalised British Subject' to their status between censuses without any evidence of a successful application for naturalisation in the Home Office records or certificate of naturalisation in TNA record series HO 334. Certainly the GRO was continually pestered by foreign embassies to supply the names and addresses of their nationals resident in the UK. But the GRO always

[47] E. A. Wrigley, 'Baptism coverage in early nineteenth-century England: the Colyton area', *Population Studies*, 29 (1975), pp. 299–306.

[48] T. MacKay, *A History of the English Poor Law, Vol. III* (London, 1904), pp. 341–66; D. H. Morgan, *Harvesters and Harvesting 1840–1900* (London, 1982), pp. 199–200; K. D. M. Snell, *Annals of the Labouring Poor: Social Change and Agrarian England 1600–1900* (Cambridge, 1985), pp. 71–84.

[49] *1891 Census Report*, p. 64.

refused such requests, and generally thought that this problem was not very serious.[50] Enumerators may have been totally mystified by the accents of Jewish immigrants, or by foreign nomenclature. This might explain the entry of 'Warsaw in Guernsey' found in the returns for Exeter in 1851. The individual probably told the enumerator that he had been born in 'Warsaw Gubernia', the latter term being well known to Yiddish speakers as a governmental district. This would have meant very little to the English enumerator, who may have plumped for the nearest approximation that made sense to him.[51]

For an example of the sort of information on immigrants that one can obtain from the census returns, see Chapter 12.

Medical disabilities

Despite the importance that the GRO placed upon the collection of information relating to medical disabilities, there are indications that the results obtained were untrustworthy. The reasons for this inaccuracy are interesting in themselves but also provide examples, writ large, of problems found elsewhere in the census data.

The first questions about medical disabilities were introduced in the 1851 census. Householders were asked to state if members of their household were deaf and dumb, or blind. The same question was asked in 1861 but 'from birth' had to be added if the affliction was congenital. In 1871 householders were also to indicate if members of the household were 'imbeciles, idiots or lunatics'. The term 'from birth' was also to be added in appropriate cases. The examples of how to fill out the form muddied the waters, however, by containing 'Blind from Small-pox' as an entry in the appropriate column. The 1881 instructions were the same as in 1871 but 'Blind from Small-pox' was removed from the example. The instructions for 1891 and 1901 were similar to those for 1881, although 'from childhood' was substituted for 'from birth', and 'feeble-minded' for 'idiot'. Householders were also warned not to use vague terms such as 'afflicted' or 'infirm'.[52]

Although the census authorities were fairly sanguine about the results in 1851, they appear to have become increasingly aware of the deficiencies as the century drew to a close. By the 1880s they no longer defended the statistics produced as accurate but simply argued that, since the level of inaccuracy was probably constant across the country, the returns could be used for comparative purposes.[53] The main problem was that parents, or other family members, were unwilling to admit that their children or relatives had medical disabilities. In the case of very young children, parents may have been unaware of any medical problems. Even as they grew older it may have been difficult for parents to admit to themselves, never mind to the census

---

[50] TNA, RG 29/9, pp. 72, 104; *1891 Census Report*, p. 66.

[51] B. Susser, *The Decennial Census: Studies in Anglo-Jewish History, No. 1* <http://www.eclipse.co.uk/exeshul/susser/southwestcensus.htm> (30 Sept. 2004).

[52] See Appendix 7 for references to examples of the household schedules.

[53] *1881 Census Report*, p. 69.

authorities, that their children were mentally or physically disabled. After the age of 15 such reluctance may have declined. In 1881 the census authorities obtained from the managers of a large asylum the addresses of the families of those persons admitted as 'idiots' in the year commencing with the day of the census. They discovered that in half the cases of those aged 5 to 14 years, no mention was made in census schedules as to the existence of any mental incapacity.[54] When 'feeble-minded' was substituted for 'idiot' in 1901, the number of persons recorded as having a mental disability rose markedly. This was put down to the fact that the former term was much less derogatory than the latter.[55] The substitution of terms makes it extremely difficult to make any comparisons between 1901 and previous censuses.

The other general problem with the returns was confusion over the exact nature of the data required. Householders, many illiterate, were being asked to give information about medical disabilities without any precise definitions of the terms employed. In the case of blindness, no indication was given as to whether a person had to be totally blind to be included, or whether a partial lack of sight could be enumerated. For practical purposes most people probably regarded someone as blind if they were unable to direct their path by means of sight. Popularly the term 'born blind' appears to have included those who had gone blind at a very early age as well as those blind at birth. Similarly, the census asked for information on those who were deaf and dumb, but people put down both relatives who were deaf and those who could not speak but retained the faculty of hearing.[56]

The exact definitions of terms such as 'lunatic', 'imbecile', 'idiot' and 'feeble-minded' are plainly extremely problematic. According to the *1881 Census Report*:

> No accurate line of demarcation can be drawn between the several conditions indicated by these terms. Speaking generally, however, the term idiot is applied in popular usage simply to those who suffer from congenital mental deficiency, and the term imbecile to persons who have fallen in later life into a state of chronic dementia. But it is certain that neither this nor any other definite distinction between the terms was rigorously observed in the schedules, and consequently no attempt has been made by us to separate imbeciles from idiots. The term lunatic also is used with some vagueness, and probably some persons suffering from congenital idiocy, and many more suffering from dementia, were returned under this name.[57]

One cannot be certain, therefore, to what extent the usage of these terms corresponded to the later distinctions made between mental illness and mental disability. Or did people adhere to the earlier definition of a lunatic as a person who had lucid periods, while an idiot did not? Within the field of mental disabilities, early-twentieth-century medical usage was that the term 'idiot' indicated someone who was incapable of attending to his or her own personal needs. An imbecile could perform some simple functions of self-help, while having only a

[54] *1881 Census Report*, pp. 68–9.
[55] *1901 Census Report*, pp. 155–6.
[56] *1861 Census Report*, pp. 47, 55; *1891 Census Report*, p. 70; *1901 Census Report*, p. 153.
[57] *1881 Census Report*, p. 66.

limited grasp of ideas. How far these definitions would have been popularly used in the nineteenth century is difficult to determine. The use of the term 'feeble-minded' in 1901 produced further complications and appears to have led to a greater willingness to record senile dementia among the elderly.

The degree of confusion in filling in this column is made plain by the insertion of information regarding afflictions other than those required. In one area of Wales, for example, the following entries were recorded: 'invalid for eight years', 'rheumatic cripple', 'unhealthy from birth', 'not well', 'helpless', 'infirmity', 'pleurisy', 'illness entire', 'tubercular' and 'cripple from birth-one leg'.[58] In at least one case, in North Ormesby in 1891, all the patients in a cottage hospital were listed with their occupations and ailments. They were mostly workers from the local iron works suffering from fractures and burns.[59] There is even the unfortunate case of the Austrian mate of the good ship *Guiseppe Guippa*, in Cardiff harbour in 1871, who was described as a 'eunuch' in the infirmities column.[60] But there is no guarantee that such states were recorded consistently. Confusion may also be caused by the use made of this column by the census clerks for ticking off birthplaces as they went through the books.

The indications are, therefore, that the information relating to medical disabilities is very untrustworthy. Aggregate analyses based on this data may have some uses for comparative purposes but the results cannot be used to estimate the overall extent, or relative importance, of the various medical disabilities suffered by Victorians.

Language spoken in Wales, Monmouthshire and the Isle of Man

In Chapter 2 the special arrangements for enumerating the Welsh-speaking population in Wales and Monmouthshire were briefly described. Household schedules in Welsh were produced from 1841 onwards. Until 1891 the enumeration books used and the questions asked in the principality were the same as those in England. In that year a new question on the language spoken was introduced but was confined solely to Wales and Monmouthshire. The household schedules (both in English and Welsh) and enumeration books used there in 1891 and 1901 have an extra column for this information as compared to those used in England. The number of Welsh speakers who were living in England cannot, therefore, be calculated. In the column in their schedules headed 'Language Spoken' householders were to put 'English' if they only spoke English, 'Welsh' if they only spoke Welsh, and 'Both' if they spoke Welsh and English.[61] In 1901, however, returns were not to be made for children under three years of age.

---

[58] A. A. Benjamin, 'Human afflictions: a study of the North Ceredigion census returns, 1851–1871', *Ceredigion*, 10 (1985), pp. 155–6.

[59] TNA, RG 12/4017, fo. 135.

[60] TNA, RG 10/5370, fo. 24.

[61] For a general introduction to the Welsh-language enquiry in the 1891 census, see G. H. Jenkins, 'The historical background to the 1891 census', in G. Parry and M. A. Williams, *The Welsh Language and the 1891 Census* (Cardiff, 1999), pp. 1–30.

A further minor complication was that the administration of the census was based on registration districts rather than on the ancient counties or contemporary sanitary districts. Some Welsh-speaking communities of the Ceiriog valley in South Denbighshire, for example, as well as areas of Radnorshire and Montgomeryshire, were administered as parts of English registration districts. As such they did not receive schedules with the Welsh language question.[62]

The results obtained by means of these questions do not appear to have been completely trustworthy. Since there was no standard laid down as to the degree of proficiency in speaking English that was required, people in certain districts believed that if they spoke Welsh preferentially or habitually, and only spoke English occasionally or poorly, they were justified in returning themselves as speaking Welsh only. It was noted that children in schools which taught English were put down as being able to speak Welsh only, as were infants of only a few months, or even days, old. The GRO hinted that this may have been due to the effects of Welsh nationalism but the usual confusion on the part of householders as to the exact information required was probably a more potent source of error.[63] In 1901 no language returns were received on 2,757 persons. By 1911 the numbers of incomplete returns had jumped considerably to 58,517. The *Census Report* of that year suggested that in 1901 the apparent deficiencies were small because local enumerators had 'adjusted' their returns, putting down everyone in a household as speaking the same language as the household head. This practice ceased in 1911 when the enumeration procedures were tightened up.[64]

The 1901 exclusion of children aged under three years may have improved the returns to some extent but they must still be handled with some caution. They can be used to obtain the total number of persons who could speak Welsh, with or without English, by combining those who were returned as speaking only Welsh with those who were bilingual. One is less justified in using them to calculate the number who could not speak English in some form or other.

In both censuses some people indicated that they spoke languages other than Welsh or English. The appropriate column in the household schedule was headed 'Language Spoken', and although it was plainly intended to relate to the Welsh-speaking question, this could be interpreted in the broader sense. In 1891, 3,076 persons in the Welsh registration division were recorded in the published tables as speaking languages other than Welsh or English, or 1.7 per 1,000 population. In 1901 the figure was 1.9 per 1,000, reaching 3.6 per 1,000 in Glamorganshire, presumably because of the presence of the ports of Cardiff and Swansea.[65] But householders were only specifically asked to indicate Welsh- or English-speaking, and many of those speaking other languages will probably have made no returns.

---

[62] W. T. R. Pryce and C. H. Williams, 'Sources and methods in the study of language areas: a case study of Wales', in *Language in Geographic Context*, ed. C. H. Williams (Clevedon, 1988), p. 173.

[63] *1891 Census Report*, pp. 81–2; *Explanatory Letter of the Registrar General of England and Wales Relative to the Census of 1891* (PP 1894 LXIX [Cd.331.]).

[64] Pryce and Williams, 'Sources and methods in the study of language areas', pp. 178–9.

[65] Pryce and Williams, 'Sources and methods in the study of language areas', p. 182.

In 1901 a question on languages spoken was inserted into the census schedules for the Isle of Man. From this the GRO was able to establish the numbers speaking Manx only, English only or both Manx and English.[66]

---

[66] *Census 1901. Islands in the British Seas* (PP 1903 LXXXIV [Cd.1473.], p. 18).

8 Occupations in the censuses

The occupational information recorded in the nineteenth-century censuses is of fundamental importance for reconstructing Victorian society and its economy. In an age before censuses of production, or large sociological investigations, this is the most comprehensive statistical source for the detailed investigation of economic and social structure. There are a considerable number of problems, however, with the occupational returns that need to be considered before the source is utilised in this manner. This is not to disparage the use of such information but merely to urge caution when dealing with certain economic or social groups.

It should be noted that, at least until 1891, householders were not asked to indicate the paid economic activities of the members of their household; they were asked to give their 'Rank, Profession, or Occupation'. This could be taken to imply personal social status, rather than a description of economic activity. The only innovation in 1891 was to drop 'Rank' from the heading. It was only in the twentieth century that the census asked for a separate description of the nature of the business of one's employer, as well as one's own personal occupation.[1]

It is also essential to examine the practices of individual enumerators in order to detect certain biases in their occupational reporting. On occasion the feelings of the enumerators shine through in their returns. In Limehouse in 1871, for example, one enumerator described every prostitute as 'fallen' in the occupational column. The men in the brothels on census night were given such occupations as 'Gentleman (Query)', and 'Jack of all trades (Nothing)'. The enumerator added 'These fallen women very often don't know either the names or ages of those men who slept with them, their ages are therefore only guessed at'.[2] Interestingly, the term 'prostitute' does not appear in the occupational dictionaries used to abstract data in the Census Office. Another euphemism for prostitute, 'unfortunate', seems to have been struck out of the census returns (see Figure 8.1).

In broader terms, all occupations were also social designations reflecting status and perceived social worth. The differing assumptions that individual enumerators made about what constituted an occupation must be taken into consideration when analysing the data. In general terms, the full-time paid work of men creates relatively few problems of interpretation. On the other hand, the recording of seasonal, casual or part-time labour is more problematic. This is especially true of the work of women and children, and in the agricultural sector of the economy. The distinctions

---

[1] Office of Population Censuses and Surveys and General Register Office, Edinburgh, *Guide to Census Reports*, pp. 53–5.
[2] TNA, RG 10/544, fos. 116–18.

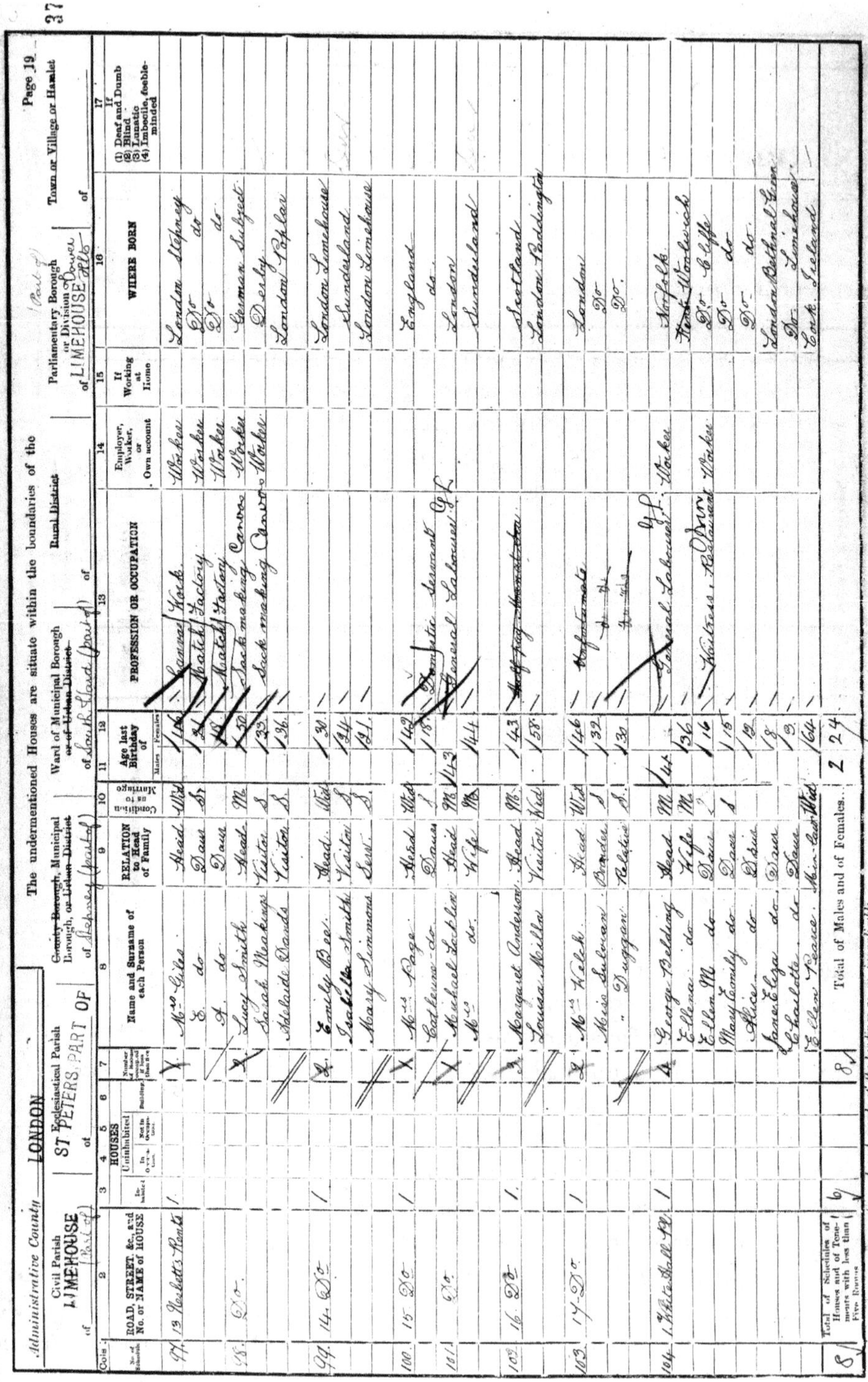

Administrative County LONDON

The undermentioned Houses are situate within the boundaries of the

Page 19

37

Civil Parish of LIMEHOUSE (Part of) | Ecclesiastical Parish of ST PETERS PART OF | ~~County Borough~~, Municipal Borough, ~~or Urban District~~ of Stepney (part of) | Ward of Municipal Borough ~~or of Urban District~~ of South Ward (part of) | Rural District of | Parliamentary Borough or Division of LIMEHOUSE (Part of) Lower Hts | Town or Village or Hamlet of

1 No. of Schedule	2 ROAD, STREET, &c., and No. or NAME of HOUSE	3 Inhabited	4 Uninhabited: In Occupation	5 Uninhabited: Not in Occupation	6 Building	7 Number of Rooms occupied if less than five	8 Name and Surname of each Person	9 RELATION to Head of Family	10 Condition as to Marriage	11 Age last Birthday of Males	12 Age last Birthday of Females	13 PROFESSION OR OCCUPATION	14 Employer, Worker, or Own account	15 If Working at Home	16 WHERE BORN	17 If (1) Deaf and Dumb (2) Blind (3) Lunatic (4) Imbecile, feeble-minded
97	13 Nesbett's Rents	1				1	Mrs Giles	Head	Wid		46	Canvas Work	Worker		London Stepney	
							E. do	Daur	S		21	Match Factory	Worker		Do do	
							A. do	Daur			18	Match Factory	Worker		Do do	
98	Do.					2	Lucy Smith	Head	M		50	Sack making Canvas	Worker		German Subject	
							Sarah Meakings	Visitor	S		33	Sack making Canvas	Worker		Derby	
							Adelaide Dands	Visitor	S		36				London Poplar	
99	14 Do	1				2	Emily Bee	Head	Wid		30				London Limehouse	
							Isabella Smith	Visitor	S		24				Sunderland	
							Mary Simmons	Serv	S		21				London Limehouse	
100	15 Do	1				1	Mrs Page	Head	Wid		42				England	
							Catherine do	Daur	S		18	Domestic Servant			do	
101	Do					1	Michael Locklin	Head	M	43		General Labourer			London	
							Mrs do	Wife	M		44				Sunderland	
102	16 Do	1				3	Margaret Anderson	Head	M		43	~~Half pay Monat[illegible]~~			Scotland	
							Louisa Millo	Visitor	Wid		58				London Paddington	
103	17 Do	1				2	Mrs Welch	Head	Wid		46	~~Unfortunate~~			London	
							Miss Sulivan	Boarder	S		32	~~do do~~			Do	
							" Duggan	Relative	S		30	~~do do~~			Do	
104	1 White Hall Pl	1				4	George Belding	Head	M	41		General Labourer	Worker		Norfolk	
							Ellena do	Wife	M		36				~~Kent~~ Woolwich	
							Ellen M do	Daur	S		16	Waitress, Restaurant	Worker		Do Cliffe	
							Mary Emily do	Daur	S		15				Do do	
							Alice do	Daur			12				Do do	
							Jane Eliza do	Daur			8				London Bethnal Green	
							Charlotte do	Daur			3				Do Limehouse	
							Ellen Pearce	Mo-in-law	Wid		64				Cork Ireland	
8	Total of Schedules of Houses and of Tenements with less than Five Rooms	6				8	Total of Males and of Females			2	24					

NOTE.—Draw your pen through such words of the headings as are inapplicable.

Figure 8.1 'Unfortunates' in Limehouse, 1901 (TNA, RG 13/322, fo. 37, p. 19)

which were drawn between making and dealing, employers and employees, and those economically active and those unemployed and retired, are all obscure. On occasion the occupations given appear somewhat bizarre, such as 'professional wizard' or 'nymph of the pavé', but such idiosyncrasies are, lamentably, rare. On occasion, poor transcription by the enumerator caused unintentional oddities, as in the case of the 'Brickslayers Labourer', the 'Nasal Architect' and the 'Rust Attendant at a Lavatory' in the 1881 census.[3]

However, such problems do not mean that the occupational data in the census returns cannot be used for statistical analysis. All historical sources are imperfect, or at least are not necessarily in the form that historians would like. With care, and based on an understanding of their limitations, census data can be used for historical research in the same manner as any other source.

It is probable, at least in the mid nineteenth century, that the census authorities were not primarily concerned with gathering occupational data for economic analysis. They were most anxious to ensure that occupational terms were accompanied by the materials being worked upon; that people showed whether they were working with cotton, metals, animals, vegetable matter, and so on. This, in turn, probably reflected a preoccupation with the effects of working with such materials on the character and life expectancy of individuals. The medical aspects of the census, as noted in Chapter 1, should always be borne in mind.

The work of men

In general terms the paid employments of men appear to be fairly accurately recorded in the census returns. The evidence of occupations from nineteenth-century street directories largely appears to agree with that found in the census. Some occupations, such as 'bull-dog burner', 'doctor maker', 'keel bulley', 'sad-iron maker', 'tingle maker', and so on, may be difficult to interpret but such cases are generally few in number. In other cases, occupational terms may have more than one meaning, or a differing meaning in differing parts of the country. A clothier in some areas meant a cloth maker, whereas elsewhere it meant a cloth dealer. A bricksetter in some regions meant a bricklayer, while in most areas it meant a man who performed certain operations in brick making. On the other hand, a bank manager might be the manager of a money bank but in mining districts the term could be used for someone who superintended operations at the pithead. An engineer might be a maker or driver of engines, or the term could be a shortened version of civil engineer.[4] Such problems with local usages and ambiguous meanings are probably not too serious, especially when data are aggregated over large areas. In the case of local studies, though, an awareness of such linguistic variations is essential.

---

[3] Lumas, *Making Use of the Census*, p. 52. The 1881 misspellings were provided by Matthew Woollard from the digitised 1881 census held at the UK Data Archive at the University of Essex.

[4] For occupational titles, see C. Waters, *Dictionary of Old Trades, Titles and Occupations* (Newbury, 2002). See also E. Higgs, 'Counting heads and jobs: science as an occupation in the Victorian census', *History of Science*, 23 (1985), p. 340.

A more serious problem was the widespread tendency to omit the branch of employment or material being worked upon. Hence the appearance of undifferentiated terms such as 'labourer', 'weaver', 'spinner', and so on. The Census Office dealt with such vague terms in the process of abstracting data for the published tables by either creating similarly vague headings such as 'Weaver (undefined)' and 'General labourer', or by assuming that such occupations should be placed under the most common industry of the area.[5] Thus, a 'weaver' might become a woollen weaver in Yorkshire, or a cotton weaver in Lancashire. How such rules were applied in areas that combined both woollen and cotton manufacture is more difficult to determine. Such qualifying terms were sometimes added by the census clerks to the occupational descriptions in the enumerators' books.

Multiple and seasonal occupations

In the nineteenth century work patterns were more fluid than those of today, although it would appear that such economic uncertainty is now returning. Even in the cities many people might have differing jobs according to the season of the year, while in the countryside the whole population could be called out to lend a hand at harvest time.[6] The alternation between work on land and sea was the classic pattern for fishing communities in the period. A late example of this more general seasonal pattern of labour can be found in hop picking, traditionally carried out by the twentieth-century Londoners of the East End. People might also have had complementary jobs such as butcher and grazier, or maltster and brewer.

The question of multiple occupations was covered in the householders' instructions from 1851 onwards.[7] In that year a person 'following more than one distinct trade may insert his occupations in the order of their importance'. The term 'distinct trade' became 'distinct business' in 1861, and 'distinct occupations' thereafter. Similarly, 'may' became 'should' in 1861, and 'must' from 1891. The masculine 'his' was dropped from the instructions in 1871. The tendency, therefore, was to strengthen the instruction while making it more generally applicable to the population. If large numbers of people were not prepared to be specific about single occupations, however, we may have some doubts about the exhaustiveness of the recording of multiple occupations. Nevertheless, Woollard has shown that multiple occupations were more common in 1881 than in 1851.[8] In the process of abstracting the data for publication the census clerks were instructed to count only the occupation which appeared 'most important', usually the first one given.[9] These occupations have sometimes been underlined by the clerks.

[5] TNA, RG 27/5, Item 69, p. 4.

[6] See, for example, R. Samuel, 'Comers and goers', in Dyos and Wolff, *The Victorian City: Images and Realities, Vol. I*, pp. 123–60.

[7] See Appendix 7 for references to examples of the household schedules.

[8] M. Woollard, 'The classification of multiple occupational titles in the 1881 census of England and Wales', *Local Population Studies*, 72 (2004), pp. 34–49.

[9] TNA, RG 27/5, Item 69, p. 2.

At the same time it must be remembered that tasks which are usually separated today into distinct occupations might be combined in the nineteenth century. Thus, a shoemaker might make shoes but also sell them; a baker could make and also sell bread; and so on. It is probable that there was a gradual dissociation between making and selling in the period, and this may make the calculation of the numbers solely employed in retailing a difficult task.

There were no specific instructions given with regard to seasonal employments in the nineteenth-century censuses. In the case of women and children, their occupations were to be recorded if they were 'regularly employed from home'. But did this include harvest work, and what of the irregular tasks of the agricultural year, such as throwing stones at the crows, collecting windfalls, and the like? In general the returns give the impression that only the regular, paid employments of men and women on census night were recorded. This is perhaps in keeping with the *de facto* nature of the census as a picture of society on one night every 10 years. Since the census was usually taken in March or April, expressly in order to avoid the movements of the population during summer and the harvest season, part of the seasonal cycle of labour appears to be missing from the returns. It is conceivable that the recording of such marginal occupations improved in 1891 because of the inclusion of questions on employment status. These may possibly have encouraged a greater degree of care on the part of householders.

The work of women

There is a considerable body of evidence that indicates some problems with the recording of the work of women in the censuses.[10] Women often worked for pay on a casual or part-time basis, and this labour often does not appear to have found its way into the returns as an 'occupation'. There are also the inevitable problems of how one treats the work of women in the home. Was such work an 'occupation', or 'merely' housework? This is especially serious when, as was very common in the nineteenth century, the home was a place of production of articles or services for sale, such as lodging houses, inns, farms and shops. Some forms of remunerative activity, such as prostitution, often went unrecorded.[11] The exact economic and social position of domestic servants also causes some problems.[12]

The domestic work of women in the family home was either directly or implicitly excluded from consideration in the census. In the examples provided on how to fill in the returns the occupational column for wives and daughters was left blank unless they had a specific paid occupation. From 1851 to 1881 a specific instruction was given that the 'occupations of women who are regularly

---

[10] For women's work in general, see S. Horrell and J. Humphries, 'Women's labour force participation and the transition to the male-breadwinner economy, 1790–1865', *Economic History Review*, 48 (1995), pp. 89–117; E. Roberts, *Women's Work, 1840–1940* (Oxford, 1988).

[11] See, for example, Emerson, 'The lodging market in a Victorian city: Exeter', p. 108, for the probable enumeration of prostitutes as 'dressmakers'.

[12] For a more general discussion of these problems, see E. Higgs, 'Women, occupations and work in the nineteenth century censuses', *History Workshop Journal*, 23 (1987), pp. 59–80; Roberts, *Women's Work 1840–1940*, pp. 18–19.

employed from home, or at home, in any but domestic duties, [are] to be distinctly recorded'. However, the large number of female kin given occupational designations such as 'housekeeper' indicates that this distinction was not always finely drawn. In 1891 the general instruction was that 'the occupations of women and children, if any, are to be stated as well as those of men'. In 1901 there was no instruction on the work of women at all.[13] The work of women in the home which created services and products for sale was probably indifferently recorded. In 1841 this whole category of work was simply excluded by the instruction that 'The profession &c of wives, or of sons or daughters living with and assisting their parents but not apprenticed or receiving wages, need not be inserted'.[14] The instruction of 1851 regarding women's work at home should have cleared up this problem but there is still some evidence that such productive labour was not regarded as an 'occupation' and went unrecorded.

In the case of farms, however, the female kin of the householder were almost automatically assumed to be helping with agricultural tasks. In the years 1851–81, the householders' examples showed the wife of the farmer described as a 'Farmer's Wife'.[15] In the same years, the householders were told that in the case of farmers, 'Sons or daughters employed at home or on the farm, may be returned – "Farmer's Son", "Farmer's Daughter"'. The instructions relating specifically to women on the farm were removed in 1891. These had apparently caused confusion among some enumerators who described women as 'butcher's daughter', 'retired paper hanger's daughter', 'cotton spinner wife', and so on. The question arises as to whether these designations represent economically remunerative work, kin relationships or multiple occupations (cotton spinner *and* wife?). There is even some evidence that the returns of women with permanent paid jobs in factories could be treated in the same manner or left blank. Could their domestic duties be seen as their proper occupation, overriding outside work? In general, however, the recording of women factory workers appears to be reliable.[16]

These considerations should be borne in mind when studying the employment of domestic servants, the largest category of employment for women in the period. In Rochdale in 1871 only one-third of the women described as being in servant occupations in the occupational column of the census were also described as servant in relationship to the head of the household. The majority of the remainder lived in the homes of their relatives. Many may have been day-servants or unemployed domestics living at home while they sought work, but large numbers of 'housekeepers' and 'nurses' were probably performing 'domestic duties' at home.[17] Anderson

---

[13] See Appendix 7 for references to examples of the household schedules and enumerators' books.

[14] TNA, RG 27/1, p. 58.

[15] For the importance of the work of farmers' wives, see N. Verdon, '"… a subject deserving the highest praise": wives and the farm economy in England, *c*.1700–1850', *Agricultural History Review*, 51 (2003), pp. 23–9.

[16] M. Anderson, 'What can the mid-Victorian censuses tell us about variations in married women's employment?', *Local Population Studies*, 62 (1999), pp. 9–30.

[17] For a more general discussion of the ambiguities relating to domestic service, see E. Higgs, 'The tabulation of occupations in the nineteenth-century census, with special reference to domestic servants', *Local Population Studies*, 28 (1982), pp. 58–66; E. Higgs, 'Domestic servants and households in Victorian England', *Social History*, 8 (1983), pp. 203–10; E. Higgs, 'Domestic service and household production', in *Unequal Opportunities: Women's Employment in England 1800–1918*, ed. A. V. John (Oxford, 1986), pp. 125–52; E. Higgs, *Domestic Servants and Households in Rochdale, 1851–1871* (New York, 1986).

has noted that the category 'housekeeper' appears to have been a particular problem of the Northern textile districts. Nor does the Census Office in London appear to have treated such women as servants when abstracting the data for the published tables from 1861 onwards.[18] Still other servants worked on farms or in shops. The majority of servant employers in Rutland in 1871 were farmers, while retailers were always the largest category of employers in mid-century Rochdale. It is conceivable that in many such households there was a strict demarcation between domestic, agricultural and retailing tasks but there is evidence that this was not the case in many small units of production.[19] Rochdale and Rutland in 1871 may have been unusual in these respects and researchers need to guard against local or temporal idiosyncrasies.

Jordan has argued that the wide regional variations in the proportion of young women aged 15–19 without stated occupations indicate that the census returns can be used to indicate spatial differences in occupational opportunities for women.[20] One may be less justified in using them to calculate absolute, as opposed to relative, levels of employment, especially among married women or in small areas. As with so many of the facets of census studies discussed here, it is essential to compare the conventions employed by enumerators in order to understand their individual biases and styles. Some enumerators appear to have been less willing than others to regard the work of women as an 'occupation'. But in the absence of alternative sources, the census enumerators' books are still our best source for understanding the economic activities of women in the Victorian period.

The work of children

The instructions in the censuses respecting the work of children were similar to those for women. Indeed, women and children are usually yoked together in the conventions to be used. The problems already noted regarding the enumeration of the work of women can also be found in the case of children. The family comprising an independent male 'breadwinner' with dependent wife and children was an aspiration which only certain sections of the population could achieve. The wages of men were often irregular, and illness and death could cause acute crises for working-class families. In these circumstances children were expected to make a contribution to the well-being of the household. This did not usually take the form of a full-time job but casual and part-time employment: looking after small children, running errands, foraging, helping in the family shop or with the family laundry business, and so on. In the countryside children might be employed casually on such tasks as leading horses, weeding, bird scaring and harvest work. The opportunities

[18] M. Anderson, 'Mis-specification of servant occupations in the 1851 census: a problem revisited', *Local Population Studies*, 60 (1998), pp. 58–64. See also R. Hancock, 'In service or one of the family? Kin-servants in Swavesey, 1851–1881, Ryde, 1881, and Stourbridge, 1881', *Family and Community History*, 21 (1999), pp. 141–8.

[19] E. Higgs, *Domestic Servants and Households in Rochdale*, pp. 124–6; J. A. S. Green, 'A survey of domestic service', *Lincolnshire History and Archaeology*, 17 (1982), pp. 65–9; M. Bouquet, *Family, Servants and Visitors: the Farm Household in Nineteenth and Twentieth Century Devon* (Norwich, 1985), pp. 75–9.

[20] E. Jordan, 'Female employment in England and Wales 1851–1911: an examination of the census figures for 15–19 year olds', *Social History*, 13 (1988), pp. 175–90.

for such work differed, of course, from area to area, and over time.[21] There is some evidence that the census authorities understood this pattern of work. Even when the occupational column was left blank, there are examples where boys aged 10–14 years have had the occupations of their fathers added by the census clerks in pencil. But, as in the case of women, such work was probably seldom seen as a formal 'occupation'.

The most common designation for children in the census was that of 'scholar', and the censuses have been used by historians to calculate the number of children receiving education in the nineteenth century.[22] The returns should, however, be used with caution for this purpose. The definition of the term 'scholar' in the census instructions was vague, and became vaguer over time. With the advent of compulsory education after the 1876 Elementary Education Act there may also have been a temptation for some working-class householders to use the term to conceal the work of their children. In 1851 parents were to record their children as 'scholars' if they were above five years of age and were 'daily attending school, or receiving regular tuition under a master or governess at home'. In 1861, however, regular tuition at home did not require the presence of a master or governess. In 1871 and 1881 children only needed to be 'attending a school, or receiving regular instruction at home' to be returned as scholars. In 1891 there was no instruction on the subject. In 1901, however, children attending school 'and also engaged in a trade or industry should be described as following the particular trade or industry'.[23]

Leaving aside the case of 1901, it would appear that the term 'scholar' became progressively less precise over time. How often or for what period of time should a scholar attend a school to be so defined? How did one define 'regular' tuition, and regular tuition in what? Did learning the family trade, or instruction in lacemaking at a 'lace-school' count? It might also be possible, or at least consistent with the instructions, for a child who only attended Sunday school to be described as a 'scholar'. The term was becoming increasingly vague at the very time when the pressures on the working classes to conceal the labour of their children was greatest. The Factory Acts of the nineteenth century had placed some restrictions, which could be evaded, on the work of children under 13 years of age in factories. From 1876 onwards, however, various Education Acts still further curtailed the legal right of parents to dispose of their children's time in this manner, and a network of school attendance officers was established to ensure that children were sent to school. This was a double blow to working-class parents since they could no longer count upon the labour of their children to help supplement the family income, and they had to pay school fees as well. Although the latter could be remitted in cases of hardship, they were only abolished in the 1890s.[24]

---

[21] A. Davin, 'Working or helping? London working-class children in the domestic economy', in *Households and the World Economy*, ed. J. Smith, I. Wallerstein and H. Evers (London, 1984), pp. 215–32; A. Davin, *Growing Up Poor: Home, School and Street in London 1870–1914* (London, 1996).

[22] See, for example, B. I. Coleman, 'The incidence of education in mid-century', in Wrigley, *Nineteenth-Century Society*, pp. 402–10.

[23] See Appendix 7 for references to examples of the household schedules.

[24] P. Horn, 'Child workers in the Victorian countryside: the case of Northamptonshire', *Northamptonshire Past and Present*, 7 (1985–6), p. 177.

In the first few decades of compulsory education the conflict between many working-class households and the school boards established to oversee the system was often severe. Truancy, frequently supported by parents, was common. Any enquiries in the census respecting the work of children might, therefore, be viewed with suspicion in some working-class areas.[25] This was certainly the view of witnesses before the 1890 Treasury Committee on the Census.[26] In London in 1871 they would have been justified in their suspicions since the census authorities, under instructions from the home secretary, broke their pledge of confidentiality and provided the London School Board with the names and addresses of all children aged between three and 13 years, their exact ages and the names and occupations of their parents.[27]

When the census totals of scholars are compared with contemporary surveys of schools certain anomalies become apparent. In 1851 the census enumerators left a separate educational schedule at every school of any description which they found in their district. The original schedules have not survived but printed summaries give the enrolment and attendance figures for boy and girl pupils at day schools and Sunday schools. This source gives a total of 1,139,300 boys enrolled at school in England and Wales, which compares almost exactly with the 1,148,100 boy scholars in the census. On the other hand there were 1,096,000 girl scholars in the latter but only 969,300 in the 1851 census of schools. The 1851 census did not cover every school, however, although the under-enumeration was probably quite small. At the same time the numbers actually attending school regularly would be less than those enrolled.[28]

A similar survey of schools was undertaken in 1871 and returns made of the number of children for whom accommodation in schools existed, and the number in attendance on the day the returns were made. Table 8.1 shows the returns for three civil parishes in Devon in which all schools made returns, and the numbers of scholars in these parishes in the 1871 census.[29]

Such returns are by no means conclusive proof of a general tendency to use 'scholar' as a blanket term for children whether they were at school or working but certainly point in that direction. The not uncommon cases of 'scholars' aged under five years should also indicate the problematic nature of the census data.

Even if children did attend schools, and were properly described as 'scholars', this did not necessarily mean that they did not perform some work. The imposition of compulsory education did not stop all remunerative work but probably displaced it into Saturday jobs and work after

[25] For such conflicts in the rural setting, see Morgan, *Harvesters and Harvesting 1840–1900*, pp. 63–73.

[26] *Report of the Treasury Committee on the Census* (QQ 821–3, 965, 1342).

[27] TNA, RG 29/2, p. 129; *Report of the Treasury Committee on the Census* (QQ 2265–6, 2480–2); Greater London Record Office, London School Board Statistical Committee, SBL 908, Minutes of 3 Apr. 1871, 15 May 1871 and 6 July 1871.

[28] Coleman, 'The incidence of education in mid-century', p. 403. See also J. M. Goldstrom, 'Education in England and Wales in 1851: the education census of Great Britain, 1851', in Lawton, *The Census and Social Structure*, pp. 224–40.

[29] *Return Relating to Elementary Education (Civil Parishes)* (PP 1871 LV [201.], pp. 72–3); TNA, RG 10/2035, Parish of Shute; TNA, RG 10/2034, Parish of Stockland; TNA, RG 10/2031, Parish of Uplyme.

Table 8.1 Returns for three parishes in Devon and numbers of scholars, 1871

Number of children for whom accommodation exists in schools	Number of children in attendance on day returns made		Number of census 'scholars'	
	Boys	*Girls*	*Boys*	*Girls*
Parish of Shute (66)	46	35	67	51
Parish of Stockland (146)	63	63	83	69
Parish of Uplyme (94)	31	23	76	74

Sources: *Return Relating to Elementary Education (Civil Parishes)* (PP 1871 LV [201.]).
TNA, RG 10/2035, Parish of Shute; TNA, RG 10/2034, Parish of Stockland;
TNA, RG 10/2031, Parish of Uplyme.

school hours, with a resulting concentration in services and trading. Patterns of school attendances fitted into this regime of weekend or seasonal work, with high rates of absences on Mondays and Fridays, and at harvest time.[30] Such work may have declined in the later years of the century as children's labour came to be marginalised. This was the result of the rise in the level of men's wages, which cut down the need for a family contribution; the cumulative effects of factory and education legislation shortening the hours of work that children could perform; the invention of the telephone, which cut down the need for messengers; and, above all, the decline of activities such as lacemaking and shoemaking as domestic industries.[31]

Given these problems, great care should be taken in using the census returns for calculating the provision of education in the period and the participation rate of children in the economy. An examination of alternative sources, such as the surveys of schools, and a comparison of the conventions of differing enumerators are of great importance. The temptation to regard all nineteenth-century children as unoccupied dependants is to be avoided.

The agricultural workforce

The nineteenth century was a crucial period in the transition of England and Wales from a predominantly agricultural economy to a modern industrialised nation. In 1801 agriculture was the largest sector in the economy. One hundred years later the majority of people lived in towns and the proportion of the population employed on the land was comparatively small. The census returns have been a principal source for the quantitative analysis of this decline.[32] There are

[30] Davin, 'Working or helping?', p. 222.

[31] Davin, 'Working or helping?', p. 226.

[32] See, for example, Charles Booth, 'Occupations of the people of the United Kingdom, 1801–81', *Journal of the Statistical Society of London*, 49 (1886), pp. 314–444; B. R. Mitchell, *Abstract of British Historical Statistics* (Cambridge, 1962), pp. 55–63; P. Deane and W. A. Cole, *British Economic Growth, 1688–1959* (Cambridge, 1969), pp. 136–73; W. A. Armstrong, 'The use of information about occupation, pt. 2: an industrial classification, 1841–1891', in Wrigley, *Nineteenth-Century Society*, pp. 226–310; C. H. Feinstein, *National Income, Expenditure and Output of the United Kingdom, 1855–1965* (Cambridge, 1972).

problems with these returns, however, which must be borne in mind when attempting to establish the size and structure of the agricultural workforce. The following analysis should be read in conjunction with the discussion of the size of the agricultural workforce as revealed in the occupational tables in the published *Census Reports* in Chapter 13.

The instructions for filling in the occupations of those working on farms changed over time.[33] In 1841 comparatively few instructions were given. The householder was told that 'The profession &c of wives, or of sons and daughters living with and assisting their parents but not apprenticed or receiving wages, need not be inserted'. This immediately removed the work of the farmer's family from consideration. At the same time the enumerator was instructed that 'Ag. Lab.' was to be used as an abbreviation for agricultural labourer, 'which may include all farming servants and labourers in husbandry'.

In 1851 much more specific instructions were given. The householders were told that

> The term FARMER is to be applied only to the occupier of land, who is to be returned – *Farmer of* [317] *acres employing* [12] *labourers'*, the number of acres, and of in and out-door labourers, on March 31st, being in all cases inserted. Sons or daughters employed at home or on the farm, may be returned – *Farmer's Son,' 'Farmer's Daughter'*.

The instructions to the enumerators repeated this guidance and added the following examples and notes:

> Farmer of 220 acres (employing 11 labourers).
> Bart; landed proprietor, farming 613 acres (employing 25 agricultural labourers).
> Farmer of 110 acres (employing 4 labourers and boy).
> Farmer of 41 acres (employing 1 in and 1 out door labourer, with a boy).
> Freeholder, farmer of 10 acres (employing no labourer).
> Farmer's son (employed on the farm).
> Farmer's daughter (employed at home).
> The *acres* occupied by the farmer are to be stated exclusive of heath, mountain, moor, marsh, or common land – the extent of which used by the farmer should be *separately* stated. The number of *labourers* returned should include waggoners, shepherds, and all kinds of workmen employed on the farm, whether they sleep in the house or not; and when *boys* or women are employed, their number should be separately given. The male and female farm servants who sleep in house will be entered in the household schedule, and their particular employments, as waggoner, dairy maid, &c., inserted in the column headed 'Occupation'.

These rather complex instructions plainly prescribed an exhaustive itemised description of the resources of the farm. In practice, however, the precise definitions of the acreage and number of labourers to be returned appear to have been lost on most farmers and enumerators.

The instructions in 1861 were much less detailed. The householder was told that

---

[33] See Appendix 7 for references to examples of the household schedules.

The term FARMER [is] to be applied only to the OCCUPIER of land. Example: *Farmer of 317 acres, employing 8 labourers and 3 boys'*; the actual number of acres, and of men and boys employed on the farm, on April 8th, being in all cases inserted. Sons or daughters employed at home or on the farm, may be returned – *'Farmer's Son,' 'Farmer's Daughter'*.

FARM SERVANTS sleeping in the Farmer's house must be described in his schedule as *'Carter', 'Dairymaid'*, &c., as the case may be.

An out-door LABOURER working on a farm must be described as *'Agricultural labourer', 'Shepherd'*, &c., as the case may be.

The 1851 instructions on the type of land to be included in the acreage were dropped. At the same time the number of women working on the farm was not mentioned.

In 1871 and 1881 the number of men, women and boys working on the farm was supposed to be returned. But only men employed on the farm and sleeping in the farmer's house were to be described as farm servants. This gradual exclusion of women was taken a stage further in 1891 when householders were instructed to return only 'SONS or other RELATIVES of FARMERS employed on the farm ... as *"Farmer's son", "Farmer's brother"*'. The daughters of farmers were no longer mentioned. The other important change in 1891 was the abandonment of any returns on the acreage of farms and the number of labourers employed. This was the first census at which people were asked to state whether they were employers or employees, and it may have been considered that a specific question regarding employment on farms was now redundant.

There are plainly some problems with these returns.[34] First, the under-enumeration of seasonal and casual work, and of the work of women and children, is probably most serious with respect to agricultural employment. As mentioned above, the exact status of female servants on the farm is especially difficult to determine. Were they domestic or agricultural workers? Such problems may be more serious in the north and west where the predominance of dairy farming provided a demand for casual and seasonal female labour. In the arable east and west the participation of women in field work was less common.[35] The instructions given also failed to define the term 'farmer'. Since no lower limit was placed on the size of a holding which could be termed a farm, 'farmers' occupying one or two acres can be found. The distinction between such 'farmers' and market gardeners is plainly difficult to draw. Some people combining farming as a subsidiary trade with another occupation, such as miller, baker, publican and even labourer, recorded themselves as occupying larger acreages. The division between agricultural and non-agricultural employment was often ill-defined. Still other 'farmers' neglected to give any acreage returns at all. Some of these will, no doubt, have been retired

[34] E. Higgs, 'Occupational censuses and the agricultural workforce in Victorian England and Wales', *Economic History Review*, 48 (1995), pp. 700–16.
[35] K. D. M. Snell, 'Agricultural seasonal employment, the standard of living, and women's work in the South and East, 1690–1860', *Economic History Review*, 2nd ser., 34 (1981), pp. 407–37.

from the land. One nineteenth-century study claimed that retired farmers were no more than two per cent of the total, although another contemporary study of Huntingdon put the figure nearer 12 per cent.[36]

There was also confusion as to what was to be returned for acreage farmed. When the acreage returns in the census have been checked against other contemporary sources, such as tithe apportionments and parish rate books, a fair degree of consistency appears to emerge.[37] It should be noted, however, that the returns for 1851 were supposed to differentiate between land in and out of agricultural use, while the instructions for later years could be taken as referring to total acreage. The extent to which this created misunderstandings, especially in 1851, is difficult to determine.

The returns for the numbers of persons employed on the farm are similarly problematic. In theory farmers were to give the total number of people working on the farm irrespective of whether they were living-in farm servants, agricultural labourers who lived out, women or children. Women, however, appear to have been excluded in 1861. Some farmers neglected to make any returns under this head at all and it cannot be assumed that they did so because they did not employ anyone. The number of women and children employed, moreover, often seems to have been left out.

It is also difficult to decide what the number of agricultural labourers in the returns refers to. Agricultural historians who have studied the question have concluded that only the number of agricultural labourers employed by the farmer but not living in his or her house were returned. Farm servants living on the farm are supposed to have been excluded.[38] But this is perhaps drawing too great a distinction between the two terms. In 1841 the term 'agricultural labourer' was expressly to be used for 'all farming servants and labourers in husbandry'. In 1851 the enumerators were told that the number of labourers was to include all 'workmen employed on the farm, whether they sleep in the house or not'. In 1861 'labourers' appears only to have related to men and boys; women were not mentioned. Thereafter the term was to apply to the total number of men, women and boys employed on the farm. One cannot assume, therefore, that the bald statement 'Farmer X employs three labourers' relates to only one category of employees. Similarly, adding up the number of persons employed by farmers in a particular parish or township and comparing this to the number of persons in agricultural occupations in

[36] D. Grigg, 'Farm size in England and Wales, from early Victorian times to the present', *Agricultural History Review*, 35 (1987), p. 181.

[37] S. Thomas, 'The enumerators' returns as a source for a period picture of the parish of Llansantffraid, 1841–1851', *Ceredigion*, 4 (1963), p. 409; S. Thomas, 'The agricultural labour force in some South-West Carmarthenshire parishes in the mid-nineteenth century', *Welsh History Review*, 3 (1966–7), p. 64. But see also D. R. Mills, 'Trouble with farms at the Census Office: an evaluation of farm statistics from the censuses of 1851–1881 in England and Wales', *Agricultural History Review*, 47 (1999), pp. 58–77.

[38] J. A. Sheppard, 'The east Yorkshire agricultural labour force in the mid-nineteenth century', *Agricultural History Review*, 9 (1961), p. 45; Thomas, 'The agricultural labour force in some South-West Carmarthenshire parishes', p. 67.

the same area is not always a meaningful exercise.[39] The two figures might not be even approximately similar if large numbers of agricultural labourers lived in one parish but worked in another. Female farm servants may well not be included in the number of labourers employed and this might explain why in some cases the total number of farm servants in an area exceeds the figure for the number of persons employed. Such analyses on a country-wide basis are perhaps less prone to such errors. It is very difficult, therefore, to say exactly what the returns relate to, since this presumably depended on the interpretation put on the complicated instructions by farmers and enumerators. As ever, a careful scrutiny of the returns for local and personal idiosyncrasies is extremely important.

An additional problem was the tendency of householders and enumerators to describe people as 'labourers' without indicating if they were agricultural workers, casual dock labourers, road workers, and so on. In thoroughly rural areas one might be justified in assuming these to be agricultural labourers but there will be problems in doing so elsewhere. The GRO got over this difficulty by placing all such persons in a vague residual category for 'General labourers'.[40]

Undoubtedly the returns of the agricultural workforce can be used for very broad regional comparisons but their use in local studies is fraught with potential dangers.

Employers and employees

The GRO was interested in distinguishing between employers and employees from the very first census under its control. Its efforts in this respect do not appear to have borne fruit, however, and this can be explained, in part, by the difficulties inherent in trying to pin down fluid nineteenth-century employment practices. The instructions also show a gradual progression from a model of an economy based on the old handicraft distinctions between 'master', 'apprentice' and 'journeyman', to one structured around the polarity of 'employer' and 'worker'.[41]

The distinction to be made in 1841 was essentially a negative one. Enumerators were told to put down people's employments, 'writing *"J."* for *Journeyman*, *"Ap."* for *Apprentice*, and *"Sh."* for *Shopman*, after the statement of the trade of those who are such. *"Master"* need not be inserted; everyone will be so considered who is not entered as journeyman or apprentice'. Comparatively few people followed this instruction and so the exact distinction between master, apprentice and day labourer was obscured.

---

[39] C. Thomas, 'Rural society in nineteenth-century Wales: South Cardiganshire in 1851', *Ceredigion*, 6 (1970), pp. 397–8; S. Thomas, 'The enumerators' returns as a source for a period picture', pp. 412–13. See also Mills, 'Trouble with farms at the Census Office'. The term 'farm service' appears particularly problematic (see N. Goose, 'Farm service in southern England in the mid-nineteenth century', *Local Population Studies*, 72 (2004), pp. 77–82).

[40] TNA, RG 27/5, Item 69, p. 4; TNA, RG 27/6, Item 61, p. 4.

[41] See Appendix 7 for references to examples of the household schedules and enumerators' books.

In 1851 fuller instructions were provided for the enumerators:

In TRADES the master is to be distinguished from the Journeyman and Apprentice, thus – *'(Carpenter, master employing [6] men)'*; inserting always the number of persons of the trade in his employment on March 31st.

Baker (master employing 4 men, 2 women).
Bootmaker (journeyman).
Ironmonger's Apprentice.
Shoemaker (master employing 15 men, 3 women).

In trades where women or boys and girls are employed, the number of each class should be separately given. Where the master is one of a manufacturing or mercantile firm, the entry should be after this form: – 'Cotton manufacturer – firm of 3, employ 512 men, 273 women, 35 boys, and 272 girls.'

On the other hand, shareholders in companies and the owners of mines were not to return themselves as employers but as 'Fundholder', 'Proprietor of iron mines', and so on.

In the 1861 instructions to the householders the master was defined in terms of being an employer: 'IN TRADES, MANUFACTURES, or other business, the employer must, in all cases, be distinguished; Example: *'Carpenter – master, employing 6 men and 2 boys'*; inserting always the number of persons of the trade in his employ, if any, on April 8th.' Fundholders and the proprietors of mines were to be treated as in 1851. In the case of firms, however, the number of persons employed only needed to be returned by one partner. In 1871 and 1881 the instructions reverted to talking of a 'Master' as opposed to an 'Employer', and in the case of firms the numbers employed were to be returned by 'the senior or some one partner only'. In these years those deriving their income from dividends were to describe themselves as such but nothing specific was said about mine owners.

In 1891 the system was radically changed by the introduction of three columns for employment status. These were headed 'Employer', 'Employed' and 'Neither employer nor employed, but working on own account'. An 'Employer' was defined as 'a master, employing under him workers in his trade or industry'. A cross was to be placed in the relevant column. Married women assisting their husbands in their trade were to be returned as 'Employed'. The occupation column was retained, however, and the enumerators' instructions still showed the terms 'Master' and 'Apprentice' being added to occupations. Those owning shares in companies were now to describe themselves as 'Living on their own means'. The growing complexity of employer/employee relations was recognised by the inclusion of instructions regarding managers, foremen and superintendents.

In 1901 only one extra column was used, in which householders were now to write 'Employer', 'Worker' or 'Own Account'. The employment of domestic servants was not to be counted. The examples of the occupational column no longer mentioned masters or apprentices. There was also no specific mention of fundholders but those 'deriving their income from private sources should return themselves as "Living on own means"'.

Despite all these elaborate instructions the returns under this heading were plainly imperfect. In the years 1851–81 many employers failed to indicate the number of persons they employed, although in some cases this may reflect the fact that householders were following the instructions relating to partnerships. Even fewer people took the trouble to describe themselves as 'apprentice' or 'journeyman', and these terms must have become increasingly inappropriate in many industries. In 1891 the census authorities expressed themselves bitterly disappointed by the entries in the three employment status columns. People put crosses in more than one column, and it was felt that many had inflated their social position by putting a cross under the heading 'Employer'.[42]

These latter problems may, however, have been exaggerated by the census authorities. There may have been perfectly good reasons why householders placed crosses in more than one column. People with more than one occupation, for example 'Farmer and agricultural labourer', might be employed in one and self-employed in another. Others may have worked in trades such as building where subcontracting was widespread. A person might be employed to complete a job and then employ others to do the work. Those in managerial roles might be the employees of a company but employ others on behalf of the firm. Even workers in the lowest social classes might be employers. Costermongers, for example, might employ children for a few pence, or for as much fruit as they could eat, to mind the stall.[43] The GRO had also been forced against its will to introduce the three columns by the 1890 Treasury Committee on the Census, and may have been unnecessarily critical of the results as a consequence.[44] It should be noted, however, that the GRO's low opinion of the returns under this heading was seconded by the National Federation of Registrars of England and Wales which believed that 'large numbers of householders quite misunderstood and confused the terms Employer, employed, etc.'[45] Such 'problems' may have been overcome in 1901, when only one column was available for such information, but this does not necessarily mean that the data supplied were any nearer to economic reality.

Retirement and unemployment

Similar difficulties are to be found in relation to the information on retirement and unemployment in the census schedules. The GRO probably wished to know the former occupations of people in such circumstances in order to calculate occupational life-tables for actuarial purposes. The problems that arose reflected, no doubt, the difficulties of defining these terms in the nineteenth-century context, and the changing instructions in the schedules themselves. It is difficult, therefore,

[42] *1891 Census Report*, p. 36.

[43] The author is grateful to Kevin Schürer of the University of Essex for these comments. See also K. Schürer, 'The 1891 census and local population studies', pp. 24–6.

[44] Higgs, 'The struggle for the occupational census', pp. 81–6; Higgs, *Life, Death and Statistics*, pp. 126–7.

[45] TNA, RG 19/2, Memorandum of Jan. 1900 from the honorary secretary of the Census Committee of the National Federation of Registrars of England and Wales to the Local Government Board.

to estimate the proportion of the population that fell under these headings. It is interesting, however, that the category in the 1831 census for those who were retired or disabled comprised nearly six per cent of all males over 20.[46]

In 1841 neither unemployment nor retirement was mentioned but in 1851 householders were instructed that:

> Persons of advanced age who have RETIRED FROM BUSINESS to be entered thus – 'Retired silk merchant', 'Retired watchmaker', &c.

> ALMSPEOPLE, and persons in the receipt of parish relief should, after being described as such, have their previous occupations inserted.

The instruction in 1861 was similar, although the clause 'of advanced age' had been dropped. Rather confusingly, however, the example on the schedule showed a woman described as 'Formerly laundress'. In 1871 and 1881 the householders' instructions dropped any specific mention of almspeople, while retaining the wording of the 1861 instructions as to the retired. Unemployment made its first specific appearance in these years with the instruction that 'Persons ordinarily engaged in some industry, but OUT OF EMPLOYMENT on April 2nd, should be so described, as *"Coal miner, unemployed"*, *"Printer, unemployed"*'. Some inconsistency crept in, however, when the example on the enumerator's schedule contained the entry, 'Ship carpenter (out of employ)'. In 1891 and 1901, with the introduction of the columns for employment status, the question regarding unemployment was dropped. The guidance regarding retirement was broadened, however, with the instruction that, 'Persons who have *retired* from their profession, business, or occupation must state their former calling with the addition of the word "Retired"'. The household schedule now contained a 'Retired laundress' in its example.

The returns under these headings were plainly imperfect. Information on unemployment was seldom given. The inmates of prisons, hospitals and workhouses often have specific occupations against their names, although they might more properly be regarded as retired or unemployed. People are sometimes described as 'annuitants' (the term could refer to someone receiving an annual allowance, as well as to a person with an investment producing an annual return), although many were probably institutionalised pensioners. Often very elderly people have no occupation recorded at all, although one might regard them as having been retired. The list of such ambiguities could be multiplied.

Part of the problem may have been the difficulty in making a definite distinction between being in employment and being retired or unemployed. When work was very casual and stoppages frequent, especially in the later years of people's working lives, the distinction might be very difficult to draw. A dock labourer, for example, might not know if he was to get work until he

---

[46] See Appendix 7 for references to examples of the household schedules. E. A. Wrigley, 'Men on the land and men in the countryside: employment in agriculture in early-nineteenth-century England', in *The World We Have Gained: Histories of Population and Social Structure*, ed. L. Bonfield, R. M. Smith and K. Wrightson (Oxford, 1986), p. 306.

turned up at the dock gates in the morning. On the other hand, someone in business or a farmer might have handed over control of the business for all practical purposes to a son, and yet still have regarded himself as the titular head of the firm or farm. Similarly, despite the introduction of the New Poor Law in the 1830s, many paupers receiving out-relief still had some employment. Hence entries such as 'in receipt of parish relief and straw-bonnet maker', or 'pauper and charwoman', or 'Carpenter (parish pay)'. The concept of a definite 'age of retirement' probably only became current after the passage of the 1908 Old Age Pensions Act, which gave people aged 70 and over a pension if they fulfilled certain criteria. But the elderly appear to have been increasingly dropping out of the labour market from the 1880s onwards, perhaps under the impact of technological change.[47]

The returns under these heading must, therefore, be used with caution. Certainly some common-sense rules have to be applied to the inmates of institutions, who cannot be regarded as part of the economically active population. The problem is, of course, to decide which of the inmates were temporarily out of the labour market and which were permanently institutionalised. In later years the GRO's own solution was to regard all such people aged 60 years and over as having retired but to count the rest as having a current occupation.[48]

Working at home

In 1901 another column was added for home-working. The instruction at the head of the column read, 'Write opposite the name of each person carrying on trade or industry at home the words *"At home"*'.[49] This instruction appears rather vague; did it include servants or housewives? The census authorities do not appear to have used this information in their tabulations consistently, and did not comment on the accuracy of the data.

Abbreviations

In the course of copying out their returns, the enumerators were given permission to use certain abbreviations for occupations.[50] This practice was most extensive in 1841 and gradually diminished thereafter. By 1871 the only abbreviation mentioned was 'Ag. Lab.' for agricultural labourer. In 1881 a more general instruction was given: 'such contractions may be used as "ag. lab." for agricultural labourer, but care must be taken that the contractions used are such as will be readily understood.' From 1891 onwards no mention was made of the possibility of using such abbreviations. Table 8.2 summarises those abbreviations mentioned in the instructions on the enumeration schedules.

[47] M. Woollard, 'The employment and retirement of older men, 1851–1881: further evidence from the census', *Continuity and Change*, 17 (2002), pp. 437–63.
[48] TNA, RG 27/6, Item 61, p. 2.
[49] TNA, RG 19/11.
[50] See Appendix 7 for references to examples of the household schedules.

**Table 8.2 Abbreviations mentioned in the instructions
on the enumeration schedules**

Abbreviation	Dates	Meaning
Ag. Lab.	1841–81	Agricultural labourer
Ap.	1841–61	Apprentice
Army	1841	Members of HM land forces of whatever rank
Cl.	1841–61	Clerk
F.S.	1841	Female servant
H.P.	1841	Members of HM armed forces on half-pay
Ind.	1841	Independent – people living on their own means
J.	1841	Journeyman
M.	1841	Manufacturer
m.	1841	Maker – as in 'Shoe m.'
M.S.	1841	Male servant
Navy	1841	Members of HM naval forces, including marines, of whatever rank
P.	1841	Pensioners in HM armed forces
Rail Lab.	1851	Railway labourer
Serv.	1861	Servant
Sh.	1841	Shopman

Sources: Census enumeration schedules, 1841–81.

9 Missing returns

Regrettably the surviving census returns are not a full record of the population of nineteenth-century England and Wales, and it may not always be possible to track down individuals, addresses and households. These omissions reflect both under-enumeration at the time of the census, and subsequent loss or damage to the returns.

Under-enumeration: special groups

In the early censuses under the GRO, certain groups, usually those not living in conventional households, were simply not enumerated by name. These included the members of the Royal Navy on board ship in 1841, and possibly in 1851; all members of the merchant marine in 1841, and various sections of it thereafter; all fishermen afloat in 1841, and sections of this group thereafter; the crews of vessels engaged in inland navigation in 1841 and 1851; and all itinerants, travellers and night workers in 1841, and probably a considerable number of the same in later years. The soldiers serving abroad were never enumerated by name. All these groups have been considered in more detail in Chapter 4.

Under-enumeration: households

Undoubtedly some individuals and households that should have been enumerated will have completely slipped through the census net. Some of these omissions might reflect clerical error as enumerators and householders made the inevitable slips in recording or copying. A house might have been omitted, perhaps because it was unoccupied on census night, and the enumerator forgot to note it down as empty; a wife might have been absent because of an enumerator's copying blunder; an elderly visitor might have been temporarily lost sight of; and so on. But in some districts, or among some social groups, it might have been difficult for hard-pressed enumerators to ensure that they had handed a household schedule to every family.

In the absence of any detailed research on the subject it is difficult to put a figure to such levels of under-enumeration. It should be noted, however, that post-enumeration surveys for the 1981 census indicated that 0.5 per cent of households were missed in that census in the whole of England and Wales. In Inner London in 1981, however, the under-enumeration may have been of the order of 2.75 per cent.[1] Under-enumeration was still higher in 1991. In 2001 there may

[1] Whitehead, 'The GRO use of social surveys', p. 46.

have been a million people, mainly young men, who were missing from the census – the difference between the actual enumeration and the total estimated from rolling forward the corrected 1991 figures. The Office for National Statistics, which incorporates the GRO, claims that the discrepancy is due to emigration that has not been picked up, although some doubt that this would explain the gender bias.

For the Victorian period we have little pertinent information on this matter. Wrigley and Schofield have calculated, for example, that the censuses of 1841–71 record approximately five per cent fewer children aged under five years than would be expected from vital registration data, although this probably reflects problems with age recording.[2] Rather more alarmingly, the findings of preliminary studies in the USA suggest that approximately 15 per cent of adults were omitted in the censuses of that country in the mid nineteenth century. Since the people so omitted shared characteristics that probably increased their chances of enumeration – they were eligible voters, property holders, or previously enumerated in a census – the average under-enumeration rate for the entire population may have been still higher.[3] Coverage in American cities may have been worse than in the countryside, especially among the poor and marginal groups such as servants.[4] Such levels of under-enumeration are perhaps exaggerated and may not be typical of nineteenth-century England and Wales, especially given the different manner in which the US censuses were administered.[5] But they do point to the need for caution when making generalisations based upon census aggregates. There were certainly suggestions at the time that the numbers of Russian and Polish Jews in the 1901 census returns were an undercount, although how far this reflected contemporary fears over immigration is difficult to say.[6]

Damaged returns

Lastly, some of the original returns, which were not always kept in optimum archival conditions in the nineteenth century, have been lost or damaged.[7] Often such damage was confined to the backs and fronts of enumerators' books, but more extensive gaps exist. Special returns, such as those for shipping, which were often appended to the back of enumerators' books, were especially liable to damage. In 1841, for example, the Kensington, Paddington, Golden Lane and Whitecross sub-districts are missing from the London returns, as are parts of Kent and Essex. In Denbighshire at the same date the books covering the hundred of Bromfield are missing, as are parts of the hundreds of Yale, Rhuthun and Isaled. In 1851 the returns for

---

[2] Wrigley and Schofield, *The Population History of England 1541–1871*, pp. 589–90.

[3] R. H. Steckel, 'The quality of census data for historical enquiry: a research agenda', *Social Science History*, 15 (1991), p. 593.

[4] D. H. Parkinson, 'Comments on the underenumeration of the US census, 1850–1880', *Social Science History*, 15 (1991), p. 514.

[5] Conk, 'Labor statistics in the American and English censuses', pp. 83–102.

[6] *Daily Express*, 26 Nov. 1901.

[7] For the archival history of the returns, see Chapter 1.

Salford and parts of Manchester have been severely damaged by water. The ships' returns for this census also seem to have been destroyed at some stage. In 1861 the Belgravia and Woolwich Arsenal sub-districts (containing 75,000 people) are missing. In 1901 the returns for Deal appear to be missing. The list of such problems could be greatly extended but this would soon become tedious. The only comprehensive guide to such gaps is to be found in the series lists at the FRC.

PART III

MAKING USE OF THE CENSUS

10 References and finding-aids

It is not the purpose of this chapter to give a detailed account of how to find a place or person in the census returns. Microfilm copies of the censuses can be found in numerous local record offices and libraries, as well as at the Family Records Centre, and it would be impossible to describe all the differing finding-aids in use. A considerable amount of work is going on in record offices, libraries and family history societies to produce new and improved indexes and guides. A description of the finding-aids extant at any one point in time would very quickly become outdated. All that will be attempted here is to describe the reference system used at the FRC that gives a unique reference to every page in the census returns, and to give a general outline of the types of finding-aids available at the FRC and in local repositories. Some general guidance on the conventions for producing these will also be given.

Public access to the census returns

The National Archives administers records in conformity with the Public Records Acts of 1958 and 1967. Under these acts, public records selected for permanent preservation are normally opened to public inspection in TNA in the January after they become 30 years old. With the approval of the lord chancellor, however, certain records may be withheld from public inspection after 30 years have elapsed under section 5(1) of the Public Records Act 1958, as amended by the 1967 Act. Before the lord chancellor gives his approval, he requires departments to satisfy him that the grounds for such closures conform to certain criteria. These are:

exceptionally sensitive papers, the disclosure of which would be contrary to the public interest whether on security or other grounds (including the need to safeguard the Revenue);

documents containing information supplied in confidence, the disclosure of which would or might constitute a breach of good faith;

documents containing information about individuals, the disclosure of which would cause substantial distress to or endanger living persons or their immediate descendants.

The census returns are closed for 100 years on the grounds that the information was supplied in confidence and its disclosure would be a breach of good faith.[1] This means that the enumerators' books for the 1901 census are the latest that are currently open to public inspection. From

---

[1] This position was re-asserted in Parliament 29 March 2004 (*Hansard*, Vol. 419, Pt. 65, 29 March 2004, cols. 1394–1402).

January 2005 the Freedom of Information Act will replace the access provisions of the Public Records Act but the position with regard to census returns is not expected to change. The 1911 returns are due to be opened in January 2012.[2]

Where to find the census returns

The pre-1841 nominal returns were probably only created in certain areas, and were unlikely to have been sent to the central authorities. Some appear to have been preserved by the local Poor Law officers and clergy who produced them, and found their way into local Poor Law records and parish chests. In many cases these records have subsequently been deposited in local record offices and libraries, although others may still remain with the parish authorities. The most comprehensive topographical listing of these returns can be found in Wall, Woollard and Moring, *Census Schedules and Listings, 1801–1831: an Introduction and Guide*.[3]

The original census returns for the period 1841–1901 are currently held by TNA at Kew, or in out-storage. These are not made available to the public except in very special circumstances, and one has to use the microfilm and microfiche copies currently housed in TNA's Family Records Centre (FRC) in central London. At Kew, the 1901 census only is available on microfiche. The census records are so heavily used that the originals would soon be destroyed if the public were allowed to consult them directly. The 1901 census is also available remotely online at the FRC or at Kew (http://www.1901census.nationalarchives.gov.uk). Access to the index is free, and one can make online searches for named persons, addresses, institutions and vessels but one has to pay to get access to the images of the returns.[4]

Many local record offices and local history libraries have now purchased copies of these returns.[5] It should be noted, however, that these local repositories usually only acquire the returns for the administrative areas within which they lie. Moreover, these modern administrative areas are usually different from the old historical counties of the nineteenth century. Sometimes, the collection in a local repository may not include the microfilms and fiche for every year. Having pinpointed a likely repository, therefore, it is always essential to check with them about their holdings before going to consult the returns. The local Church of Jesus Christ of Latter-day Saints (LDS) Family History Centres will borrow microfilms from their headquarters in Utah for any parts of the censuses requested.[6]

[2] Information on access to public records can be found on The National Archives website <http://www.nationalarchives.gov.uk> (30 Sept. 2004).

[3] Wall, Woollard and Moring, *Census Schedules and Listings, 1801–1831*. See also C. Chapman, *Pre-1841 Censuses & Population Listings in the British Isles* (Dursley, 1994).

[4] For an introduction to this form of remote access, see Lumas, *Making Use of the Census*, pp. 49–53.

[5] J. Gibson and E. Hampson, *Census Returns 1841–1891 in Microform: a Directory to Local Holdings in Great Britain; Channel Islands; Isle of Man* (Birmingham, 1994). See also the Familia website <http://www.familia.org.uk> (30 Sept. 2004).

[6] They can be contacted at the Genealogical Society of Utah British Isles Family History Centre, 185 Penns Lane, Sutton Coldfield, West Midlands. One can also visit their website for the location of their libraries, and to access their catalogue <http://www.familysearch.org> (30 Sept. 2004).

Census holdings in electronic form

For historians who are interested in undertaking national or regional studies on computer, it may be unnecessary for them to collect their own data from the census. AHDS History at the UK Data Archive at the University of Essex has archived numerous local computerised datasets derived by historians and social scientists from the original census returns. It holds a complete digitised version of the 1881 census, and a two per cent clustered sample of the 1851 returns for England, Wales and Scotland. This sample, the work of a team at the University of Edinburgh under Professor Michael Anderson, is available, whole or in sub-sets. Details of these datasets, and the scale of charges for access, are available from AHDS History and its website.[7] The Church of Jesus Christ of Latter-day Saints also makes available a digitised version of the 1881 census, and parts of other enumerations.[8] Numerous local societies have made their own transcripts, and will make them available online or via CD-ROM, although these may have to be used with caution. CD-ROM images are also sold by S & N British Data Archive Ltd., and other companies with non-exclusive licences from TNA.

TNA references

Public records usually take the form of series of like records produced for a common purpose: a series of letter books, a file series, a set of census returns, and so on. They are usually designated as series within TNA and have a series code made up of the letter code and a number. HO 45, for example, is the main registered file series in the Home Office, while RG 18 is a series of maps from the GRO showing the boundaries of registration districts in the nineteenth and early twentieth centuries. Table 10.1 gives TNA series references for the census returns from 1841 to 1901.

Table 10.1 TNA series references (1841–1901)

Series Reference	Years
HO 107	1841 and 1851
RG 9	1861
RG 10	1871
RG 11	1881
RG 12	1891
RG 13	1901

Every series is broken down into a number of pieces, each piece being a single orderable item within the record office. Each piece has a reference made up of the series reference, an oblique stroke, and usually a number. The first orderable unit in the 1861 census returns is therefore RG

[7] AHDS History, UK Data Archive, University of Essex, Wivenhoe Park, Colchester, Essex CO4 3SQ. See also the AHDS History website <http://www.ahds.ac.uk/history/> (30 Sept. 2004).

[8] See the Church of Jesus Christ of Latter-day Saints website <http://www.familysearch.org> (30 Sept. 2004).

9/1. It should be noted that a piece reference does not necessarily refer to a single artefact – it may relate to a bundle of letters, a box of miscellaneous papers, a sack of rolls, and so on. It is basically only a stock reference. Within the piece the structure of the records will define the internal system of references used. A single volume may have page numbers; the letters within a file may be referred to by the names of the correspondents and the date; each of the papers in a box may have a registered number which forms their references within the piece; and so on.

The structure of the various sets of census returns varies, and so do the reference systems used to identify pieces of information within them. The records for each census are arranged in the topographical order outlined in Chapter 3. This means that the 1841 records are in a very different order from those produced later, since they are mainly arranged according to hundreds and parishes rather than by registration districts. Counties are arranged alphabetically, rather than topographically as in later years. But the main difference in the reference systems lies in the manner in which the returns have subsequently been boxed and numbered. What follows is an attempt to describe the typical arrangement of the records. There are, undoubtedly, numerous local idiosyncrasies and variations that will crop up from time to time.

In 1841 each piece is a box containing folders. Each piece contains the folders covering a hundred or series of parishes forming part of a hundred, and has a reference such as HO 107/1. Each folder in turn contains several enumerators' books, and has the numbers of the enumeration districts that these cover on the front. Each folder has a reference dependent upon its position within the piece. The first folder in the box is number 1, the second is number 2, and so on. This number is found at the top of the front cover of the folder. Each folder is therefore identified by the piece number and this sub-number, in the form HO 107/1/1 or HO 107/670/2. On the microfilm copies of these records, these references appear on each frame of the film. Part of this extended reference can be found on the bottom of the folder covers in the form 670/2. To complicate matters somewhat TNA has traditionally called each folder an 'enumeration book', and each enumerator's book an 'enumeration district'.

Within each folder, or 'enumeration book', each folio is numbered from 1 to x in the top right-hand corner from the front cover to the end of the folder. Consequently, a single enumerator's book may cover folios 38–56 within a folder. The enumerators' books have their own internal numbering system, of course, with the pages for nominal information numbered 1 to x. This means that the exact reference for each page of the 1841 returns is made up of five pieces of information: the series code, the piece number, the book (i.e., folder) number, the folio number and the page number, for example HO 107/504, bk. 9, fo. 5, p. 2.

In the case of the 1851 returns, each piece is again a box containing folders. Each piece usually covers a registration district or a number of sub-districts forming part of one. The returns continue the piece numbering of the 1841 series, so the first piece number for the 1851 returns is HO 107/1466. This number is, as before, on each frame of the microfilm copies. Each folder, again called an 'enumeration book' at TNA, contains a number of enumerators' books. The contents of each piece are again foliated. But whereas in 1841 each folder was separately foliated, in 1851 the piece is foliated as a whole, starting with the first folio of the first enumerator's book in the first folder, and ending with the last folio in the last enumerator's book in the last folder. One folder may have the reference HO 107/1698, fos. 161–394, and an enumerator's book within it the reference HO 107/1698, fos. 205–30. Each enumerator's book has its district number in the top right-hand corner of the front page, and its own internal pagination. Each page in the 1851 returns, therefore, has a reference such as HO 107/1798, fo. 52, p. 4, made up of four elements: the series number, the piece number, the folio number and the page number.

In the period 1861–1901, each piece is the folder containing a number of enumerators' books. The piece usually covers a sub-district rather than a district. Each set of returns forms a separate series, with pieces numbered 1 to *x*. The first folder in the 1881 returns is therefore RG 11/1. Again, the folder is referred to as an 'enumeration book' at TNA. Each piece, or folder, is foliated from the first folio in the first enumerator's book to the last folio in the last enumerator's book. An enumerator's book could, therefore, cover folios 15–38 within the piece. Each enumerator's book has its district number at the top right-hand corner of the front page, and its own internal pagination. Each page in the returns, therefore, has a reference in the form RG 9/38, fo. 18, p. 3.

The reference system used at TNA uniquely identifies each page in the returns, and should always be used when referring to census data. It should be noted, however, that it refers solely to the actual manuscripts rather than to the microfilm copies which most people use. Each reel of microfilm may contain copies of several pieces, and even parts of pieces, although the extent of the latter can still be deduced from their TNA foliation on the film.

Finding a place or address

Since the census returns are arranged topographically, generally in the order that places appear in the published population tables, the finding-aids at TNA are similarly arranged, and are available on its web-based catalogue (http://www.nationalarchives.gov.uk).[9] They are laid out by parishes, hundreds or registration districts. To use the census returns it is necessary to have some geographical information, such as the name of a street, parish or township. People with the name Smith are not grouped together, nor is it easy to identify areas that are meaningful in a sociological sense, such as those occupied by distinct social groups, prior to consulting the returns themselves.

At TNA, the finding-aids for the censuses were originally marked-up copies of the published population tables. These have been superseded by typed lists reproducing, roughly, the order and layout of the published tables. In order to find the piece reference for the returns covering a particular place, it is necessary to use special place-name indexes to find the page of the 1841 list or, for later censuses, the number of the registration sub-district in which they can be found.

[9] For a description of the finding-aids at TNA's Family Records Centre, see Lumas, *Making Use of the Census*, pp. 11–30.

There are different indexes for each census. The place-name indexes for 1841–91 are only available at the FRC. For 1901, they may be consulted both at the FRC and at TNA, Kew. One can then go to the series lists to find the relevant entry. The places within a particular hundred or registration district will be given broadly in the order in which they appear in the returns. To the side of the entry will be a reference to the appropriate TNA piece number that is used to order the microfilm of the record.

An example may help to elucidate this procedure. The 1871 place-name index indicates that the parish of Friston in Suffolk then lay in the registration district of Plomesgate (district number 215), in sub-district 5. The number of the registration sub-district was therefore 215:5. Going to the RG 10 list, one can look up the 215th district, and the fifth sub-district within it. This is the sub-district of Aldeburgh, and Friston is shown as the first place within it. The list shows that the piece reference for the returns for this area is RG 10/1765. This is then used to locate the appropriate reel of microfilm.

Many local record offices and libraries have used TNA's reference system explained above to produce their own indexes to the returns that they have on microfilm. Some repositories, however, have indexed their holdings according to the references that they have given to the reels of census microfilm purchased from TNA. Rather than giving the full TNA reference, a place is said to be on 'Reel 1' or some other reference meaningful to the repository. This system of numbering is an unfortunate one since such references do not uniquely identify each frame of the microfilm, and it is unlikely that any replacement microfilm purchased in due course will contain exactly the same pieces and folios.

For very small places that are not mentioned in the place-name indexes it may be necessary to use topographical gazetteers to discover within which larger administrative area they fall. This may be especially relevant in the case of ecclesiastical areas overlapping civil administrative boundaries. Care should be taken to ensure that the gazetteer used is as near contemporary as possible to the relevant census since boundary changes may affect administrative areas. In those cases where places cannot be found in gazetteers, recourse can be had to contemporary maps, especially those produced by the Ordnance Survey. Local repositories will usually have a collection of maps of the area. A particularly useful set of such documents can be found in TNA record series RG 18.[10] This is a series of maps showing the boundaries of the registration districts and sub-districts for various dates in the late nineteenth and early twentieth centuries.

In the case of many towns, the Family Records Centre, and other repositories, hold street indexes. Not every town has an index for every census year. Street indexes can be very complicated and a description of their workings is best left until one actually consults them at the archive. They are often arranged by registration district, sub-district and enumeration district numbers, rather than by TNA piece, folio and page references, and it is necessary to use tables to convert the former into the latter. Streets might run through several enumeration districts, and several different

---

[10] Reference Maps of Registrars' Districts (TNA, RG 18).

pieces may have to be consulted to find the right address. The problems associated with addresses outlined in Chapter 5 should, however, be borne in mind.

Many local family history societies have produced surname indexes for particular areas. The FRC has a collection of many of these but recourse may also be had to the local societies themselves. The addresses of local societies can be obtained through the Federation of Family History Societies.[11] The Society of Genealogists[12] attempts to acquire all census transcripts and indexes as they become available. Some locally produced surname indexes are defective in certain respects. Some fail to give TNA references, preferring idiosyncratic references of their own, or quoting the reel numbers in local repositories. This makes it impossible to use these indexes in the FRC, or in other local record offices and libraries. Some only refer to the names of heads of households, or to surnames without Christian names. It becomes extremely tedious to go through a large number of entries for families called 'Smith', before coming across the household required. Some online indexes are available through, for example, Ancestry.co.uk

In the case of the 1901 census, searching the returns has been made much easier by the online address search facility.

---

[11] See the Federation of Family History Societies website <http://www.ffhs.org.uk> (30 Sept. 2004).
[12] 14 Charterhouse Buildings, Goswell Road, London EC1M 7BA. See also the Society of Genealogists website <http://www.sog.org.uk> (30 Sept. 2004).

11 Some historical skills for census analysis

This chapter is an introduction to some of the methods that historians have used to analyse the census returns, and points to some of their strengths and limitations. Given the range of research that has been undertaken on the returns, only some of the relevant skills can be mentioned, and then in a very preliminary fashion. The aim here is to give an indication of possibilities for those setting out on historical research, rather than to give an exhaustive account. The chapter also aims to indicate some of the issues that researchers need to consider before applying certain methodologies in census research. References are given in the footnotes to sources of detailed methodological guidance. In Chapter 12 examples of the application of some of these and other techniques to the analysis of the census returns are given. For those in higher education institutions who can obtain an Athens password, a more detailed introduction to many of the methods of analysis discussed here can be found on the CHCC website, *British History and the Census*.[1]

Quantification and computing

Many people when they first venture into historical research are tempted to regurgitate verbatim what they find in the sources. Some studies based on the census enumerators' books, for example, take the form of the information in the returns rendered in a descriptive manner – so and so lived next to so and so, there were five labourers in the village, two households ran shops, and so on. This has some value but hardly goes beyond providing a transcript of the original, and indeed lacks the latter's comprehensiveness. Much more information can be conveyed using quantitative techniques which either summarise the returns, thus allowing comparisons with other findings, or which enable the modelling of relationships between variables. It is much more useful to be able to say that 90 per cent of the household heads worked on the land, which was four times the national average, or that there was a statistically significant positive relationship between social status and the employment of servants.

It will not be possible here to go into great detail as to the quantitative methods available for research but an indication of their nature and use might be helpful at this point.[2] Most people

---

[1] Collection of Contemporary Census Data and Materials (CHCC) website, *British History and the Census* <http://chcc.arts.gla.ac.uk> (30 Sept. 2004).

[2] For those wishing such detailed guidance there are numerous relevant works (see R. Floud, *An Introduction to Quantitative Methods for Historians* (London, 1990); K. H. Jarausch and K. A. Hardy, *Quantitative Methods for Historians: a Guide to Research, Data and Statistics* (London, 1991); D. Greenstein, *A Historian's Guide to Computing* (Oxford, 1994), pp. 114–32; M. Drake, D. Mageean and W. T. R. Pryce, 'Quantitative techniques', in *Sources and Methods for Family and Community Historians: a Handbook*, ed. M. Drake and R. Finnegan (Cambridge, 1994), pp. 175–202; P. Hudson, *History by Numbers: an Introduction to Quantitative Approaches* (London, 2000)).

are familiar with the use of summary statistics – averages, percentages and other ratios being obvious examples. Such statistical measures help one to describe the characteristics of data in a shorthand manner. However, the differences between measurements of 'central tendency', such as the mean and the median, and concepts such as the mode, are often not grasped.[3] Measurements of dispersal about the central tendency of a set of data, such as the inter-quartile range and the standard deviation, are also less commonly understood. Thus, it is quite possible for the mean household income of one population to be the same as that of another, but for the gap between the richest and poorest in the two societies to be very different. Put Bill Gates down in a typical Indian village and one will get a very high mean income, even if the vast majority live in the direst poverty. Measurements of 'spread' are useful for summarising such differences.

On the other hand, if one wants to discover the *relationship* between variables, it is possible to resort to techniques such as regression or correlation analyses. Such techniques allow researchers to say that changes in the magnitude of one variable are associated with changes in the magnitude of another, with some unexplained residuum. Thus, for example, one might use regression techniques to measure the positive relationship which existed between increases in the size of farms, as given in the census, and in the number of labourers employed therein.

The use of such statistical techniques need not be an onerous undertaking. Modern computer software exists to enable the capture of census data and their analysis using various statistical processes. Given the ubiquity of personal computers, and commercial software designed for office and home use, the quantitative analysis of census data need no longer be difficult or time-consuming. Due to the vast range of products now available, the problem is more that of selecting the right software for the historian's requirements.[4] This does not mean, of course, that it is not possible to undertake useful quantitative research with a pocket calculator. Calculating and comparing percentages of individuals or households falling into certain categories, for example, can be an effective technique but hardly requires very sophisticated computer software.

None of this detracts, however, from the need for historians to understand the nature and limitations of the statistical techniques that they are using. As was noted above, with respect to household income and wealth distribution, summary statistics can obscure as much as they can illuminate, and are sometimes used consciously to do the former.[5] Statistical techniques are merely tools to do a job, and, as in all such cases, it is necessary to match the tools to the task at

---

[3] The mean is what is commonly referred to as the average – the sum of the values of individual cases divided by the number of cases. The mode is simply the value among the individual cases which appears most often. The median is that value of a variable which splits the cases into two halves, so that there are as many cases with values below the median value as there are with values larger than the median value.

[4] See Greenstein, *A Historian's Guide to Computing*; Hudson, *History by Numbers*, pp. 218–46; M. J. Lewis and R. Lloyd-Jones, *Using Computers in History: a Practical Guide* (London, 1996); E. Mawdsley and T. Munck, *Computing for Historians: an Introductory Guide* (Manchester, 1993); and K. Schürer, 'Computing', in Drake and Finnigan, *Sources and Methods for Family and Community Historians*, pp. 203–20. That much of the detail in these commentaries may now be obsolete reflects the speed with which information technology is developing. But they should give a good introduction to the general approach to historical computing.

[5] D. Huff, *How to Lie with Statistics* (London, 1991).

hand. It is also important to realise what one is doing when one uses such techniques – any tool can be used inappropriately, and the more powerful the tool, the more ridiculous may be the results. In addition, one must remember that statistical relationships do not necessarily imply causal relationships. There is, no doubt, a strong positive relationship between the consumption of ice cream and the use of suntan lotion, but this does not mean that eating ice cream results in the desire to apply such lotions to one's person. These variables are not causally linked to one another, they are linked independently to a third variable, the length and intensity of exposure to sunlight. In other cases apparent statistical relationships may merely reflect coincidence. Advanced statistical methods exist for investigating such effects. In short, statistics are interpretative devices rather than 'facts'.

Lastly, and perhaps inevitably, it should always be remembered that no amount of statistical sophistication or computing power can make up for unquantifiable deficiencies in the original data.[6] If a sample is biased, or a source is deficient in some other unrecognised respect, then the result of any statistical analysis may also be biased or misleading. All the limitations and deficiencies of nineteenth-century census data rehearsed in previous chapters should be taken into consideration when using quantitative techniques in this field. One should always bear in mind the acronym GIGO, standing for the old computing adage 'Garbage In, Garbage Out'. This is not to dissuade researchers from applying such techniques, merely to advocate their informed use.

Sampling strategies

One of the main problems associated with the study of census returns is their sheer bulk. If the aggregate information which the historian seeks has already been abstracted and published in contemporary *Census Reports* (see Chapter 13), all to the good. However, the aggregation of census data in the *Reports* only goes down to certain geographical levels, and often does not include the cross-tabulation of census variables that would interest historians. If, for example, one wants to study the relationship between household structure and the occupation of household heads in selected portions of differing cities, this information is not ready-tabulated. On the other hand, capturing and analysing data from all the households in the selected populations may well be beyond the resources of the individual researcher. In such circumstances recourse to sampling may be necessary.

The term 'sample' causes endless confusion because it has several meanings. A 'sample' can be a selection of items, or a single item, which stands as an example. The 'samples' that used to be carried by commercial sales representatives, or selected forms used in a bureaucratic process preserved in an archive as an 'administrative epitome', might be included here.[7] These are rather

---

[6] This is not to say that is impossible make good the deficiencies of data if one has a good idea of the nature of their bias or shortfall (see Wrigley and Schofield, *The Population History of England, 1541–1871*, pp. 15–156).

[7] The National Archives record series RG 27 (GRO: Forms and Instructions for taking the Census) is just such a 'sample'.

different from sampling in the statistical sense, in which a sub-set of the members of a population is selected, and then inferences drawn, within certain bounds of probability, from the characteristics of that sample as to the characteristics of the population as a whole. Opinion polls are a classic example of sampling in the statistical sense. Intuitively it is possible to grasp that one does not have to have seen every human being in the world in order to gain a reasonable idea of what human beings look like. Since, in this sense, the part can stand for the whole, with some room for possible error, historians need only analyse some of the individuals or households in a census population in order to gain a picture of the characteristics of all such entities.

Statistics can also give an idea of the margin of error of any conclusions drawn from such samples. This error is dependent on the variability of the characteristics in the population to be sampled, and the size of the sample. Thus, if one wanted to know how many heads all living human beings had, excluding Siamese twins, a sample of one would be sufficient and there would be no margin of error. The variability of this characteristic is zero. On the other hand, if information is sought on the distribution of money incomes by household on a world-wide basis, a far larger sample would be required, and the results of such an exercise would be liable to some uncertainty. If the size of the population to be sampled, and the variability of the characteristics within it, are known, mathematical procedures exist which will allow one to establish the size of sample to draw.

Similar procedures also allow the reliability of any results from such a sample to be established; that, for example, one can be 95 per cent certain that the mean value of a characteristic in a sample will be the same as that in the population as a whole, plus or minus a certain amount. In general terms, the larger the sample the more reliable the results in terms of the narrower the bounds within which a certain level of probability is valid. Since the measurement of several characteristics of the same population may be required, some of which may be more variable than others, a sample size that may be adequate for one purpose may be inadequate for another. If a sample is to be used to examine more than one characteristic in a population, then the sample size needs to be large enough to allow significant results to be derived for the most variable characteristic. The sample size also has to be large enough to enable statistically significant results to be derived for the smallest sub-set of the population to be analysed. A sample of households may, for example, allow one to say something significant about the mean size of all households but it might not give one enough cases to say anything significant about the sub-set of houses headed by a small number of women.

It may be necessary, therefore, to take a pilot sample in order to get some idea of the relative frequency of the appearance or variability of certain characteristics.[8] It should be noted here

---

[8] It will not be possible to go in any depth into the statistical procedures used in sampling but these can be found in many texts on statistics, such as W. G. Cochran, *Sampling Techniques* (New York, 1977). Introductions to the theory of sampling, with historians specifically in mind, can be found in Floud, *An Introduction to Quantitative Methods for Historians*; Greenstein, *A Historian's Guide to Computing*, pp. 203–10; Hudson, *History by Numbers*, ch. 7; Jarausch and Hardy, *Quantitative Methods for Historians*, ch. 4; and R. S. Schofield, 'Sampling in historical research', in Wrigley, *Nineteenth-Century Society*, pp. 146–90.

that the sample size is a number of cases sampled rather than a percentage of the population. A random sample of 100 cases drawn from a population of 10,000 may give as accurate a picture of that population as a sample of 1,000 cases. A 10 per cent sample may be no better than a one per cent sample.

This whole statistical edifice is based on the concept of randomness, that each item in the population has an equal chance of appearing in the sample. A conscious selection made of all the tall people in a population would not enable one to say anything about the average height of the population as a whole. The most statistically valid method for drawing a random sample is first to assign a number to each entity in the population to be sampled (the census households in a registration district, for example)[9] and then to use a random number table to draw a sufficiently large sample. A random number table is essentially a list of numbers generated by a computer in a random manner. Often people take every *n*th element in the population as a simple way of drawing a sample. This procedure, usually termed systematic sampling, can substitute for a random sample, but only if there is no underlying structure in the data. Thus, if all the streets in a town contained 20 houses, and the house at the end of every street was a corner shop, and all shops were corner shops, a systematic sample of every 20th house would contain either all shopkeepers, or none at all. If practical, purely random sampling is always advisable.

Other, more sophisticated, types of sampling, such as cluster and stratified analysis, are, of course, possible. Thus, in cluster sampling, a number of complete census enumerator's districts might be selected randomly to represent the population of a whole city or country. Alternatively, in stratified sampling, a sample could be taken from particular sections of the population which had been predefined. The case records of hospital patients, for example, might first of all be sorted into groups according to ailments, and then sampled differently within each grouping. One might sample one per cent of those relating to common disorders, 10 per cent of less common ones, and all of the extremely unusual ailments. Both types of sampling have their uses, but have different implications for calculations of likely levels of confidence in results drawn from them.

A variation on the stratified sample is to draw one random sample from a stratum within a population and then to draw another random sample from the complete population. The latter acts as a 'control', showing how the sub-set in the stratum varies from the population as a whole. An example might be sampling households with servants in a particular town, and then comparing the results from this with another sample drawn from all households in the area under consideration.[10] Since the results from both samples can only be said to be true with some margin of error (say they are 95 per cent likely to fall within a certain range), then it is only possible to claim to be 95 per cent certain that the ranges do not overlap and that there is, therefore, a true difference. This type of analysis can also be used to examine the characteristics of the same stratum over time, by comparing the results of analysing samples drawn randomly from the same stratum in the census returns of differing censuses.

---

[9] This is the creation of a 'sampling frame'.

[10] This was the procedure used in Higgs, *Domestic Servants and Households in Rochdale, 1851–1871*.

Because of the complexities of sampling methods, they should only be used if the questions to be answered require the analysis of large populations. If the population to be analysed is that of a parish or a small township, it may prove just as convenient to input all households.

Industrial classifications and occupational coding

Historians are usually not very interested in occupations for their own sake but for the information that they give on economic structure. In the nineteenth century this tends to mean the division of the working population into the three great sectors of classical economics: the primary extractive sector made up of agriculture and mining; the manufacturing sector; and the tertiary or commercial sector of retail, transport, service and white-collar workers. Lurking here is the old economic distinction between land and capital, and between 'productive' and 'unproductive' labour. The movements of labour from the primary sector to the secondary and tertiary sectors are also seen as having immense implications within theories of 'modernisation' and urbanisation. Statements that a particular community was 'agricultural', 'industrial' or 'commercial', are usually based on implicit or explicit occupational groupings of this nature.

It is often convenient to consolidate occupations into larger groupings on purely pragmatic grounds, since this facilitates comparisons between populations and over time. Classification is inevitable, given that human beings can only process so much information at a time. A listing of the number of people in 500 separate occupations only becomes meaningful if these occupations are grouped in some manner. But this has to proceed via some principles that may or may not be very sensible or clear. Classification is, therefore, a step away from the original data, but an inevitable one.[11] More will be said about the problems inherent in classification in Chapter 13.

Various classifications of occupational data have been devised for these purposes.[12] The GRO used its own classification systems when abstracting and tabling occupations in the published *Census Reports*, which were based on rather different principles from those with which social scientists are familiar today. The most widely used system today for studying the Victorian censuses is probably that elaborated by Charles Booth in the 1880s. Booth took the occupational headings in the *Census Reports* and arranged them in the following main groupings:

[11] For some further consideration of the issue of classification, see E. Higgs, 'The General Register Office and the tabulation of data, 1837–1939', in *From Sumer to the Spreadsheets: the Curious History of Tables*, ed. M. Campbell-Kelly, M. Croarken, R. Flood and E. Robson (Oxford, 2003), pp. 209–34; E. Higgs, 'The linguistic construction of social and medical categories in the work of the English General Register Office', in *The Qualitative Dimension of Quantitative Demography*, ed. S. Szreter, A. Dharmalingam and H. Sholkamy (Oxford, 2004), pp. 86–106.

[12] For an introduction to the main industrial classifications, see D. R. Mills and K. Schürer, 'Employment and occupations', in Mills and Schürer, *Local Communities in the Victorian Census Enumerators' Books*, pp. 139–50. See also Wrigley, 'The occupational structure of England in the mid-nineteenth century', pp. 129–203.

Agriculture, breeding and fishing
Mining and quarrying
Building and contracting
Manufacture
Transport
Dealing
Industrial service (Commercial)
Industrial service (General and unspecified labour)
Public service and professional
Domestic service
Property owning, indefinite and 'dependent'

A description of the structure of Booth's schema, and a detailed breakdown of the headings in Booth's occupational groupings, with some minor revisions, has been supplied by W. A. Armstrong.[13]

There are certain practical difficulties with using such a classification schema. First, the Booth-Armstrong system only goes down to the level of the hundreds of occupational headings given in the published *Census Reports*. There are, however, thousands of actual occupational titles in the census returns, and it is not always easy to interpret their meaning, although this can sometimes be inferred from the local context. A much more serious problem is not deciding where an occupation should go in the classification but whether individuals should be regarded as occupied or not. For example, does the wife of a farmer work in agriculture? Booth's original schema was also problematic because his distinction between those who made things, and those who sold them, was sometimes arbitrary. This was, however, a distinction that could often not be made in practice. Perhaps, above all, such schema only work if individuals are given meaningful occupational titles to begin with. Some of these issues are considered in more detail in Chapter 13.

When entering occupational data on computer, historians have often used codes corresponding to the headings in occupational classification systems, rather than the original descriptions themselves. A particular occupational term is entered as '026.07', or some other such code. This goes back to the days when data were entered into computers by being punched on 80-column cards, each variable describing a family or individual being allocated a fixed field of so many characters. With modern database packages and other types of computer software these restrictions no longer apply. It is advisable, therefore, to enter full occupational titles on computer, including spelling variants, then to have a separate field for standardised occupational titles, and finally to code the latter in a third field. This allows greater flexibility, and the comparative luxury of being able to revise the coding system later, if necessary.[14]

---

[13] Armstrong, 'The use of information about occupation', pp. 260–310.

[14] K. Schürer, 'The historical researcher and codes: master and slave or slave and master', in *History and Computing III: Historians, Computers and Data – Applications in Research and Teaching*, ed. E. Mawdsley, N. Morgan, L. Richmond and R. Trainor (Manchester, 1990), pp. 74–82. The whole subject is discussed in greater detail in *The Use of Occupations in Historical Analysis*, ed. K. Schürer and H. Diederiks (St Katharinen, 1993).

Socio-economic groupings

Historians and sociologists have also used the occupational data in the censuses to construct various measurements of the status of households.[15] These usually draw upon the social classifications of occupations put together by the GRO in the twentieth century, based on the principle that census households can be assigned to specific social strata, or classes, according to the occupation of the household head. These are further conceived as a small number of ordered grades forming a hierarchy of status, which are assumed to exist throughout society in essentially the same form regardless of locality or community. Some type of ordering of this nature may be a useful prerequisite for analysing aspects of social structure but it is important to realise that the GRO's social classifications rest upon certain debatable assumptions that reflect their historical origins.

As Simon Szreter has shown, the GRO's original 1911 classification was an attempt to establish hierarchies of status in order to examine eugenicist claims that contemporary declines in fertility were due to a decrease in family size among the 'higher' classes. The assumption was made by both the eugenicists and the GRO that society could be ordered into an occupational hierarchy that would measure 'intelligence' or 'skill'. Inevitably, the civil servants at the GRO placed themselves in the highest social class in their own classification. What was originally a very *ad hoc* system of groupings became, over time, a rigid five-part structure which was supposed to capture accurately levels of education. These, in turn, were used to underpin a defusionist view of family limitation based on access to information respecting mechanical means of birth control.[16] Such schema should, therefore, be used with some caution, and, if possible, in conjunction with other proxies for wealth, such as income or the levels of rent or rates paid.

Following the work of Armstrong on the 1841 and 1851 censuses, the most frequently used schema for such assignments in the Victorian period has been his revised version of that drawn up by the GRO for use in the census of 1951.[17] By the use of occupational dictionaries each occupation is assigned to one of five classes:

Class I   Professional, etc., occupations
Class II   Intermediate occupations
Class III Skilled occupations
Class IV   Partly skilled occupations
Class V   Unskilled occupations

---

[15] For an introduction to some of the social classification systems most frequently used by historians, see Mills and Schürer, 'Employment and occupations', pp. 150–9.

[16] S. R. S. Szreter, 'The genesis of the registrar-general's social classification of occupations', *British Journal of Sociology*, 35 (1984), pp. 522–46; S. Szreter, *Fertility, Class and Gender in Britain 1860–1914* (Cambridge, 1996), pp. 67–282. See also, Higgs, *Life, Death and Statistics*, pp. 141–9. It may well be that occupation and local labour markets, and their impact on relationships between men and women, were more important determinants of family size than socially stratified 'intelligence' or education.

[17] Armstrong, 'The use of information about occupation', pp. 198–225; Armstrong, *Stability and Change in an English County Town*, pp. 13–15. A condensed version of this schema can be found in D. Mills and M. Drake, 'The census, 1801–1991', in Drake and Finnegan, *Sources and Methods for Family and Community Historians*, pp. 48–9.

An accountant, and his family, would, for example, be placed in Class I, and a road labourer in Class V.

Armstrong modified the 1951 attribution lists in the following manner for use with the 1851 census data:

1) all employers of 25 or more persons were raised to Class I, whatever their classification in the registrar-general's 1951 list;

2) all 'dealers', 'merchants', except those distinctly described as brokers or agents (Class II) or hawkers (Class V), and all persons engaged in retail board, lodging and catering were initially classed as III, despite the fact that the registrar-general's list placed them variously;

3) from Class III (or in a few cases IV), upon consideration of individual cases, those who employed at least one person, other than their own family, were then raised to Class II. In boarding, catering, etc., the employment of one or more servants was taken to count for this purpose;

4) house and land proprietors, those 'living off interest' or 'of independent means', annuitants and paupers were placed in Classes I, I, I, II and V respectively;

5) uninformative entries such as 'husband away', or 'spinster' were placed in a residual Class X, and retired persons were classified on the basis of their previous occupations.

Armstrong had to modify his schema still further for the analysis of the 1841 census because at that date individuals were not asked to state whether or not they were employers, or their number of employees. He again used the 1951 attributions as his point of departure but used the following modifications:

Class I	as in 1851, fewer unidentified large entrepreneurs;
Class II	individuals who would have been assigned to Classes II and III according to the 1851 procedures, provided that they employed at least one servant;
Class III	the same, where no servants were employed;
Classes IV and V	according to the initial attribution list.

This schema has been criticised on the grounds that it is inappropriate to use a twentieth-century social classification to order nineteenth-century data. The Armstrong classification also assigns a very large number of households to Class III.[18] Similarly, Armstrong depends upon information on the employment of servants to assign households to socio-economic groups. As was noted in Chapters 7 and 8, however, the exact employment status of 'servants' can be obscure. In 1841 there was no column for relationship to head, so there is no way of telling if a person with a

---

[18] Armstrong, *Stability and Change in an English County Town*, p. 15.

servant occupation was in service in the household in which they resided. They may have been day or unemployed servants living with relatives or in lodgings. The relationship between servant employment and social status is also not as clear cut as one might assume.[19] Armstrong 'proves' the validity of his schema, in part, by showing that the employment of servants was greater on average the higher one goes up his social scale.[20] But this is, to some extent, a circular argument, especially in 1841, because he uses the employment of servants to assign households to his higher social categories. As noted above, some of these problems might be overcome by linking census data to other sources.[21]

There are also problems over the use of the number of hands employed. Some employers neglected to give this information, and they would have been perfectly correct to do so from 1861 onwards if they were one of the partners in a firm. The Armstrong system breaks down after 1881 because in 1891 and 1901 employers were not required to state the number of hands that they employed. The classification can only be used with any degree of confidence for the 30-year period from 1851 to 1881.[22]

Life-cycle stages

Another problem with such socio-economic classification systems is that they assign households to status groups according to the occupation of the, usually male, household head. However, as Seebohm Rowntree showed in the early twentieth century, prosperity was often determined among the working classes by the total family income, including that brought in by wives and children, and the total number of dependants to be fed.[23] This has led some historians to group households, for the purposes of analysis, into life-cycle stages according to the relative number of children in and out of employment. A working-class household with a large number of children not at work is assumed potentially to be in more difficult financial circumstances than one without children, or with children at work. The use of such classifications for the analysis of nineteenth-century census data was pioneered by Anderson,[24] who distinguished, for married couples only, the following stages:

---

[19] Higgs, *Domestic Servants and Households in Rochdale*, pp. 102–9.

[20] Armstrong, 'The use of information about occupation', pp. 211–12.

[21] For further discussion of the problems of using such systems of social stratification, see W. A. Armstrong, 'The interpretation of census enumerators' books for Victorian towns', in *The Study of Urban History*, ed. H. J. Dyos (London, 1968), pp. 67–86, and the subsequent discussions therein. See also S. A. Royle, 'Social stratification from early census returns: a new approach', *AREA*, 9 (1977), pp. 215–19; R. S. Holmes and W. A. Armstrong, 'Social stratification', *AREA*, 10 (1978), pp. 126–9; D. R. Mills and J. Mills, 'Occupation and social stratification revisited: the census enumerators' books of Victorian Britain', in *Urban History Yearbook 1989* (Leicester, 1989), pp. 63–71.

[22] For an example of the use of use of a schema for social stratification in a local study, see M. Warwick and D. Warwick, 'Burley-in-Wharfedale in the nineteenth century: a study of social stratification and social mobility', *Local Population Studies*, 54 (1995), pp. 40–55.

[23] B. S. Rowntree, *Poverty: a Study of Town Life* (London, 1901), pp. 28–9; B. S. Rowntree, *Poverty and Progress: a Second Social Survey of York* (London, 1941), pp. 155–71.

[24] Anderson, *Family Structure in Nineteenth Century Lancashire*, p. 202.

1. Wife under 45, no children at home.
2. Wife under 45, one child under one year old at home.
3. Children at home, but none in employment.
4. Children at home, and some, but under half, in employment.
5. Children at home, and half, or over half, in employment.
6. Wife 45 and over, no children, or one only over 20, at home.

The analysis of households arranged in this schema is a much more subtle use of sociological methodology. There are still problems, however, with the construction of such groupings. The work of women is obscured in this classification, and it is dependent upon the employment of children being given consistently. As was noted in Chapter 8, this is just the sort of occupational data that the census often obscures. At best, life-cycle stages, as well as socio-economic groupings, must be regarded as relatively crude analytical tools.[25]

Record linkage

The Victorian censuses are unique among historical sources from that period in that they place individuals in a temporal, spatial and social context. Historians can establish exactly where a person was on a particular night, and show the relationship of that person both to the household in which he or she lived, and to the broader society in which he or she worked and migrated. Individuals, families and whole communities can be traced across censuses. Given the wealth of information contained in the census enumerators' books it is perhaps understandable that many people using the returns never venture beyond the source. This is a pity, since the information that they contain, especially with respect to names and addresses, can be extremely useful in linking these records to other historical sources. In the present work there have been several examples of the usefulness of such procedures. In a sense the comparison of the same household in two censuses, based on similarities of name, relationship to head, addresses, and so on, is an example of such linkage. Numerous other kinds of historical record, such as maps, rate books, employment records, trade directories and civil registration data, can be associated with the census returns in an analogous manner.[26]

It is often quite easy to establish that two records relate to the same family or individual, as, for example, when in two censuses households live at the same address and have the same, or consistent, information with respect to the names, ages, birthplaces, and so on, of their members. But what of the man living alone at differing addresses with the same name and birthplace but a different occupation and an age discrepancy of three years? Some characteristics such as occupation, marital status and medical disabilities plainly change over time, and are difficult to

---

[25] See Mills and Schürer, *Local Communities in the Victorian Census Enumerators' Books*, section 5, for a discussion of the various approaches to using census data to study family and household.

[26] For the range of local sources available, see, for example, W. B. Stephens, *Sources for English Local History* (Chichester, 1994); Drake and Finnegan, *Sources and Methods for Family and Community Historians*.

use for purposes of inter-censal identification. Some occupational changes, however, are suggestive of occupational mobility, as in the case of a shift from bricklayer's labourer to bricklayer, or a move between related occupations such as brewer and maltster. On the other hand, few Victorians moved from working as an agricultural labourer to practising as a physician in 10 years!

Other characteristics, such as age or birthplace, should not change between censuses, or progress in units other than 10, but often do. Perhaps age discrepancies of plus or minus two or three years can be allowed, as, possibly, can birthplace changes involving adjacent parishes or the substitution of place of residence for another birthplace. Names might usually be taken as invariant, unless examples appear to represent obvious misspellings, or phonetic variations. The comparison of census returns for whole households, containing a majority of easily identifiable persons, may enable the establishment of a link between two individuals across censuses even where the anomalies in the returns might disqualify a link if they lived alone. Similar issues arise when linking census data with other sources, such as parish registers or poll books. Much of this type of linkage, which was once done by hand, can now be undertaken by computer algorithms.

Plainly some linkages are more certain than others, and it is important to make explicit what counts as evidence that two individuals or families are the 'same' in any exercise of this nature. Useful pointers as to how this can be done can be found in the extensive literature respecting family reconstitution; the linking of ecclesiastical records relating to baptisms, marriages and burials; and the application of computing techniques to record linkage.[27]

---

[27] *Identifying People in the Past*, ed. E. A. Wrigley (London, 1973); R. J. Morris, 'In search of the urban middle class. Record linkage and methodology: Leeds, 1832', in *Urban History Yearbook 1976* (Leicester, 1976), pp. 15–20; *History and Computing: Special Issue on Record Linkage*, 4 (1992); *History and Computing: Special Issue on Record Linkage, II*, 6 (1994); I. Winchester, 'What every historian needs to know about record linkage for the microcomputer era', *Historical Methods*, 25 (1992), pp. 149–65; C. Harvey, E. Green and P. Corfield, 'Record linkage theory and practice: an experiment in the application of multiple pass linkage algorithms', *History and Computing*, 8 (1996), pp. 78–89; P. Tilley, 'Creating life histories and family trees from nineteenth century census records, parish registers and other sources', *Local Population Studies*, 68 (2002), pp. 63–81. The articles in the *History and Computing* volumes contain numerous other useful references. For a helpful introduction to the whole subject, see A. Todd, *Nuts and Bolts: Family History Problem Solving Through Family Reconstitution Techniques* (Bury, 2003).

12 An introduction to using the census in historical research

In recent years the emphasis within the teaching of history at all levels has shifted from the imparting of knowledge to the imparting of skills, although there is plainly debate over what is the correct balance between the two. Many universities now include formal teaching in historical and research methodologies as part of their first and further degree courses. In a world dominated by the need to find employment, the teaching of the skills of locating, evaluating, interpreting and processing evidence is plainly of importance. This explains why grant awarding bodies in higher education, such as the Economic and Social Research Council (ESRC) and the Arts and Humanities Research Board (AHRB), only reward funding for doctoral research to students who have received training in historical skills. In this respect the use of census data to reconstruct past societies, especially through the use of quantitative and computer techniques, is good training both in historical research and in transferable skills in general.

With this in mind, this chapter is an attempt to put to work some of the procedures that can be used to study Victorian communities from the census returns. These can be employed by those undertaking their own local studies but will also be helpful for those teaching or seeking to understand research methodologies. The focus here will be local and communal, as is appropriate in an introduction to research methods. A fairly narrow geographical focus also facilitates linkages with a wider range of alternative sources. Where appropriate, references will be made to other relevant sections in the handbook. The chapter includes an analysis of some contrasting communities in the 1901 census, in order to show the application of some of the skills and methodologies outlined in Chapter 11.

Reconstructing communities: preparation

The first, and in many ways the most important, question to answer before embarking on a local study is what is meant by the 'community' to be analysed. Local historians have naturally tended to define their domains of study in spatial terms but how big should the unit of analysis be? It might be argued that this depends on the time and resources available. The use of sampling techniques, however, makes this a somewhat redundant argument, since a comparatively small number of households, if randomly chosen, can stand as proxy for a much larger community. It might be more sensible to define the area to be studied in terms of the questions being addressed. If one wants to know what a village or town was like 100 years ago, the geographical area covered by that entity today could be the unit of analysis. If working-class housing conditions in a city are the subject to be investigated, a smaller area might be studied than if one were interested in the spatial segregation of social classes in the same entity. What is important is not the size of the area, or even its population, but the need to avoid abstracting and analysing census data that are not germane to the investigation being undertaken.

Given the manner in which the census returns are arranged, registration areas, districts or sub-districts are often the simplest geographical areas to handle. When comparing the same population in two censuses, it is important to ensure that the areas covered by the registration districts in question are constant over time. The tables of population in the published *Census Reports* (see Chapter 13) often contain notes on boundary changes. In some cases, however, especially where the unit of analysis is small, it may be necessary to compare the descriptions of the enumerations districts at the front of the books, or even list the streets in the returns. These procedures sound somewhat pedantic but are necessary to ensure that changes in the characteristics of a population of a named district reflect more than the omission or inclusion of some habitations. If one collects information from administrative units other than registration districts – civil parishes for example – one must not assume that the results from any analysis of that data will match the population totals for registration units given in the *Census Reports*.

When choosing an area for analysis, it is always important to consider what other sources are available for that district. What contemporary maps, newspapers, directories, voting records, rate books, photographs, and so on, exist, and are they easily accessible? An initial trawl through the local record office or public library is always advisable prior to collecting and analysing census data. Such institutions may have bibliographies of secondary material that could be of use. They will also have the addresses of local and family history societies, which can provide other useful guidance.

Before embarking on the proposed analysis, it is always a good idea to undertake a pilot, in which relevant questions are asked of a small portion of the available census data. This allows one to determine the feasibility of the chosen research strategy, and to establish the amount of time a full analysis would take. At this stage it can be discovered whether or not the census returns will answer the sort of questions it is intended to ask of them, or if the resources required for data input dictate a recourse to sampling. Researchers often underestimate the amount of time that data preparation and inputting takes, and miscalculations at this stage can play havoc with timetables for the completion of a project. It is necessary, of course, to weigh the time saved in inputting through sampling with the extra time needed to learn and apply the sorts of statistical techniques noted in Chapter 11. If one does not feel equal to the latter, it may be necessary to reduce the amount of census data analysed by diminishing the scope of the project instead.

Reconstructing communities: analysis

When moving from the study of the life histories of individuals or families to that of the structure of communities over time, one tends to move from the particular to the aggregate.

Although database management systems can be used to match individuals in differing censuses, they, and the statistical routines that they can deploy, come into their own when handling data relating to larger entities. Since the principles upon which such software packages work, and the functions that they can perform, differ, it would be unhelpful to attempt to describe them here in any detail. As such, the suggestions in this section for types of analysis with respect to census communities should be read in conjunction with the more detailed sources of advice on quantification and computing referenced in Chapter 11. It is also important to ensure that the information input is as close as possible to the original returns, and that coding is undertaken at a secondary stage, as recommended in the section on industrial classifications and occupational coding in the same chapter. This is not to say that the analysis of local populations cannot be undertaken using index cards and a pocket calculator, merely that the speed of analysis is greatly reduced, as is, therefore, the range of questions that can be asked within the time at one's disposal.

For the purposes of demonstrating the sort of analysis that can be undertaken via the census enumerators' books, the author was supplied by QinetiQ with a digitised version of the returns for four communities in the 1901 census:[1] East Tuddenham in Norfolk, parts of Salford in Lancashire, Senghenydd in Glamorganshire, and parts of Spitalfields in the East End of London.[2] Since the data were already in a standard digitised format, with the columns of data delineated by commas, it was a comparatively simple procedure to input this information into a database package. This obviated the tasks of data abstraction and input, and allowed the work to proceed immediately to data analysis. As already noted, if data is available ready-digested, this cuts out the most tedious part of any research project. But it is important to ensure that the original data inputting has been done to a satisfactory standard.

The four selected communities were very different places, whose contrasting structures and characteristics are easily shown by a quantitative analysis.[3] East Tuddenham was a typical Norfolk farming village, some nine miles west of Norwich. Salford was an industrial town near Manchester in Lancashire based on the cotton industry, and was still growing rapidly in 1901, at which time its population had reached 220,957. In 1901, Senghenydd was a newly developed mining village, some four miles from Caerphilly in South Wales. Its colliery produced coal for use by ships, and was owned by the Universal Colliery Company, which had been established as recently as 1889. Spitalfields in East London had by 1901 become home to a large population of Jewish immigrants, mainly from Russia and Eastern Europe. The area had the reputation of being the poorest and most dangerous in the East End of London, and had been the stalking ground of Jack the Ripper in the 1880s.

---

[1] QinetiQ funded the transcription of the 1901 census and the 1901 Census Online website <http://www.1901census.nationalarchives.gov.uk> (30 Sept. 2004).

[2] TNA, RG 13/1870, fos. 7–87; TNA, RG 13/3737, fos. 119–58; TNA, RG 13/5000, fos. 1–66; TNA, RG 13/298, fos. 1–70.

[3] They are also the subject of a website on the 1901 Census maintained by TNA on 'Pathways to the past' <http://www.nationalarchives.gov.uk/pathways/census/> (30 Sept. 2004).

Paul Glenister, a research student of the author, created a database of the census returns for these communities, and produced tabulations for each of the four places showing the following:

1) age pyramids of the numbers of males and females in 5 year age spans, and the percentage in each cohort;

2) the percentage of the working population in occupational sectors by sex, based on the Booth-Armstrong classification (see Chapter 11);

3) the percentage of the total population in occupational sectors by sex, based on the Booth-Armstrong classification (see Chapter 11);

4) for birthplaces – the percentage born in the place of enumeration; the percentage born in the rest of England and Wales; the percentage born in Ireland; the percentage born in Scotland; the percentage born outside UK; and a list of the places of birth outside the UK;

5) for birthplaces of household heads – the percentage born in the place of enumeration; the percentage born in the rest of England and Wales; the percentage born in Ireland; the percentage born in Scotland; the percentage born outside UK; and a list of the places of birth outside the UK.

These tabulations were later manipulated by the author, using a standard spreadsheet package, to create the tables in Appendix 9.

The first thing that can be seen from Tables 1 and 2 in Appendix 9 is the difference in terms of migration into these communities. East Tuddenham was a place in which the majority of people, and of household heads, had been born in the village. A quick scan of the original data reveals that most of those who had migrated into East Tuddenham had done so from within East Anglia. This short-range migration pattern was typical of much of rural England in the Victorian period, as had been noted by Ernest George Ravenstein as early as the 1880s.[4] This pattern might have been shown more clearly, however, if an additional category, 'Born in the same county', had been introduced into the analysis. Alternatively, although this would have meant a great deal of extra labour, the distance of birthplaces from East Tuddenham could have been calculated and presented in ranges of miles.[5] Deciding on how to group data is not always an easy matter, and one may want to rework material to get the most informative results. This is not massaging the data, merely presenting underlying patterns in the most telling manner. The question that needs to be asked is, rather, whether the extra work involved would give sufficient extra information, and thus merit the expense in terms of effort forgone elsewhere.

---

[4] E. G. Ravenstein, 'The laws of migration', *Journal of the Statistical Society of London*, 48 (1885), pp. 167–235.
[5] Higgs, *Domestic Servants and Households in Rochdale, 1851–1871*, p. 67.

The Spitalfields data presents a very different picture. Here only a small minority of the household heads had been born locally, and a majority had been born outside the United Kingdom. Even in the population as a whole, including children, just over 40 per cent had been born abroad. Unlike the 2001 census, the 1901 enumeration did not ask for information on the ethnicity or religion of individuals. However, the large number of people with Jewish names from Poland, Romania and Russia indicates that these people may well have been economic migrants or refugees fleeing pogroms in those countries. This is, of course, confirmed by other contemporary sources.

The birthplaces of family members can give one an insight into the journeys made by these families. Take the case, for example, of the Rosen family of 79 Rothchilds Building, Block C.[6] The head of the family, Lazarus, was a cap maker aged 42, who was married to Leah, aged 36. Both had been born in 'Russia, Wilna', which is presumably Vilnius in modern-day Lithuania. However, very early in their marriage they had moved to Norway, because they had a daughter and a son, aged 19 and 17 respectively, who had been born there. But they had stayed in Norway for only a short period because they then had two more daughters, aged 15 and 14, who were again born in Vilnius. At some date in the next eight years they had moved to London, because another daughter, Sarah, who was six years old, was born there. A daughter, Fanny, aged three, and a son, Abraham, six months old in 1901, and both born in London, completed the family. One might speculate on why there was an eight-year gap between the birth of the last child in Vilnius and that of Sarah in London – had the family been temporarily broken up in some way, or had some children died? Only additional written sources, or perhaps family traditions, could explain what happened.

Yet again, at 10 Godfrey House in Thrawl Street one finds the Heidelman household, headed by Joseph Heidelman, a cabinet maker from Russia. Joseph, said to be a Russian subject, was married to Minnie, who was also born in Russia. They were aged 30 years and 29 years respectively, and their eldest son, Woolf, aged 11, had been born in Whitechapel. But he had two brothers, Myer and Solomon, aged seven and five, who had been born in Nottingham. By the time of the birth of their daughter Esther, aged three, they had moved back to London, to Spitalfields. Here, their last daughter, Sarah, had also been born 10 months before census night. Compared to the population of East Tuddenham, where no-one had been born outside the United Kingdom, such people were highly mobile on an international scale.

The Salford districts and Senghenydd also show interesting migration patterns. Both populations had comparatively low levels of household heads born in the place of enumeration. But the Welsh coal-mining community also had the lowest proportion of all the four areas when it came to the proportion of the community as a whole, barely 18 per cent, who had their birthplaces in Senghenydd itself. Even very few children had been born there. This reflects the fact, no doubt, that Senghenydd was a new community built around a recently opened pit, while Salford, although a place of in-migration, was much better established. In both cases the in-migration was mostly from nearby settlements – Manchester and Lancashire in the case of Salford, and other mining

---

[6] TNA, RG 13/298, fo. 12, p. 17.

communities in Glamorganshire and Monmouthshire in the case of Senghenydd. However, Salford was unique in the four settlements in terms of the high proportion of the Irish in the community. This was a reflection of the long-standing migration from Ireland, dating from before the time of the Irish Famine, that Friedrich Engels had noted in his *Condition of the Working-Class in England* in the 1840s.[7]

The four communities were also very different in the nature of their occupational structures. As Tables 3 and 4 in Appendix 9 show, the men in both East Tuddenham and Senghenydd were following a comparatively narrow range of occupations, while comparatively few women had any jobs at all. Nearly 90 per cent of all men with jobs in East Tuddenham in 1901 were working in agriculture, while a not dissimilar proportion of the male workforce in Senghenydd was employed as coal miners. Most of the women with jobs in the Norfolk community were domestic servants, while the very few employed women in Senghenydd were also servants, or dressmakers. One has, of course, to be a little careful about such pronouncements, given the possibility of seasonal employment in agriculture, and elsewhere, as discussed in Chapter 9. Such patterns were, however, typical of agricultural and mining communities in this period. The preponderance of a declining industry such as agriculture in East Tuddenham would explain why there was so little migration into the area in comparative terms. The lack of work for women in mining communities has also been put forward as the reason for the high fertility in such places – lacking the independence that employment and wages brought, women may not have been able to insist on sexual abstinence within marriage to control pregnancies.[8]

Salford and Spitalfields, on the other hand, had a wider range of occupations for both men and women. In the Salford districts examined, over a third of men worked in textile manufacture, although there were also large numbers involved in transport and warehousing, and in the manufacturing of machinery. These latter sectors in the local economy may, of course, have been dependent upon the textile industry. As will be noted in the next chapter, it is not always possible to establish in which particular industries people worked from their occupations alone. It was only in the twentieth century that a question on industry of employment was introduced into the census enumeration. In the Salford districts over a quarter of all women had jobs, mainly in textiles, and this has been given as a possible reason for the low fertility in the cotton towns in Lancashire. With their own sources of income, Lancashire women were able to take an independent line on the size of their families.[9]

In the Spitalfields districts examined there was an even more extensive range of occupations, although 45.7 per cent of men and 43.5 per cent of women were employed in the making of dress, as tailors, cap makers, dressmakers, and the like. There were, however, large numbers employed in furniture making, the manufacture of pipes for smoking, in dealing, and in domestic

---

[7] F. Engels, *The Condition of the Working-Class in England from Personal Observation and Authentic Sources* (Moscow, 1973), pp. 116–19.

[8] Garrett, Reid, Schürer and Szreter, *Changing Family Size in England and Wales*, pp. 299–313.

[9] Garrett, Reid, Schürer and Szreter, *Changing Family Size in England and Wales*, pp. 299–313.

service. This range of occupations was perhaps typical of London in this period. The metropolis was a vast, complex economy, which provided highly specialised employment niches, and jobs in the luxury and seasonal trades.[10] This, and the importance of the Port of London, has always made the great city a magnet for refugees and other long-distance migrants. However, one occupation for women – prostitution – is absent from the census returns. It was said at the time that many unemployed domestic servants and dressmakers obtained at least some of their income from this, the oldest, profession.[11] This points to the difficulties in interpreting the census entries relating to the occupations of women, although it is unlikely that such ambiguities would greatly alter the picture given of the economy of the district.

As already noted, the economic structure of theses communities helps to explain the history of the migration, or lack of it, into them. But it also helps to explain their age and sex structures. As can be seen from Table 5 in Appendix 9, the proportion of the population under 10 years of age, or 60 years and over, is very similar in the case of Salford, Senghenydd and Spitalfields. East Tuddenham, however, had rather fewer children than the other communities, and a much larger proportion of the elderly in the population. This was a reflection of the dynamics of migration in the period. Since agriculture was in decline much migration was from the countryside into the town, and was especially typical among young, unmarried adults. This meant that there were fewer young families in places such as East Tuddenham, and a large number of elderly farm workers who had been left behind. Similarly, the rather odd sex structure of Senghenydd (Table A9.6) – there were significantly fewer women than men – may reflect the very recent foundation of the settlement, and the comparatively limited work opportunities for women.

The sort of information that can be extracted from census data by such analyses could be endlessly multiplied. Little has been said here about family or household structure, for example. Some idea of the range of possibilities can be derived from examining works of historical research that have used the source, such as Anderson on Preston in the mid nineteenth century, or Armstrong on York.[12] It is hoped that enough has been done here to show how useful such quantitative analysis is, and also some of the methodological issues that it raises.

Reconstructing communities: record linkage

As noted in Chapter 11, one of the most useful features of the census returns is that they can be easily linked to other sources, especially via the addresses given. This can enable one to

---

[10] G. Stedman Jones, *Outcast London: a Study in the Relationship between Classes in Victorian Society* (Harmondsworth, 1984), pp. 19–158.

[11] Higgs, 'The linguistic construction of social and medical categories in the work of the English General Register Office', pp. 86–7.

[12] Anderson, *Family Structure in Nineteenth Century Lancashire*; Armstrong, *Stability and Change in an English Country Town*. See also the essays in Mills and Schürer, *Local Communities in the Victorian Census Enumerators' Books*; and the articles published in the journal *Local Population Studies*. For a bibliography of census-based studies, see Mills and Pearce, *People and Places in the Victorian Census*.

build up a much richer picture of selected communities. As an example, it is possible to link the 1901 census returns described in the section above with the Inland Revenue Valuation Office's Field Books, which contain details of the valuation of land under the Finance (1909–10) Act 1910. The latter was a piece of legislation introduced by Lloyd George for the purposes of levying a tax on the value of property as it increased over time. These records, held at TNA, Kew, as record series IR 58, normally contain names of occupiers and owners; dates of the erection of buildings; details of extent, owner's interest, tenure and market value; and information about such matters as liability for rates and taxes.[13] The finding-aids to these records are a series of 'Record Sheet Plans', which give the assessment numbers for the various properties.[14]

The relevant plan for part of Spitalfields in 1910 can be found in TNA, Kew, at reference IR 121/20/25,[15] and is reproduced below as Figure 12.1. This shows the assessed properties leading off Brick Lane, and in particular properties 848 and 851. According to the relevant Valuation Office Field Book,[16] the latter property was 19a Brick Lane. In the 1901 census this was the abode of Abraham Lipman, a wholesale confectioner aged 36, who had been born in Poland. His wife, Anne, was aged 28, and had also been born in Poland. They had two live-in employees, Abraham Deitz, who had been born in Spitalfields, and was described as a 'Van Guard', and a 20-year-old servant, Betsy Ruby, also from Poland.[17] The Field Book, compiled nine years later, indicates that at that date the property was owned leasehold by James Smith, and the occupier paid a weekly rent of £2 5s 0d. Smith seems to have taken over the lease in 1893 for 80 years, so would have been the Lipman family's landlord in 1901. The street plan shows the property surrounded by other properties in Flower and Dean Street and in Brick Lane, and this rather haphazard arrangement is also indicated by the description of the block in the Field Book. This speaks of a 'Lodging house in rear forming one block of red brick shops, with chambers over a common lodging house in rear. Front 4 floors and basement. Back building 3 floors throughout but rambling from irregular levels'.

Plainly, this was a rough neighbourhood, little changed from when Jack the Ripper stalked these streets, and indicating the conditions in which immigrants had to live. This supposition is supported by the results of Charles Booth's poverty maps of the 1890s. Booth surveyed the whole of London and drew coloured maps showing the class of people who lived in particular streets. These are now available online at the Charles Booth Online Archive at the London School of Economics and Political Science (LSE). Here the corner of Flower and Dean Street and Brick Lane is picked out in the darkest black, corresponding to the lowest social class A, described by Booth in a somewhat prejudiced fashion as 'Vicious. Semi-criminal'.[18]

[13] TNA, IR 58, Board of Inland Revenue, Valuation Office, Field Books.

[14] TNA, IR 121–35, Board of Inland Revenue, Valuation Office, Record Sheet Plans.

[15] TNA, IR 121/20/25, Board of Inland Revenue: Valuation Office: Finance Act 1910, Record Sheet Plans: London Region: Tower Hamlets District.

[16] TNA, IR 58/84294.

[17] TNA, RG 13/298, fo. 69, p. 45.

[18] Charles Booth Online Archive website <http://booth.lse.ac.uk> (30 Sept. 2004).

Figure 12.1 Board of Inland Revenue: Valuation Office: Finance Act 1910, Record Sheet Plans: London Region: Tower Hamlets District (TNA, IR 121/20/25)

The other property, number 848 on Figure 12.1, is marked 'P.H.', indicating a public house. The Valuation Field Book[19] indicates that this is the Frying Pan Public House, whose leasehold had been owned since 1890 by the brewers Truman, Hanbury and Buxton. They ran one of the oldest breweries in London, The Black Eagle Brewery in Spitalfields, which covered an area of over six acres. It had been founded by Thomas Bucknall, who in 1669 erected a brewhouse on 'Lolsworth Field at Spittlehope'. The business passed in 1694 into the hands of Joseph Truman the elder, and the Hanburys and Buxtons came into the business in the course of the eighteenth century.[20] The Field Book gives a rather downbeat description of the property – 'Fair repair. Rough cast front. 3 floors and basement' – perhaps fitting for a haunt of Polly Nichols, one of Jack the Ripper's victims. In 1901 the only resident on census night was the manageress, Mary Ann Muford, a 59-year-old widow from Suffolk.[21] Today, however, the pub is a listed building and currently houses an Indian restaurant, evidence of yet another wave of migration into the area.

---

[19] TNA, IR 58/84294.
[20] *Victoria History of the County of Middlesex, Vol. II* (London, 1911), pp. 168–78.
[21] TNA, RG 13/298, fo. 69, p. 45. For Polly Nichols, see <http://www.casebook.org/victims/polly.html> (30 Sept.

This sort of record linkage could be expanded greatly but it is hoped that enough has been done here to show how the census returns can be used as a 'front end' to a wealth of other historical sources.

13 Historians, the published census tables and occupational structure

A wealth of ready-aggregated material exists for use by historians in the tables of the published *Census Reports* of the Victorian period, which cover most of the elements of information collected in the census enumerators' books. The most complete listing of these, and their contents, can be found in the *Guide to Census Reports, Great Britain 1801–1966*, published jointly by the Office of Population Censuses and Surveys and the General Register Office, Edinburgh. Extracts from this work can also be found in Lawton's *The Census and Social Structure: an Interpretative Guide to Nineteenth Century Censuses for England and Wales.*[1] The tables can be used to place local studies from the enumerators' books in a broader regional or national context. Most university or central public libraries will have, or should be able to obtain, copies of the *Census Reports* in either the bound or microfiche versions of British Parliamentary Papers. The only apparent limitation to the use of such information is the dearth of data for areas smaller than registration and sanitary districts, or 'principle towns'. The Joint Information Systems Committee (JISC), funded by the British further and higher education funding councils, is supporting a project to place all the *Census Reports* for England, Wales and Scotland for the period 1801–1931, along with other related material, online.[2]

It should be pointed out, however, that the quality of the published census tables depends upon the quality of the original data aggregated. Many of the limitations of the latter, which have been rehearsed in previous chapters, will have been carried over into the published summations of the *Census Reports*. This makes it imperative that all those using the published census tables should have a grasp of the processes that created the original enumerators' returns. In many cases, of course, biases in the census data will cancel each other out, but in others there will still be important limitations to the published tables. But such limitations are, of course, inherent in all statistical series, and the tables can be used fruitfully, if with care.

Historians should also be aware that the processes of aggregation and tabulation within the Census Office in the Victorian period were not simple mechanical operations devoid of intellectual input. The tables were created for specific purposes within particular cultural and conceptual frameworks, which changed over time. This was especially true of the processes of occupational classification that have been briefly touched upon in Chapter 11. The occupational tables contained in the *Census Reports* are not, therefore, simple 'facts', or pieces of 'data' given to users unproblematically; they are culturally mediated texts which need to be interpreted in the same

---

[1] Lawton, *The Census and Social Structure*, pp. 289–319.
[2] Online Historical Population Reports Project website <http://www.histpop.org/> (30 Sept. 2004).

manner as any other historical sources.[3] It will be the aim of the rest of this chapter to describe the processes by which the occupational tables were created in the Census Office, and to make an attempt to outline some of the shifts in the conceptual frameworks that underpinned the occupational tables. This will be done via case studies of the changing treatment of the agricultural workforce and of the tertiary sector. This is not an attempt to dissuade historians from using the *Census Reports*, rather it is to enable researchers to use the tables in a more informed and sophisticated manner.

Tabulating data in the Victorian Census Office

Until 1911, when the GRO introduced machines to undertake data analysis, all of the tables in the *Census Reports* and in the *Annual Reports of the Registrar-General* were based on manual processing using tabling sheets and the 'ticking' method. In the case of occupational abstraction, the tabling sheets were large pieces of paper with occupational headings down one side and age ranges across the top. These headings were ruled across the sheet, creating a matrix of boxes into which the census clerks were to place a tick for an occurrence in the enumerators' returns of a person of the relevant age and occupation. The ticks in the columns were then added up, and the results placed in another series of columns on another sheet, giving the raw numbers of people under particular occupational headings within particular age ranges. Sheets were created in this manner for each registration sub-district.

In order to create tables by registration districts, the sheets for sub-districts had to be folded at the column to be totalled and then lined up so that they overlapped, and the figures were then read off on to district sheets. Figures were then transferred from district to county sheets in a similar manner. The staff in the GRO could call upon the help of calculating machines for the purposes of computation but not for data processing. This was extremely fiddly work, and the constant leaning over tables was fatiguing for the tabler, and necessitated frequent stops for rest. This cumbersome process helps to explain why the GRO sought to keep the census as simple as possible in the Victorian period, and was one of the reasons why the Office's statistical output was restricted to tables with simple cross-tabulations. In this, the British GRO lagged far behind the US census authorities, who had introduced machine tabulation as early as 1890.[4] An example of a portion of a tabling sheet for occupations can be found in Appendix 8.

It should be noted, however, that the tabling sheets did not list all the manifold occupational titles given by householders. The sheets only contained a few hundred headings, rather than the thousands of occupational terms recorded in the original census returns. This both facilitated

---

[3] For a more detailed discussion of some of the theoretical issues involved, see Higgs, 'The General Register Office and the tabulation of data, 1837–1939'; Higgs, 'The linguistic construction of social and medical categories in the work of the English General Register Office'.

[4] A description of the manual process with respect to cause of death tables in the *Annual Reports of the Registrar-General* can be found in TNA, T 1/6028B/12646. For the politics of the introduction of machine tabulation, see Higgs, *Life, Death and Statistics*, ch. 6.

the mechanics of abstraction, since a sheet with thousands of occupational headings would have been unwieldy, and simplified the eventual published tables. The Office was always wary of creating published tables that would be too complex for the public to understand. The clerks in the GRO ticked the occurrence of individual occupational terms under these broader categories on the tabling sheets using occupational dictionaries.[5] Thus, in 1861, the terms 'cloth bleacher', 'cloth boiler' and 'cloth brusher' would all have been ticked in the column headed 'Woollen Cloth Manufacture'.[6] This process was, in a fundamental sense, arbitrary, that is, it was one of arbitration, and the rules for placing occupational titles in the various cells of the census tables could, and did, alter from census to census. This can make it difficult to compare the data in the census tables over time.

An example, that of 'scientific persons', might help to clarify this point. In the instructions to the clerks abstracting occupational data in 1871[7] can be found the following list of occupations to be placed under this general heading:

Agricultural chemist	Geographer	Nosologist
Analytical chemist	Geologist	Observatory assistant
Antiquarian	Geometer	Ornithologist
Astronomer	Hydrographer	Philosopher
Botanist	Laboratory assistant	Doctor in philosophy
Chronologist	Lexicographer	Professor in philosophy
Entomologist	Mathematician	Philosophical practitioner
Experimentalist	Metallurgist	Phrenologist
Expert	Microscopic anatomist	Physiologist
Fly gatherer	Mineralogist	Statist
Genealogist	Naturalist	Topographer

The definition of 'science' here is plainly different from that of the early twenty-first century, including disciplines that do not fall into the modern category of the empirical and applied sciences. Terms such as 'chemist', 'biologist' and 'physicist' are conspicuous by their absence, as is, of course, 'scientist'. The classification was inconsistent in that it included professors of 'philosophy' in this category while professors of 'natural philosophy' (i.e., science) were abstracted as teachers. The equivalent list in 1881 includes the terms 'scientist', 'physicist' and 'biologist', while 'genealogist', 'topographer' and others had disappeared. This reflected a linguistic change as the meaning of 'science' narrowed in the late nineteenth century. Originally the term simply meant a body of knowledge and practice worked out on rigorous principles, hence the 'science of art' or 'scientific socialism'. But in the course of the Victorian period the use of the term was increasingly restricted to the natural sciences and applications of the 'scientific method'. Such

---

[5] Examples of the coding dictionaries for 1871 and 1881 are held in TNA, RG 27/4, Item 85; TNA, RG 27/5, Item 69. Some sample pages from the coding dictionaries can be found in Appendix 8.

[6] These are taken from a copy of the 1861 occupational dictionary in the author's possession.

[7] TNA, RG 27/4, Item 85.

changes make it unwise to use the published tables from the various *Census Reports* to reconstruct the changing size of the scientific community over time.[8]

This is a minor example but, as will be shown below, the general principles involved here have implications for the analysis of economic change in Victorian England and Wales. Much of our knowledge of changes in occupational, and therefore economic, structure of the second half of the nineteenth century is based upon this source. The numbers in economic sectors have also been used, in conjunction with sectoral outputs, to calculate relative rates of labour productivity. If changes in the census tables over time merely reflect shifts in terminology or classificatory principles, then some readjustments may be necessary to the current historiography.

The evolution of occupational classification systems

The manner in which the individual occupations were placed in broader occupational categories according to the occupational dictionaries reflected certain underlying principles. This process gives the picture of the distribution of occupations in the economy presented in the population tables a certain structure. As has already been described, one of the main organising concepts underlying the collection and arrangement of occupational data in the mid-Victorian censuses was the nature of the materials being worked upon, which were assumed to be linked to the mortality regimes of particular trades. Householders filling in their census schedules were instructed by the census authorities to qualify occupations with the substances being worked on, and this information was used to apportion workers to occupational categories based on those 'working with vegetable matter', working with metals, animals, and so on. The census data were used, in conjunction with registered deaths, to draw up actuarially sound occupational life-tables for insurance purposes.[9]

This may help to explain why, prior to 1881, many women were placed in the same occupational categories as their male relatives, under headings such as 'farmer's wife' or 'shopkeeper's wife', when, as in the case of farms, shops and lodging houses, the home was a productive unit. They presumably came into contact with the same substances as their kin and were thus regarded as having a similar mortality regime. Women who were recorded as having specific job titles, such as farmer or shopkeeper, could still be placed under such headings if they shared that occupation with their male relatives. If insufficient information was given as to materials, individuals were placed in residual categories, such as general labourer, to avoid introducing possible inaccuracies into the calculation of the occupational life-tables. What was important was not that a particular category should be exhaustive but that it should adequately capture the effects of working with particular substances.[10] The GRO itself recognised that many in this vast residual category,

---

[8] Higgs, 'Counting heads and jobs', pp. 335–49.

[9] Higgs, 'Disease, febrile poisons, and statistics'.

[10] For a general discussion of these medical concerns, see Higgs, 'Disease, febrile poisons and statistics', pp. 471–5.

numbering over half a million in 1871,[11] should have been placed in substantive categories such as agriculture for the purposes of economic analysis. Similarly, many workers in the tertiary sector – clerks, warehousemen, dealers and the like – were also placed in the relevant manufacturing sectors. Thus, a clerk in an iron mill would not appear in the census tables in the clerical category but under iron manufacture.

From 1881 onwards, under the impact of changes in GRO personnel, and pressure from other government departments, economists and social scientists, the distribution of occupations to categories began to shift.[12] The most striking modification was perhaps the establishment of a more pronounced 'unoccupied' section in the tables, and the removal to that category of many of the women formerly abstracted under the occupations of male relatives. There were, however, other less obvious changes, such as the gradual removal of clerks, warehousemen and dealers to distinct occupational categories in the tertiary sector.

These changes led Charles Booth, the noted social investigator, to present a reworking of the census data to the Statistical Society of London (soon to become the Royal Statistical Society) in 1886, in which he claimed to provide a more consistent occupational time series for the Victorian period up to 1881. One of the major reallocations he advocated was the removal to the unoccupied category of all women in censuses prior to 1881 who had previously been abstracted as occupied under their male relatives' occupations. Booth wanted to establish the relationship between occupation, family size and poverty, and made the assumption that women could be treated as dependent on their husbands.[13] His revisions, if not his reasoning, have been followed by those historians who have attempted to create occupational time series for the period,[14] even though this probably removed large numbers of active women from the occupied population. Many of the changes in the census tables were, moreover, taking place at a structural level to which Booth did not have access. As Armstrong has noted, Booth only worked with the published tables, rearranging the occupational headings rather than the job titles amalgamated therein.[15] Booth also never appears to have understood the medical influences on the pre-existing occupational classification system.

An attempt to produce a unified coding scheme for occupations in the censuses of 1851–1911 has been undertaken by scholars working at the Cambridge Group for the History of Population and Social Structure. This seeks to show where occupational terms were placed in the occupational tables in each of the relevant *Census Reports*.[16] Some of the implications of these classificatory shifts will now be worked through in respect of Victorian agriculture, and changes in the size of the tertiary sector of the economy.

[11] Armstrong, 'The use of information about occupation', p. 274.

[12] Higgs, 'The struggle for the occupational census', pp. 79–86.

[13] Booth, 'Occupations of the people', *passim*.

[14] Deane and Cole, *British Economic Growth, 1688–1959*, pp. 139–40; and Feinstein, *National Income*, pp. 223–4.

[15] Armstrong, 'The use of information about occupation', p. 230.

[16] Preliminary results can be found in K. Schürer, 'Understanding and coding the occupations of the past: the experience of analysing the censuses of 1891–1921', in Schürer and Diederiks, *The Use of Occupations in Historical Analysis*, pp. 101–62. See also, Mills and Schürer, 'Employment and occupations', pp. 149–50.

Measurements of labour inputs into agriculture

High labour productivity in British agriculture has been stressed as a crucial factor in that complex of changes we associate with the term 'the Industrial Revolution'. It is argued that agricultural efficiency allowed a constant rural population to feed and reproduce an ever-expanding urban, industrial proletariat that in itself did not have a great productive advantage over its European rivals.[17] According to Crafts, for example, 'Britain did not attain particularly high levels of output per worker in industry, and as a useful crude approximation it can be said that the triumph of the industrial revolution lay in getting a lot of workers into industry rather than obtaining high productivity from them once there'.[18] A proven shortfall in the census totals for those working on the land, if large enough, might force a reassessment of the role of agricultural productivity in the processes of industrialisation.

It is quite possible that the original census tables, and the revised versions produced by Booth, considerably underestimate the numbers working on the land. As was noted in Chapter 8, the census-taking process probably missed much seasonal and casual employment in agriculture, especially among women. The families of agricultural labourers turned out *en masse* to help bring in the harvest, and they were joined by tens of thousands of migrants from Ireland and the large cities. As late as 1906, farmers replying to the Census of Production recorded 161,000 migrant summer hop-pickers, 109,000 in Kent alone, most of whom came from the East End of London.[19] The same source also indicates large numbers of women employed as agricultural labourers who, for reasons of delicacy, did not record themselves as such in the population census.[20] Similarly, some of the work of the vast numbers of general servants employed by farmers, who may well have been abstracted as domestic servants, would have gone into agricultural production.[21] By adding to these the large numbers of agricultural labourers enumerated as 'labourer' who may have been placed under the heading 'General labourer' rather than agriculture, one begins to amass evidence of considerable under-enumeration of the agricultural workforce. Booth's reworking of the census tables probably muddied the waters still further by removing from the occupied totals many female relatives of farmers who undertook at least some agricultural tasks.

By making some, and it is hoped not too rash, assumptions about the possible size of these underestimations, one might possibly be able to increase the levels of labour inputs into the agricultural sector of the economy of England and Wales in the mid-Victorian period by as much as 30 or 40 per cent. This is equivalent to over half a million extra hands employed on the

---

[17] P. O'Brien and C. Keyder, *Economic Growth in Britain and France, 1780–1914* (London, 1978), p. 90; Wrigley, 'Men on the land and men in the countryside', pp. 295–336.

[18] N. F. R. Crafts, *British Economic Growth during the Industrial Revolution* (Oxford, 1987), p. 156.

[19] *The Agricultural Output of Great Britain* (PP 1912–13 X), pp. 547–8.

[20] *The Agricultural Output of Great Britain*, p. 545.

[21] A quarter of all servants were employed by farmers according to M. Anderson, 'Households, families and individuals: some preliminary results from the national sample from the 1851 census of Great Britain', *Continuity and Change*, 3 (1988), p. 427.

land in each of the census years 1851–71. These revised estimates raise the agricultural sector from 20 per cent of the occupied population to 25 per cent in 1851. Since much of this excess labour is, in fact, that of women, this also has important implications for the economic participation rate for women in the period.[22] Much work still needs to be done to substantiate such revisions but this points to the need for some caution when using the published tables. However, it should also be noted that even if the proportion of the occupied population in agriculture in 1851 was 25 per cent, this still made England and Wales unique at this date. Few other societies in the world could compare with it in terms of levels of industrialisation and urbanisation. The census gives a very useful picture of the economy, even if it is a little more rough and ready than one might suppose.

The expansion of the tertiary economic sector

The tertiary sector of the economy – those involved in trade, transport, domestic and personal services, public administration and the professions – appears to have expanded in the Victorian period as rapidly as agriculture declined. According to Deane and Cole, while agriculture dropped from 21.7 per cent of the British labour force in 1851 to 8.7 per cent in 1901, the tertiary sector rose from 35.5 to 45.1 per cent. Much of this increase in the tertiary sector was provided by workers in trade, commerce and transport.[23] This can be seen as a veritable 'tertiary economic revolution'.[24] Although there were plainly important structural changes going on here, shifts over time in the conventions for abstracting the occupational data in the censuses create difficulties of interpretation and chronology.[25] Many tertiary workers were placed in manufacturing sectors in the censuses of 1851–71 but these were shifted to distinct 'white-collar' categories thereafter. There were also shifts between categories within the tertiary sector. These movements reflected, in part, the revisions to the principles underlying census abstraction noted above. The nature of some of these shifts will now be illustrated with reference to clerks, warehousemen, carters and dealers.

According to Armstrong, following Booth, the number of commercial clerks in England and Wales increased from 37,500 in 1851 to nearly a quarter of a million in 1891. The percentage growth was most rapid between 1871 and 1881, when the numbers doubled from 91,000 to 181,500.[26] But the category 'commercial clerk' was not the same in the two years. Householders were always instructed to describe the branch of business in which a clerk worked.[27] Up to and including 1871 the census clerks were instructed to abstract clerks in the following manner:

---

[22] Higgs, 'Occupational censuses and the agricultural workforce in Victorian England and Wales', pp. 700–16.

[23] Deane and Cole, *British Economic Growth, 1688–1959*, p. 142.

[24] For such a claim relating to clerks, see G. Anderson, *Victorian Clerks* (Manchester, 1976), p. 2.

[25] Deane and Cole recognise these problems but imply that these shifts only represent some one or two percentage points in the share of the tertiary sector between censuses.

[26] Armstrong, 'The use of information about occupation', p. 274.

[27] See Appendix 7 for references to examples of the householders' schedules.

clerks in banks were to be ticked to 'Bank service';
clerks to 'Professional men', army agents, auctioneers and railway contractors to 'Commercial service';
law clerks were distributed to the legal category; but
'All persons engaged in any Manufacture or Trade are to be ticked against that manufacture or trade ...'[28]

A decade later, however, the instructions to the census clerks stated that, 'Clerks employed in any branch of Commerce or Industry are to be ticked, not to the special branch, but to the Heading "Commercial Clerk"'.[29] As the *1881 Census Report* noted:

> The Commercial Clerks numbered 181,457, and were also twice as many as were so classed in 1871, but the term was used in different ways on the two occasions. In 1871 the clerks in factories were placed to the account of the special manufacture in the office of which they were engaged. For instance, a clerk in a cotton warehouse was placed to Cotton Manufacture; but in 1881 all clerks, employed in any branch of commerce or industry, were assigned, not to that special class, but to the general heading "Commercial Clerk" ... The returns, therefore, for 1881 and 1871 are not comparable.[30]

The full import of this shift appears not to have been understood by Charles Booth. The rise of the clerks over the Victorian period may thus be overstated in the existing historiography, with far more clerical workers in the mid-Victorian period.[31]

Changes were also going on in the warehousing sector. Prior to 1871 there do not appear to have been any specific instructions relating to warehousemen. In 1871, although there was no general guidance respecting warehousemen, the occupational dictionary gave a number of examples of specific cases which were to be abstracted under industrial headings. Thus a 'Warehouseman (drugs)' was to go under Manufacturing Chemist. The dictionary also included rather bald statements indicating that all warehouse proprietors and porters, and each 'Warehouseman (not Manchester)', were to be placed under the general heading 'Warehouseman'. In 1881, however, more definite instructions indicated that with respect to this term:

(a) When persons are apparently meant, who are simply accessories in some manufactory or house of business, being employed in its store department, they are to be ticked by the nature of the manufactory or industry to which they are attached.

(b) When the term 'Warehouseman' appears to be simply another name for dealer or shopkeeper, for example in 'Fancy-goods Warehouseman', 'Manchester Warehouseman', and the like, the tick must also follow the special kind of goods dealt in.

---

[28] TNA, RG 27/4, Item 85, p. 5.
[29] TNA, RG 27/5, Item 69, p. 3.
[30] *1881 Census Report*, p. 34.
[31] This problem is noted in the Office of Population Censuses and Surveys and General Register Office, Edinburgh, *Guide to Census Reports*, p. 31. Feinstein appears to believe that prior to 1911 commercial clerks were *not* classified by industry, which seems to indicate some confusion on his part (Feinstein, *National Income*, p. 226).

(c) When, however, persons are meant who keep places (or assist in the management or work of places) distinct from manufactories and simply as store-housing establishments, they are to be ticked to the heading 'Warehouseman' ...[32]

The obvious problem here was how the census clerks were supposed to differentiate between (c), and (a) and (b), and there may have been a tendency to place warehousemen in industrial sectors where possible. This might explain why Booth's figures for warehousemen not dealing in Manchester goods rose from 22,600 in 1861 to 44,000 in 1871, before falling back to 30,900 in 1881.[33]

One of the apparent anomalies of Victorian occupational structure is the manner in which, during the heyday of the 'Railway Age', road transport appears to have increased in importance. According to Armstrong's reworking of Booth's figures, the numbers involved in such work rose from 74,000 in 1851 to 224,600 in 1891. Road transport workers thus increased from 21 per cent of all those involved in transport at mid-century to 27 per cent 40 years later. Much of this expansion came under the category 'Carmen, carriers, carters and draymen', who numbered 44,300 in 1851 and 170,300 in 1891. Of this increase, 50,000 took place between 1871 and 1881.[34] However, the conventions with respect to carters shifted over time in an intriguing manner which may undermine attempts to reconstruct changes in the numbers active in road transport in the Victorian economy.

In 1871 the census clerks were instructed that: '"Carters" (not otherwise described) if in large manufacturing or commercial towns, will generally be referred to "CARMAN, &c." ... but in ordinary provincial towns to "AGRICULTURAL LABOURER"'.[35] Ten years later the distinction was drawn between carters in a 'large manufacturing or commercial town' and those in 'a rural district or small town'. This seems to imply a narrower population from which carters placed in agriculture could be drawn, those in large provincial towns now being more likely to be placed in the transport sector. By 1891 the distinction based on geography or settlement type had disappeared altogether with the instruction that: 'Carters, or Waggoners, if returned as engaged on farms or in agriculture, are to be ticked to "Horsekeeper, Horseman Teamster", in the Agricultural Class, ... But all Carters and Waggoners not so described are to be ticked to "Carter, Waggoner", in order 6, sub-order 2 [i.e., in transport]'. The general carter was now assumed to work in the transport sector wherever he lived.

Thus, some of the apparent increase in the numbers of those in road transport probably reflected changes in abstraction practices at the GRO. Depending on how the 'proper' economic role of carters working on the farm is viewed, as either primary or tertiary workers, there were either too many counted under transport in the later decades of the century, or too few in the mid-Victorian period. If it is believed that agricultural carters should be placed in the tertiary sector, then this

---

[32] TNA, RG 27/5, Item 69, pp. 3–4.

[33] Armstrong, 'The use of information about occupation', p. 269.

[34] Armstrong, 'The use of information about occupation', p. 270.

[35] TNA, RG 27/4, Item 85, p. 5.

would have a knock-on effect on the proposed under-enumeration of the agricultural workforce described above.

In the case of dealers it has long been recognised that the figures in the census tables are an underestimate of their numbers. In the Victorian period, dealing and manufacturing were often inseparable; bakers, for example, both making and selling bread. Indeed, the industrial categories in the *Census Reports* were defined in terms of those 'working and dealing' in certain substances or items.[36] Charles Booth did attempt some redistribution of industrial workers to dealing, such as allocating a quarter of hatters to that heading, but this was plainly not done consistently. His figures for dealers are probably an underestimate of labour inputs into this sector.[37] Booth's reallocation of the female relatives of shopkeepers to his unoccupied category involved, in 1871, 61,553 wives of innkeepers, publicans and beersellers; 3,327 wives of lodging/boarding house keepers; 12,256 wives of shopkeepers; and 32,529 wives of butchers. This must also have led to the removal of some women who worked in dealing.[38]

One also needs to consider here the large numbers of domestic servants who worked in the homes of shopkeepers, many of which would have been retailing units. In Rochdale in Lancashire, for example, between a quarter and a third of all servants were employed by retailers, especially in the drinks trade, in the period 1851–71.[39] Similarly, Pamela Horn, in a study of the market towns of Wantage, Thame and Fakenham, concludes that in this period, two-fifths of her servant employers were small tradesmen, 'drapers, grocers, plumbers, coal merchants, corn dealers and the like'.[40] Many of the women employed as 'general servants' by small shopkeepers may have worked at least part of the time in the retailing portion of the home. This is likely to imply a still greater underestimate of labour inputs into the dealing sector.

This section has, so far, been mainly concerned with changes in systems of classification in the GRO. It is possible, however, that changes in nomenclature were going on in the occupational terms found in the enumerators' books, quite separate from these developments. One might reflect, for example, on the possible effect of the spread of the lock-up shop in the late Victorian period on the relative number of domestic servants and female shop assistants. Did the differentiation of the home and the retailing outlet lead to a similar separation of domestic and non-domestic labour? Were some of the women who would formerly have been living in shopkeepers' homes, employed part-time in the shop, and described in the census as 'general servant', now living in their own homes and working as 'shop assistants' in lock-up premises? Similarly, how far did the wives and daughters of small entrepreneurs, who helped with the clerical work of the family business in the early nineteenth century, come to fill the female clerical posts of large concerns at the end of the century?[41] Do

---

[36] Deane and Cole, *British Economic Growth, 1688–1959*, p. 140; Feinstein, *National Income*, p. 226.

[37] Armstrong, 'The use of information on occupation', pp. 231–5

[38] *1871 Census Report* (PP 1873 LXXI Pt. 1 [c.872.], pp. xliii–xlviii).

[39] Higgs, *Domestic Servants and Households in Rochdale*, p. 101.

[40] P. Horn, *The Rise and Fall of the Victorian Servant* (Dublin, 1975), p. 18.

[41] On the work of women in family businesses in early-nineteenth-century England, see L. Davidoff and C. Hall, *Family Fortunes: Men and Women of the English Middle Class 1780–1850* (London, 1987), pp. 272–89.

these developments represent new types of work, or old work with new names? Such changes are very difficult to substantiate and interpret, and are plainly subjects for further research.

On this basis, what might be the overall size of the underestimation of the tertiary sector in the mid nineteenth century? On the basis of the reconstruction of the processes of data abstraction presented here, only the most tentative conclusions can be drawn. If, however, one allowed for the sake of argument that:

the 90,000 increase in the number of commercial clerks, and the 50,000 increase in the number of carters, between 1871 and 1881 were solely a reflection of changes in classification;

the 110,000 wives of dealers were also fully employed in the tertiary sector in 1871; and

20 per cent of general servants in that year worked half-time in dealing, equivalent to 78,000 full-time women;[42]

the resulting figure of 328,000 extra workers in 1871 would represent an increase to the workforce involved in trade and commerce of some 16 per cent.[43] This estimate is undoubtedly an exaggeration but any adjustment downwards might be compensated for by the numbers of dealers placed in the manufacturing category. These shifts represent an increase in the numbers in the mid-Victorian tertiary sector as a proportion of the entire occupied population of some two to three per cent.[44] How far this adjustment is significant depends, of course, on the purpose to which the data are to be put.

Conclusion

The general conclusion to be drawn from this analysis is that although the published occupational returns from the censuses are a vital historical source, they should be used with some caution. The attempts made by Charles Booth and others to harmonise the census returns over time may not have succeeded in removing these anomalies, and may indeed have made the situation worse. The chronology and scale of sectoral shifts in economic structure revealed therein may need to be revised somewhat, although the overall shape of the British economic structure in the period is only changed marginally. The country still had fewer workers in agriculture and more in tertiary employments than other major European countries. Changes in the numbers in particular occupational categories may, however, prove to be the consequence of shifts in classification systems.

[42] *1871 Census Report* Pt. 1, pp. xliii–xlviii.

[43] Defined as Booth-Armstrong's Transport, Dealing, Industrial Service, and Public Service and Professional Sectors minus general labourers (Armstrong, 'The use of information about occupation', pp. 269–78).

[44] Based on the figures in Deane and Cole for the total occupied population plus the addition of working wives in dealing (Deane and Cole, *British Economic Growth, 1688–1959*, p. 143). No attempt has been made here to calculate a new total for occupied workers based on returning all the female relatives of farmers, shopkeepers, lodging-house keepers, and so on, to the 'economically active' population.

It will be noted that the above process of revision calls into question the underlying principle upon which the use of occupational structure for economic analysis is based – that a person marked in the census as having a particular occupation represents one 'person year' of activity in a particular economic sector. Once it is allowed that the work of a 'general servant' might be spread across several economic sectors, or that one month of the annual labour of a docker in London might be spent on the land in Kent, then many of the current orthodoxies of economic analysis begin to seem less solid. Certainly, crude calculations of labour productivity based upon annual output per sector divided by labour inputs calculated on this basis appear less robust.

These strictures should not be construed as an attempt to dissuade historians from using the published tables in the *Census Reports*. For many purposes the tables are a faithful summary of the original manuscript returns. They should not be seen, however, as indisputable 'facts' since they are the end products of shifting processes of construction for particular purposes and within changing cultural settings. As such, they need to be used with sensitivity, and with a due appreciation of the processes by which they were created. In other words, statistical tables need to be evaluated in the same manner as any other historical texts.

PART IV

APPENDICES

Appendix 1 Census Acts and census days, England and Wales, 1841–1901

Census		Census Act	
Year	Day	Reference	Date
1841	Sunday 6 June	3 & 4 Vict., c. 99	10 August 1840
		4 & 5 Vict., c. 7	6 April 1841
1851	Sunday 30 March	13 & 14 Vict., c. 53	5 August 1850
1861	Sunday 7 April	23 & 24 Vict., c. 61	6 August 1860
1871	Sunday 2 April	33 & 34 Vict., c. 107	10 August 1870
1881	Sunday 3 April	43 & 44 Vict., c. 37	7 September 1880
1891	Sunday 5 April	53 & 54 Vict., c. 61	18 August 1890
1901	Sunday 31 March	63 & 64 Vict., c. 4	27 March 1900

Appendix 2 The overall structure of the enumerators' books

1841

Unnumbered pages at beginning of book:

Page i   Geographical information – both ancient divisions (county, hundred, parish, etc.) and those for registration purposes (superintendent registrar's district, registrar's district, number of enumeration district). Description of enumeration district.

Page ii   Blank.

Page iii   Extract from Census Act regarding the penalty for refusing information or giving false answers.

Page iv   Directions for filling up the book.

Page v   Example of how to fill up the book.

Pages 1–*x*   Pages for the insertion of nominal information numbered 1 to *x*.

The last three pages continue the numbering of the above, and this was therefore dependent upon the number of such pages in the book:

First page   Summary table of the total number of houses and persons in each of the foregoing pages.

Second page   Summary tables regarding itinerants, the temporary increase and decrease of the population, and emigration.

Third page   Declarations signed by the enumerator, registrar and superintendent registrar.

Overall dimensions: 33 cm. high by 21 cm. wide (13 in. x 8.25 in.).

1851

Page i	Description of enumeration district with geographical data.
Page ii	Summary table of the total number of houses, occupiers and persons in each of the pages for nominal information.
Page iii	Summary tables for the number of itinerants and the temporary increase and decrease of the population.
Page iv	Declarations signed by the enumerator, registrar and superintendent registrar.
Page v	Directions for filling up the book.
Pages vi–vii	Example of how to fill up the book.
Pages 1–x	Pages for inserting nominal information.

Overall dimensions: 20.3 cm. high by 31.75 cm. wide (8 in. x 12.5 in.).

1861

Page i	Description of enumeration district with geographical data.
Page ii	Directions for filling up the book.
Page iii	Example of how to fill up the book.
Page iv	Summary tables for the number of itinerants and the temporary increase and decrease of the population.
Page v	Summary table of the total number of houses, persons and schedules in each of the pages for nominal information.
Page vi	Declarations signed by the enumerator, registrar and superintendent registrar.
Pages 1–x	Pages for inserting nominal information.

Overall dimensions: 23.5 cm. high by 36.8 cm. wide (9.25 in. x 14.5 in.).

1871

Page i   Description of enumeration district with geographical data.

Page ii   Directions for filling up the book.

Page iii   Example of how to fill up the book.

Page iv   Summary tables for the temporary increase and decrease of the population, and the number of houses, persons and schedules by geographical division.

Page v   Summary table of the total number of houses, persons and schedules in each of the pages for nominal information.

Page vi   Declarations signed by the enumerator, registrar and superintendent registrar.

Pages 1–*x*   Pages for inserting nominal information.

Overall dimensions: 23.5 cm. high by 36.8 cm. wide (9.25 in. x 14.5 in.).

1881

Page i   Description of enumeration district with geographical data.

Page ii   Directions for filling up the book.

Page iii   Example of how to fill up the book.

Page iv   Summary tables for the temporary increase and decrease of the population, and the number of houses, persons and schedules by geographical division.

Page v   Summary table of the total number of houses, persons and schedules in each of the pages for nominal information.

Page vi   Declarations signed by the enumerator, registrar and superintendent registrar.

Pages 1–*x*   Pages for inserting nominal information.

Overall dimensions: 23.5 cm. high by 36.8 cm. wide (9.25 in. x 14.5 in.).

1891

Page i   Description of enumeration district with geographical data.

Page ii   Directions for filling up the book.

Page iii   Example of how to fill up the book.

Page iv   Summary tables for the number of houses, tenements of less than five rooms, persons and schedules by geographical division.

Page v   Summary table of the total number of houses, persons, schedules and tenements of less than five rooms in each of the pages for nominal information.

Page vi   Declarations signed by the enumerator, registrar and superintendent registrar.

Pages 1-*x*   Pages for inserting nominal information.

Overall dimensions: 28.6 cm. high by 43 cm. wide (11.25 in. x 17 in.).

1901

Page i   Description of enumeration district with geographical data.

Page ii   Directions for filling up the book.

Page iii   Example of how to fill up the book.

Page iv   Summary tables for the number of houses, tenements of less than five rooms, persons and schedules by geographical division.

Page v   Summary table of the total number of houses, persons, schedules and tenements of less than five rooms in each of the pages for nominal information.

Page vi   Declarations signed by the enumerator, registrar and superintendent registrar.

Pages 1-*x*   Pages for inserting nominal information.

Overall dimensions: 27.5 cm. high by 43 cm. wide (11 in. x 17 in.).

Appendix 3 The structure of the nominal page

1841

Column	Heading	Subheading	Comments
1	Place		i.e., address
2	Houses	1 uninhabited or being built 2 inhabited	
3	Names		
4	Age and sex	1 males 2 females	
5	Profession, trade, employment or of independent means		
6	Where born	1 whether born in same country 2 whether born in Scotland, Ireland or foreign parts	'Y' or 'N' for yes or no 'S', 'I' or 'F' for Scotland, Ireland, or foreign parts

1851

Column	Heading	Subheading	Comments
1	Number of schedule		numbered from 1 consecutively
2	Name of street, place or road and name or number of house		
3	Name and surname		
4	Relation to head of family		
5	Condition		i.e., marital status
6	Age	1 males 2 females	
7	Rank, profession or occupation		
8	Where born		county: place
9	Whether blind or deaf-and-dumb		

1861

Column	Heading	Subheading	Comments
1	Number of schedule		numbered from 1 consecutively
2	Road, street, etc., and number or name of house		
3	Houses	1 inhabited 2 uninhabited	'U' for uninhabited: 'B' for being built
4	Name and surname		
5	Relation to head of family		
6	Condition		i.e., marital status
7	Age	1 males 2 females	
8	Rank, profession or occupation		
9	Where born		county: place
10	Whether blind or deaf-and-dumb		

1871

Column	Heading	Subheading	Comments
1	Number of schedule		numbered from 1 consecutively
2	Road, street, etc., and number or name of house		
3	Houses	1 inhabited 2 uninhabited	'U' for uninhabited: 'B' for being built
4	Name and surname		
5	Relation to head of family		
6	Condition		i.e., marital status
7	Age	1 males 2 females	
8	Rank, profession or occupation		
9	Where born		county: place
10	Whether 1 Deaf-and-dumb 2 Blind 3 Imbecile or idiot 4 Lunatic		

1881

Column	Heading	Subheading	Comments
1	Number of schedule		numbered from 1 consecutively
2	Road, street, etc., and number or name of house		
3	Houses	1 inhabited 2 uninhabited	'U' for uninhabited: 'B' for being built
4	Name and surname		
5	Relation to head of family		
6	Condition as to marriage		i.e., marital status
7	Age last birthday	1 males 2 females	
8	Rank, profession or occupation		
9	Where born		county: place
10	Whether 1 Deaf-and-dumb 2 Blind 3 Imbecile or idiot 4 Lunatic		

1891

Column	Heading	Subheading	Comments
1	Number of schedule		numbered from 1 consecutively
2	Road, street, etc., and number or name of house		
3	Houses	1 inhabited 2 uninhabited	'U' for uninhabited: 'B' for being built
4	Number of rooms occupied if less than five		
5	Name and surname		
6	Relation to head of family		
7	Condition as to marriage		i.e., marital status
8	Age last birthday	1 males 2 females	

Column	Heading	Subheading	Comments
9	Profession or occupation		
10	Employer		insert 'X'
11	Employed		insert 'X'
12	Neither employer nor employed		insert 'X'
13	Where born		county: place
14	Whether		
	1 Deaf-and-dumb		
	2 Blind		
	3 Lunatic, imbecile, or idiot		

1901

Column	Heading	Subheading	Comments
1	Number of schedule		numbered from 1 consecutively
2	Road, street, etc., and number or name of house		
3	Houses	1 inhabited	insert '1'
		2 in occupation	insert '1'
		3 not in occupation	insert '1'
		4 being built	insert '1'
4	Number of rooms occupied if less than five		
5	Name and surname		
6	Relation to head of family		
7	Condition as to marriage		i.e., marital status
8	Age last birthday	1 males	
		2 females	
9	Profession or occupation		
10	Employer, worker, or own account		answer to be written
11	If working at home		answer to be written
12	Where born		county: place
13	Whether		
	1 Deaf-and-dumb		
	2 Blind		
	3 Lunatic		
	4 Imbecile, feeble-minded		

The following illustrations of census pages are not examples of the actual manuscript returns. Rather, they are copies of the printed examples given at the beginning of enumerators' books to show them how to fill in their returns.

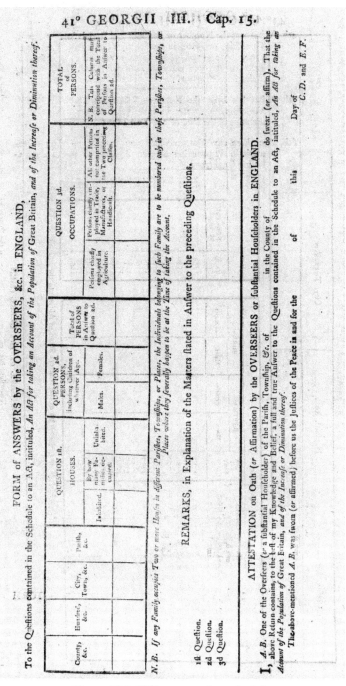

Figure A3.1 1801 enumeration schedule

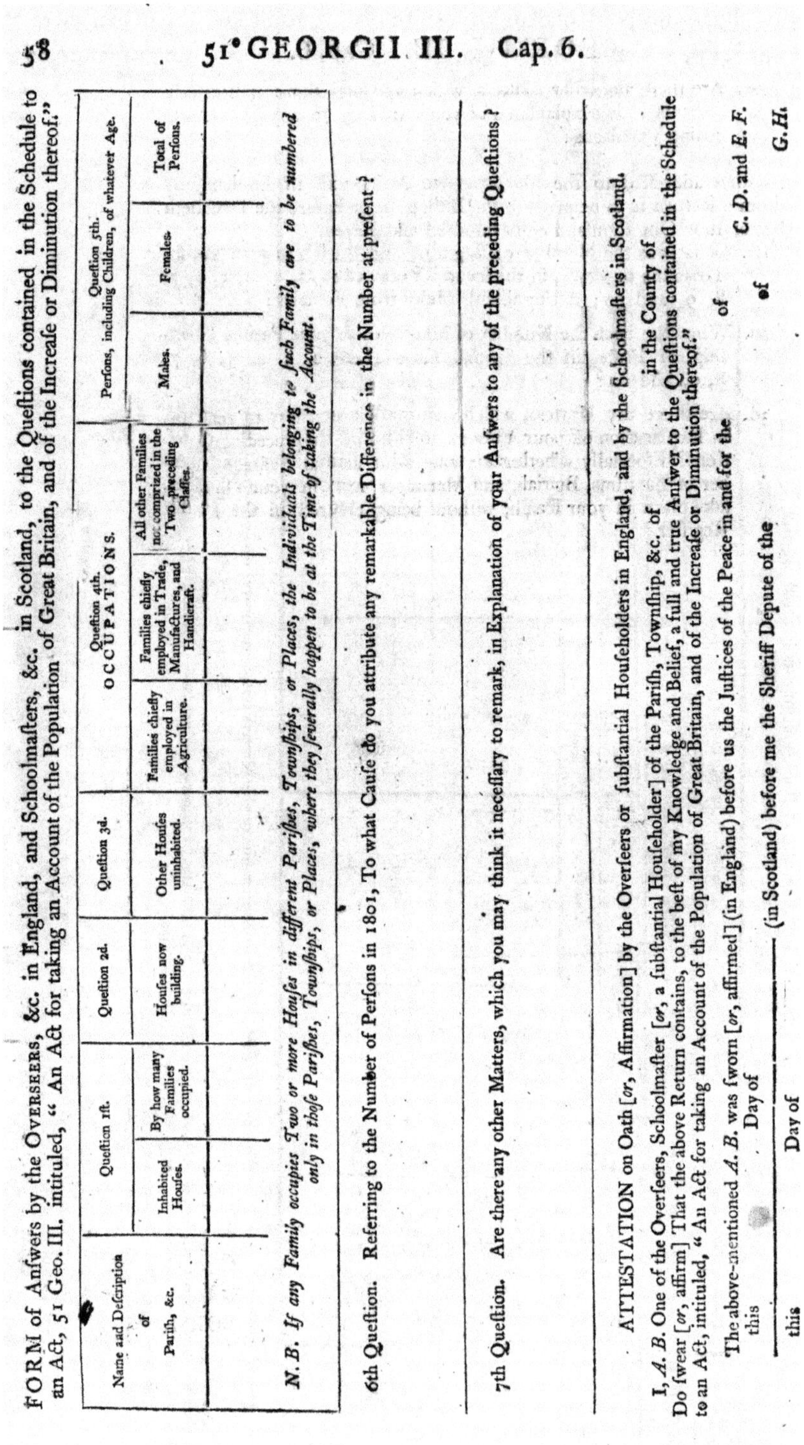

58   51° GEORGII III.   Cap. 6.

FORM of Answers by the OVERSEERS, &c. in England, and Schoolmasters, &c. in Scotland, to the Questions contained in the Schedule to an Act, 51 Geo. III. intituled, "An Act for taking an Account of the Population of Great Britain, and of the Increase or Diminution thereof."

Name and Description of Parish, &c.	Question 1st.		Question 2d.	Question 3d.	Question 4th. OCCUPATIONS.			Question 5th. Persons, including Children, of whatever Age.		
	Inhabited Houses.	By how many Families occupied	Houses now building.	Other Houses uninhabited.	Families chiefly employed in Agriculture.	Families chiefly employed in Trade, Manufactures, and Handicraft.	All other Families not comprized in the Two preceding Classes.	Males.	Females.	Total of Persons.

N.B. If any Family occupies Two or more Houses in different Parishes, Townships, or Places, the Individuals belonging to such Family are to be numbered only in those Parishes, Townships, or Places, where they severally happen to be at the Time of taking the Account.

6th Question. Referring to the Number of Persons in 1801, To what Cause do you attribute any remarkable Difference in the Number at present?

7th Question. Are there any other Matters, which you may think it necessary to remark, in Explanation of your Answers to any of the preceding Questions?

ATTESTATION on Oath [*or*, Affirmation] by the Overseers or substantial Householders in England, and by the Schoolmasters in Scotland.

I, *A. B.* One of the Overseers, Schoolmaster [*or*, a substantial Householder] of the Parish, Township, &c. of   in the County of   Do [swear [*or*, affirm] That the above Return contains, to the best of my Knowledge and Belief, a full and true Answer to the Questions contained in the Schedule to an Act, intituled, "An Act for taking an Account of the Population of Great Britain, and of the Increase or Diminution thereof."

The above-mentioned *A. B.* was [worn [*or*, affirmed] (in England) before us the Justices of the Peace in and for the   of   *C. D.* and *E. F.*
this   Day of

___ (in Scotland) before me the Sheriff Depute of the   of   *G. H.*
this   Day of

Figure A3.2 1811 enumeration schedule

1° GEORGII IV. Cap. 94. 771

FORM of Answer by the OVERSEERS, &c. in England, and Schoolmasters, &c. in Scotland, to the Questions contained in the Schedule to an Act, 1st Geo. IV., intituled "An Act for taking an Account of the Population of Great Britain, and of the Increase or Diminution thereof."

Name and Description of Parish, &c., and within what County, Hundred, Town Corporate, or other Division situate.	Question 1st.		Question 2d.	Question 3d.	Question 4th. OCCUPATIONS.		Question 3th. Persons, including Children, of whatever Age.		
	Inhabited Houses.	By how many Families occupied.	Houses now building.	Other Houses uninhabited.	Families chiefly employed in Agriculture.	Families chiefly employed in Trade, Manufactures, and Handicraft.	All other Families not comprised in the Two preceding Classes.	Males.	Females.	Total of Persons.

N. B. If any Family occupies Two or more Houses in different Parishes, Townships, or Places, the Individuals belonging to such Family are to be numbered only in those Parishes, Townships, or Places, where they severally happen to be at the Time of taking the Account.

6th Question. Referring to the Number of Persons in 1811, To what Cause do you attribute any remarkable Difference in the Number at present?

7th Question. Are there any other Matters, which you may think it necessary to remark, in Explanation of your Answers to any of the preceding Questions?

ATTESTATION on Oath [or, Affirmation] by the Overseers or substantial Householders in England, and by the Schoolmasters in Scotland.

I, A. B. One of the Overseers, Schoolmaster [or, a substantial Householder] of the Parish, Township, &c. of   in the County of   do swear [or, affirm] That the above Return contains, to the best of my Knowledge and Belief, a full and true Answer to the Questions contained in the Schedule to an Act, intituled "An Act for taking an Account of the Population of Great Britain, and of the Increase or Diminution thereof."

The above-mentioned A. B. was sworn [or, affirmed] (in England) before us the Justices of the Peace in and for the   of   C. D. and E. F.
this   Day of
                (in Scotland) before me the Sheriff Depute or Substitute of the   of   G. H.
this   Day of

Figure A3.3 1821 enumeration schedule

11° GEORGII IV. Cap. 30.

FORM of ANSWER by the OVERSEERS, &c. in England, and SCHOOLMASTERS, &c. in Scotland, to the Questions contained in the Schedule to an Act, 11th George 4th, intituled "An Act for taking an Account of the Population of Great Britain, and of the Increase or Diminution thereof."

Name and Description of Parish, &c. and within what County, Hundred, Town Corporate, or other Division situate.	QUESTION 1st.		QUESTION 2d. Houses now building.	QUESTION 3d. Other Houses uninhabited.	QUESTION 4th. OCCUPATIONS.			QUESTION 5th. Persons, including Children, of whatever Age.		
	Inhabited Houses.	By how many Families occupied.			Families chiefly employed in Agriculture.	Families chiefly employed in Trade, Manufactures, and Handicraft.	All other Families not comprised in the Two preceding Classes.	Males.	Females.	Total of Persons.

N. B. — *Individuals are to be numbered only in those Parishes, Townships, or Places where they severally happen to be at the Time of taking the Account.*

QUESTION 6th. Total Number of Males Twenty Years old.	QUESTION 7th. Males employed in Agriculture.			QUESTION 8th. Males employed in Manufacture, or in making Manufacturing Machinery.	QUESTION 9th. Males employed in Retail Trade, or in Handicraft, as Masters or Workmen.	QUESTION 10th. Wholesale Merchants, Capitalists, Bankers, Professional Persons, and other Educated Men.	QUESTION 11th. Labourers employed by the Three preceding Classes, and in other Labour not Agricultural.	QUESTION 12th. Twenty Years old (except Servants), including retired Tradesmen, superannuated Labourers, and Males diseased or disabled in Body or Mind.
	Occupiers of Land employing Labourers.	Occupiers of Land not employing Labourers.	Labourers employed in Agriculture.					

Figure A3.4 1831 enumeration schedule, Part 1

11° GEORGII IV. Cap.30. 315

QUESTION 13th. — HOW many Servants, distinguishing Males upwards of Twenty Years old ————, Males under Twenty Years old ————, Females ————?

QUESTION 14th. — IF you have entered any Males in answer to the 8th Question, be pleased to specify the Manufacture or Manufactures in which they are employed? And what Proportion of the Number of those entered in answer to Question 11th, are employed in any Quarry, Mines, Coal Pits, Fishery, or Public Work now in progress?

QUESTION 15th. — REFERRING to the Number of Persons in 1821, to what Cause do you attribute any remarkable Difference in the Number at present?

QUESTION 16th. — ARE there any other Matters which you may think it necessary to remark, in explanation of your Answers to any of the preceding Questions?

ATTESTATION on Oath [*or* Affirmation] by the Overseers or substantial Householders in England, and by the Schoolmasters in Scotland.

I, *A. B.* One of the Overseers, Schoolmaster, [*or* a substantial Householder] of the Parish, Township, &c. of ———— in the County of ———— do swear [*or* affirm], That the above Return contains, to the best of my Knowledge and Belief, a full and true Answer to the Questions contained in the Schedule to an Act, intituled " An Act for taking an Account of the Population of Great Britain, and of the Increase or Diminution thereof."

The above-mentioned *A. B.* was sworn [*or* affirmed] (in England) before us, the Justices of the Peace in and for the ̔ *C. D.* and *E. F.* of ———— this ———— Day of ————

(In Scotland) The above-mentioned *A. B.* was sworn before me, the Sheriff Depute or Substitute of the ———— of ———— *G. H.* this ———— Day of ————

The above Answers, collected and arranged by *A. B.*, are [*or* are not] (in my Opinion) correct.   *I. K.* Minister of the Parish of ———— .

Figure A3.5 1831 enumeration schedule, Part 2

~~City or~~ Borough of *Southwark* **36**

Parish ~~or Township~~ of *St. Saviour*

Example of Enumeration Schedule, shewing how Entries may be made.

PLACE.	HOUSES: Uninhabited or Building.	HOUSES: Inhabited.	NAMES of each Person who abode therein the preceding Night.	AGE and SEX: Males.	AGE and SEX: Females.	PROFESSION, TRADE, EMPLOYMENT, or of INDEPENDENT MEANS.	Where Born: Whether Born in same County.	Where Born: Whether Born in Scotland, Ireland, or Foreign Parts
George Street		1	James Johnson	40		Chemist	Y.	
			Jane do.		35		N.	
			William do.	15		Shoem. Ap.	Y.	
			Anne do.		13		Y.	
			Edward Smith	30		Chemist's Sh.	N.	
			Sarah Robins		45	F. S.		I.
do.	1U	1	John Cox	60		Publican	N.	
do.	1B		Mary do.		45		Y.	
do.	1B		Ellen do.		20		N.	
			James Macpherson	25		M. S.		S.
			Henry Wilson	35		Army	N.	
			n. k.	above 20				
Extra Parochial Place, named The Close.		1	William Jones	50		Farmer	Y.	
			Elizabeth do.		40		Y.	
			William do.	15		Navy	Y.	
			Charlotte do.		8		Y.	
			n. k. do.		5 months		Y.	
			Richard Clerk	20		Ag. Lab.	N.	
do.	1U	1	Robert Hall	45		Tailor	Y.	
			Martha do.		30		Y.	
			John Multer	25		Tailor J.		F.
			Ann Williams		20	F. S.	N.	
Chapel Row.		1	Edward Jackson	35		Ind.	N.	
			Charles do.	30		Cl.	N.	
			James Leary	20		M. S.		I.
TOTAL in Page	2U 2B	5		15	10			

B b

Figure A3.6 1841 enumerator's return

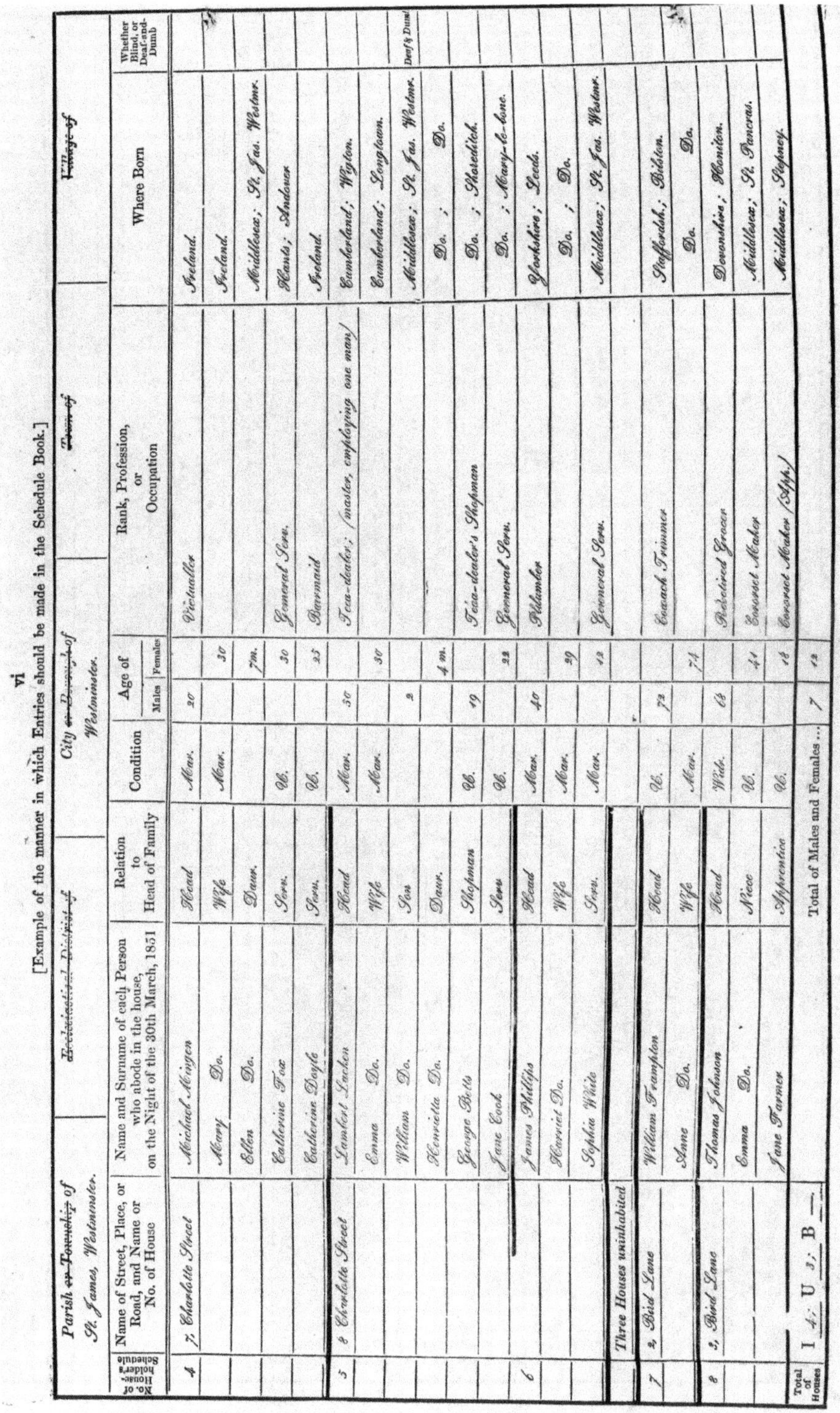

[Example of the manner in which Entries should be made in the Schedule Book.]

Parish or Township of St. James, Westminster. — Ecclesiastical District of — City or Borough of Westminster. — Town of — Village of

No. of Householder's Schedule	Name of Street, Place, or Road, and Name or No. of House	Name and Surname of each Person who abode in the house, on the Night of the 30th March, 1851	Relation to Head of Family	Condition	Age of Males	Age of Females	Rank, Profession, or Occupation	Where Born	Whether Blind, or Deaf-and-Dumb
4	7 Charlotte Street	Michael Mingen	Head	Mar.	20		Victualler	Ireland.	
		Mary Do.	Wife	Mar.		30		Ireland.	
		Ellen Do.	Daur.			7m.		Middlesex; St. Jas. Westmr.	
		Catherine Fox	Serv.	U.		30	General Serv.	Hants; Andover.	
		Catherine Doyle	Serv.	U.		23	Barmaid	Ireland.	
5	8 Charlotte Street	Lambert Lachen	Head	Mar.	50		Tea-dealer; master, employing one man	Cumberland; Wigton.	
		Emma Do.	Wife	Mar.		30		Cumberland; Longtown.	
		William Do.	Son		2			Middlesex; St. Jas. Westmr.	Deaf & Dumb
		Henrietta Do.	Daur.			4 m.		Do. Do.	
		George Betts	Shopman	U.	19		Tea-dealer's Shopman	Do.; Shoreditch.	
		Jane Cook	Serv.	U.		23	General Serv.	Do.; Mary-le-bone.	
6		James Phillips	Head	Mar.	40		Policeman	Yorkshire; Leeds.	
		Harriet Do.	Wife	Mar.		39		Do. Do.	
		Sophia White	Serv.	Mar.		13	General Serv.	Middlesex; St. Jas. Westmr.	
	Three Houses uninhabited								
7	2 Bird Lane	William Frampton	Head	U.	72		Coach Trimmer	Staffordsh.; Bidston.	
		Anne Do.	Wife	Mar.		74		Do. Do.	
8	3 Bird Lane	Thomas Johnson	Head	Wid.	63		Retired Grocer	Devonshire; Honiton.	
		Emma Do.	Niece	U.		14	Servant Maiden	Middlesex; St. Pancras.	
		Jane Farmer	Apprentice	U.		13	Corset Maker (App.)	Middlesex; Stepney.	
		Total of Males and Females			7	13			

Total of Houses: 1 4; U 3; B —

vi

Figure A3.7 1851 enumerator's return

iii

The undermentioned Houses are situate within the Boundaries of the

| | | Township] of St Saviour | City or Municipal Borough of Southwark | Municipal Ward of High Street | Parliamentary Borough of Southwark | Town [not being a City or Borough] of | Hamlet or Tything, &c., of | Ecclesiastical District of Christchurch | |

No. of Schedule	Road, Street, &c., and No. or Name of House	HOUSES Inhabited	HOUSES Uninhabited (U.), or Building (B.)	Name and Surname of each Person	Relation to Head of Family	Condition	Age of Males	Age of Females	Rank, Profession, or Occupation	Where Born	Whether Blind, or Deaf-and-Dumb
[Example]											
4	7, Charlotte St. "Queen's Arms"	1		Michael Morrison	Head	Mar.	31		Victualler	Middlesex; Islington.	
				May A. Do.	Wife	Mar.		29		Salop, Condover.	
				Ellen Do.	Daur.			1 mo.		Surrey; St Saviour, Southwark.	
				Ann Fox	Serv.	Un.		28	General Serv.	Hants; Andover.	
				Catherine Doyle	Serv.	Un.		24	Barmaid	Ireland	
5	8, Charlotte St.	1		Lambert Newton	Head	Mar.	39		Grocer; (master, employing 2 men)	Cumberland; Wigton.	
				Emma Do.	Wife	Mar.		36		Cumberland; Longtown.	
				William Do.	Son		12		Scholar	Surrey; St Saviour, Southwark.	
				Henrietta Do.	Daur.			9	Do.	Do. Do.	Deaf & Dumb from birth.
6				George Bacon	Shopman	Un.	19		Grocer's Shopman	Middlesex; Shoreditch.	
				Jane Cook	Serv.	Un.		22	General Serv.	Do.; Marylebone.	
				James F. Phillips	Head	Mar.	44		Bowler's Cl.	Yorkshire; Leeds.	
				Rachel Do.	Wife	Mar.		29		Do.; Bradford.	
		3 U		Sophia White	Serv.	Un.		16	General Serv.	Middlesex; St Ins, Westminster.	
7	9, 10, 11, Do. 1, Bird Lane	1		William Tampton	Head	Mar.	72		Coach Trimmer	Staffordshire; Brixton.	
				Anne Do.	Wife	Mar.		69		Do.	
8	2, Bird Lane	1		Thomas Johnson	Head	Wid.	68		Retired Grocer	Devon; Honiton.	
				Emma Do.	Niece	Un.		44	Court Maker	Middlesex; St Pancras.	
				Jane Faint	Septentin	Un.		18	Court Maker (Ar.)	Middlesex; Stepney.	
		2 B		Walter Johnson	Lodger	Un.	23		Ship Carpenter	Durham; Sunderland.	
9	Do.								End of Christchurch Ecclesiastical District		
	Total of Houses... 4	4 U	2 B			Total of Males and Females...	8	12			

Figure A3.8 1861 enumerator's return

[Example]

iii.

The undermentioned Houses are situate within the Boundaries of the

| Civil Parish [or Township] of St. Mary | City of Municipal Borough of Shrewsbury | Municipal Ward of Loyd Street | Parliamentary Borough of Shrewsbury | Town [not being a City or Borough] of | Village or Hamlet, &c., of | Local Board [or Improvement Commissioners District] of Shrewsbury | Ecclesiastical District of St. Michael |

No. of Schedule	Road, Street, &c. and No. or Name of House	HOUSES Inhabited	HOUSES Uninhabited or Building (B.)	Name and Surname of each Person	Relation to Head of Family	Condition	Age of Males	Age of Females	Rank, Profession, or Occupation	Where Born	Whether 1. Deaf-and-Dumb 2. Blind 3. Imbecile or Idiot 4. Lunatic
4	1, Charlotte St. (Queen's Arms)	1		Michael Mattison	Head	Mar.	31		Licensed Victualler	Middlesex; Islington	
				Mary J. Do.	Wife	Mar.		29		Salop; Condover	
				Ellen Do.	Daut.			one		Salop; Shrewsbury	
				Elizabeth Mattison	Mother	W.		58	Annuitant	Yorks; Audawer	
				Ann Fox	Serv.	Unm.		24	General Serv.	Yorks; Audawer	
				Catherine Doyle	Serv.	Unm.		24	Barmaid	Ireland	Lunatic
5	8, Charlotte St.	1		Lambert Newton	Head	Mar.	39		Grocer; (master, employing 2 men)	Cumberland; Wigton	
				Emma Do.	Wife	Mar.		36		Do.; Longtown	
				William Do.	Son		12		Scholar	Salop; Pullam	
				Henrietta Do.	Daut.			9	Do.	Do.; Do.	Deaf-and-Dumb from Birth.
6				George Bacon	Shopman	Unm.	19		Grocer's Shopman	Middlesex; Shoreditch	
				Jane Cook	Serv.	Unm.		22	General Serv.	Scotland	
				James T. Phillips	Head	Mar.	41		Draper's Clerk	Yorkshire; Leeds	
				Harriet Do.	Wife	Mar.		29		Do.; Bradford	
				Sophia White	Serv.	Unm.		16	General Serv.	Salop; Bridgnorth	
7	4, Bird Lane	1		William Frampton	Head	Mar.	72		Coach Trimmer	Staffordsh.; Bilston	
				Ann Do.	Wife	Mar.		69		Do.; Tamworth	
8	2, Bird Lane	1		Thomas Johnson	Head	Wid.	68		Retired Grocer	Devon; Honiton	
				Henry Johnson	Son	Unm.	39		Organist	Salop; Shrewsbury	
				Emma Do.	Alice	Unm.		44	Cowel Maker	Middlesex; St. Pancras	Blind from Small Pox.
9	Do.	B.		Jane James	Apprentice	Unm.		18	Cowel Maker (Apprentice)	Salop; Pullam	
				Walter Campbell	Lodger	Unm.	23		Ship Carpenter (out of employ)	Durham; Sunderland	
				End of St. Michael Ecclesiastical District							
	Total of Houses... 4	4	1 Uninh. 1 B.			Total of Males and Females...	9	13			

Figure A3.9 1871 enumerator's return

[Example]

iii.

The undermentioned Houses are situate within the Boundaries of the

| Civil Parish [or Township] of *St. Mary.* | City or Municipal Borough of *Shrewsbury.* | Municipal Ward of *Welsh.* | Parliamentary Borough of *Shrewsbury.* | Town or Village or Hamlet of — | Urban Sanitary District of *Shrewsbury.* | Rural Sanitary District of **51** | Ecclesiastical Parish or District of *St. Michael.* |

No. of Schedule	ROAD, STREET, &c., and No. or NAME of HOUSE	HOUSES (In-habit-ed)	HOUSES (Unin-habited U. or Build'g B.)	NAME and Surname of each Person	RELATION to Head of Family	CON-DITION as to Marriage	AGE last Birthday of Males	AGE last Birthday of Females	Rank, Profession, or OCCUPATION	WHERE BORN	If (1)Deaf-&-Dumb (2)Blind (3)Imbecile or Idiot (4)Lunatic
4	7, Charlotte St. ("Queen's Arms")	1		Michael Mattison	Head	Mar.	31		Licensed Victualler	Middlesex; Islington	
				Mary J. Do.	Wife	Mar.		29		Salop; Condover	
				Ellen Do.	Daur.			7mo.		Salop; Shrewsbury	
				Elizabeth Mattison	Mother	W.		58	Annuitant	Salop; Shrewsbury	Lunatic
				Ann Fox	Serv.	Unm.		28	General Serv.	Lands; Andover	
				Catherine Doyle	Serv.	Unm.		24	Barmaid	Ireland	
5	8, Charlotte St.	1		Lambert Newton	Head	Mar.	39		Grocer; (master, employing 2 men)	Cumberland; Weston	
				Emma Do.	Wife	Mar.		36		Do.; Longtown	
				William Do.	Son		12		Scholar	Salop; Ludlow	
				Henrietta Do.	Daur.			9	Do.	Do.; Do.	Deaf-and-Dumb
				George Bacon	Shopman	Unm.	19		Grocer's Shopman	Middlesex; Shoreditch	
				Jane Cook	Serv.	Unm.		22	General Serv.	Scotland	
6	Do.	1		Thomas F. Phillips	Head	Mar.	41		Banker's Clerk	Yorkshire; Leeds	
				Harriet Do.	Wife	Mar.		20		Do.; Bradford	
				Sophia White	Serv.	Unm.		16	General Serv.	Salop; Minsterworth	
7	1, Bird Lane	1		William Brampton	Head	Mar.	72		Coach Trimmer	Staffordsh.; Bilston	
				Anne Do.	Wife	Mar.		69		Do.; Tamworth	
8	2, Bird Lane	1		Thomas Johnson	Head	Wd.	68		Retired Grocer	Devon; Honiton	
				Henry Johnson	Son	Unm.	37		Organist	Salop; Shrewsbury	
				Emma Do.	Niece	Unm.		41		Middlesex; St. Pancras	
				Jane Barnes	Apprentice	Unm.		18	Corset Maker (Apprentice)	Salop; Ludlow	
9	Do.			Walter Campbell	Lodger	Unm.	23		Ship Carpenter (out of employ)	Durham; Sunderland	
						End of St. Michael			End of Ecclesiastical District		
	Total of Houses... 4	1 Uc.	2 U.B.		Total of Males and Females..		8	13			

Figure A3.10 1881 enumerator's return

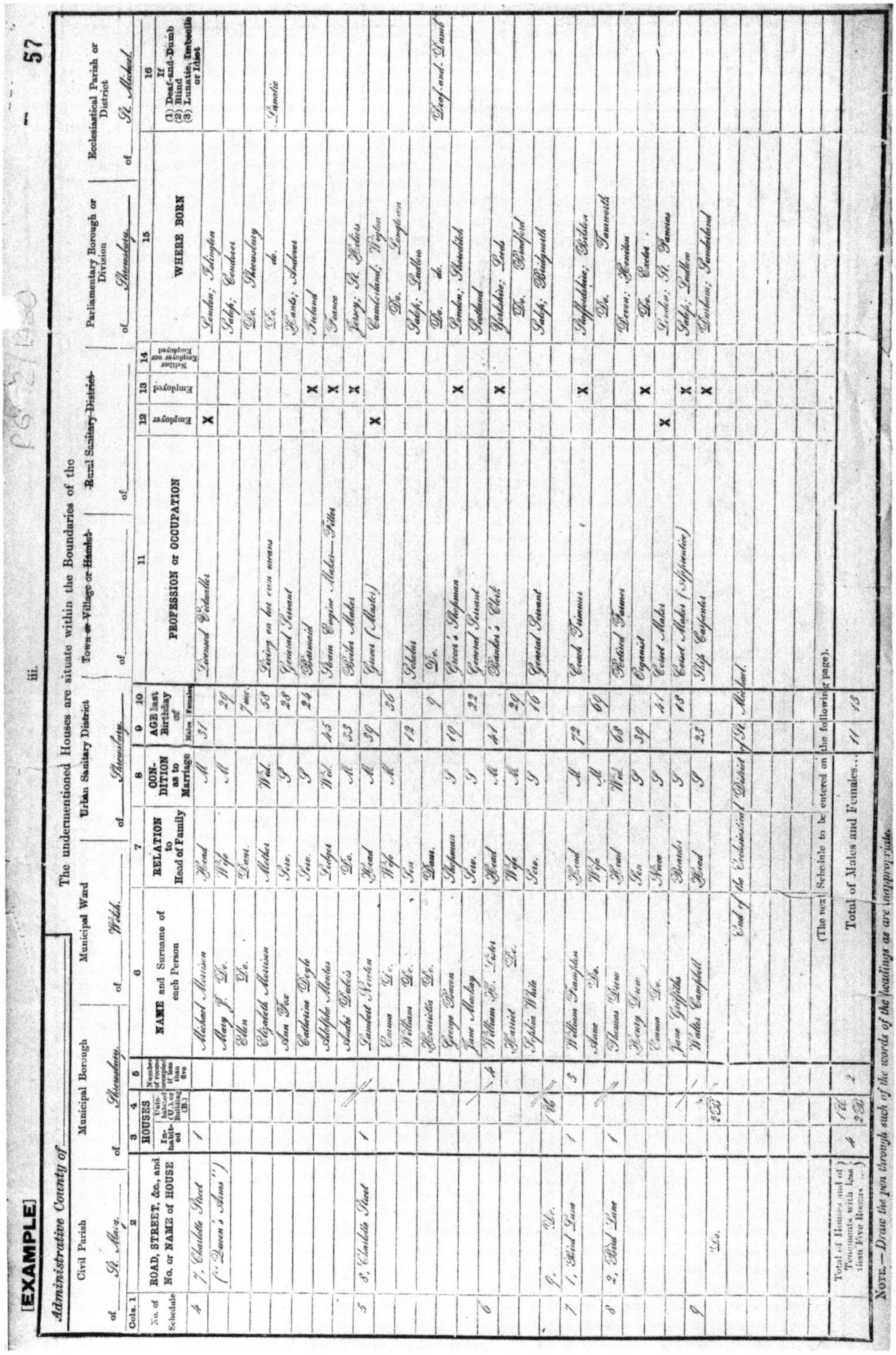

[EXAMPLE] iii. 57

Administrative County of

The undermentioned Houses are situate within the Boundaries of the

Civil Parish of St. Mary | Municipal Borough of Shrewsbury | Municipal Ward of Welsh | Urban Sanitary District of Shrewsbury | ~~Town or Village or Hamlet~~ of | ~~Rural Sanitary District~~ of | Parliamentary Borough or Division of Shrewsbury | Ecclesiastical Parish or District of St. Michael

Cols. 1 No. of Schedule	2 ROAD, STREET, &c., and No. or NAME of HOUSE	3 HOUSES In-habit-ed	4 HOUSES Unin-habited (U.), or Building (B.)	5 Number of rooms occupied if less than five	6 NAME and Surname of each Person	7 RELATION to Head of Family	8 CONDITION as to Marriage	9 AGE last Birthday of Males	10 AGE last Birthday of Females	11 PROFESSION or OCCUPATION	12 Employer	13 Employed	14 Neither Employer nor Employed	15 WHERE BORN	16 If (1) Deaf-and-Dumb (2) Blind (3) Lunatic, Imbecile or Idiot
4	7, Charlotte Street	1			Michael Morrison	Head	M	31		Licensed Victualler	X			London; Islington	
	("Queen's Arms")				Mary J. Do.	Wife	M		29					Salop; Condover	
					Ellen Do.	Daur.			7 mo.					Do. Shrewsbury	
					Elizabeth Morrison	Mother	Wid.		58	Living on her own means				Do. do.	Lunatic
					Ann Fox	Serv.	S		28	General Servant				Hants; Andover	
					Catherine Doyle	Serv.	S		24	Barmaid		X		Ireland	
					Adolphe Montas	Lodger	Wid.	45		Steam Engine Maker—Fitter		X		France	
					André Dubois	Do.	M	33		Boiler Maker		X		Jersey; St. Heliers	
5	8, Charlotte Street	1			Lambert Newton	Head	M	39		Grocer (Master)	X			Cumberland; Wigton	
					Emma Do.	Wife	M		36					Do. Longtown	
					William Do.	Son		12		Scholar				Salop; Ludlow	
					Henrietta Do.	Daur.			9	Do.				Do. do.	Deaf-and-Dumb
					George Bacon	Shopman	S	19		Grocer's Shopman		X		London; Shoreditch	
					Jane Mackay	Serv.	S		22	General Servant				Scotland	
6				4	William H. Lister	Head	M	41		Banker's Clerk		X		Yorkshire; Leeds	
					Harriet Do.	Wife	M		29					Do. Bradford	
					Sophia White	Serv.	S		16	General Servant				Salop; Bridgnorth	
	9, Do.		1 U												
7	1, Bird Lane	1		3	William Frampton	Head	M	72		Coach Trimmer		X		Staffordshire; Bilston	
					Anne Do.	Wife	M		69					Do. Tamworth	
8	2, Bird Lane	1			Thomas Drew	Head	Wid.	68		Retired Farmer				Devon; Honiton	
					Henry Drew	Son	S	39		Organist		X		Do. Exeter	
					Emma Do.	Niece	S		41	Corset Maker	X			London; St. Pancras	
					Jane Griffiths	Boarder	S		18	Corset Maker (Apprentice)		X		Salop; Ludlow	
9					Walter Campbell	Head	S	23		Ship Carpenter		X		Durham; Sunderland	
	Do.		2 B												
					End of the Ecclesiastical District of St. Michael.										
					(The next Schedule to be entered on the following page).										
	Total of Houses and of Tenements with less than Five Rooms	4	1 U 2 B	2	Total of Males and Females...			11	13						

NOTE.—Draw the pen through such of the words of the headings as are inappropriate.

Figure A3.11 1891 enumerator's return

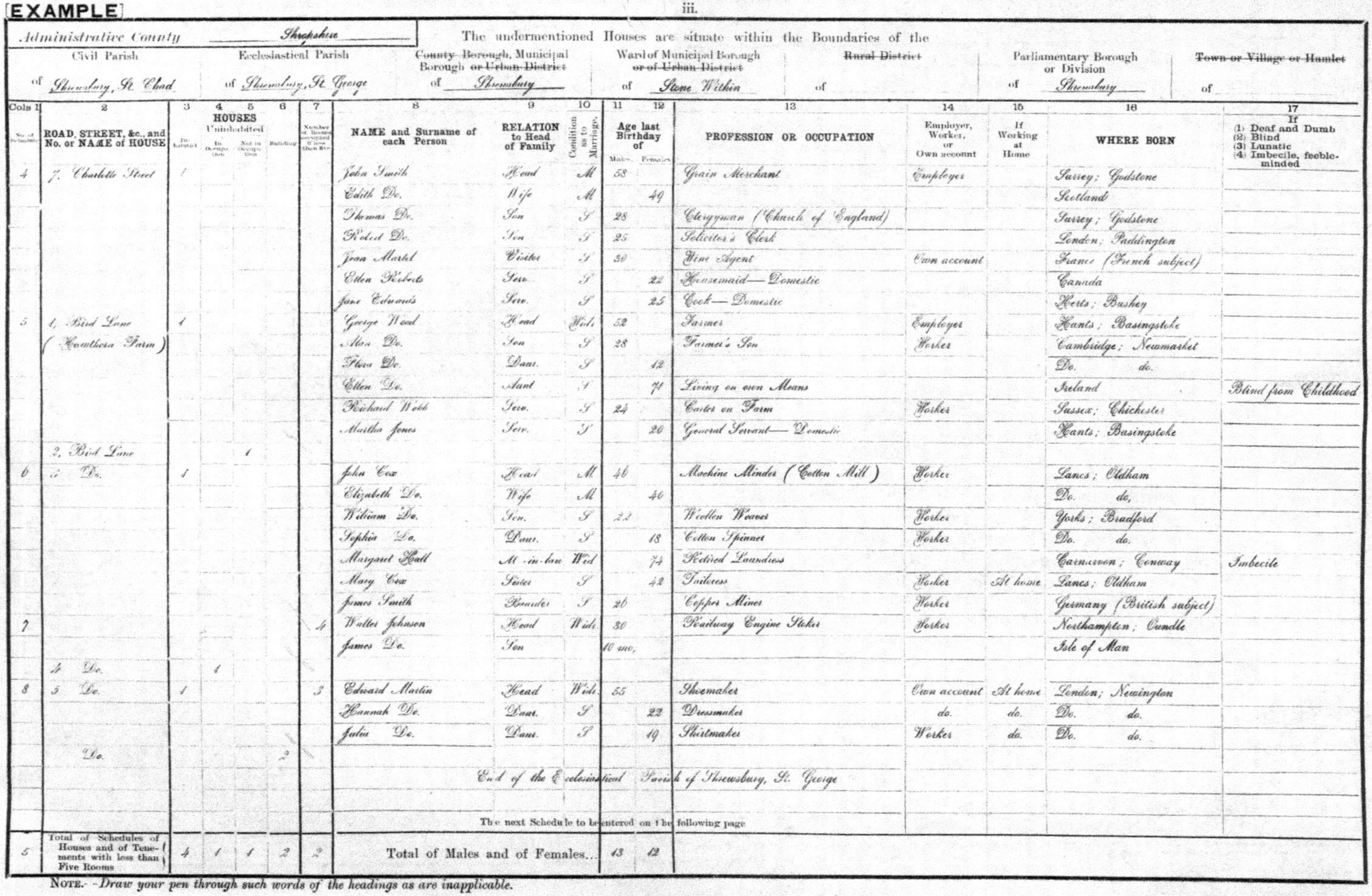

[EXAMPLE]

The undermentioned Houses are situate within the Boundaries of the —

| Administrative County ... | Civil Parish ... | Ecclesiastical Parish ... | County Borough, Municipal Borough or Urban District ... | Ward of Municipal Borough or of Urban District ... | Rural District ... | Parliamentary Borough or Division ... | Town or Village or Hamlet ... |

Cols. 1	2	3	4 5 6	7	8	9	10	11	12	13	14	15	16	17
No. of Schedule	ROAD, STREET, &c. and No. or NAME of HOUSE		HOUSES (Inhabited / Uninhabited / Building)	Number of Rooms occupied if less than Five	NAME and Surname of each Person	RELATION to Head of Family	Condition as to Marriage	Age last Birthday (Males)	(Females)	PROFESSION OR OCCUPATION	Employer, Worker, or Own account	If Working at Home	WHERE BORN	If (1) Deaf and Dumb (2) Blind (3) Lunatic (4) Imbecile, feeble-minded
4	1 Charlotte Street	1			John Smith	Head	M	53		Gents Merchant	Employer		Surrey; Godstone	
					Edith Do.	Wife	M		49				Scotland	
					Thomas Do.	Son	S	28		Clergyman (Church of England)			Surrey; Godstone	
					Robert Do.	Son	S	25		Solicitor's Clerk			London; Paddington	
					Jean Abel	Visitor	S		30	Fine Agent	Own account		France (French subject)	
					Ellen Nicholls	Servant	S		22	Housemaid—Domestic			Canada	
					Jane Colverd	Serv.	S		25	Cook—Domestic			Herts; Bushey	
5	1 Bird Lane (Wentleton Farm)	1			George Wood	Head	Wd.	52		Farmer	Employer		Cambridge; Boxingdale	
					Peter Do.	Son	S	28		Farmer's Son	Worker		Cambridge; Newmarket	
					Mary Do.	Daur.	S						do.	
					Ellen Do.	Aunt	S		74	Living on own Means			Ireland	Blind from Childhood
					Richard Webb	Serv.	S	24		Carter on Farm	Worker		Sussex; Chichester	
					Martha Jones	Serv.	S		20	General Servant—Domestic			Kents; Basingstoke	
6	2 Bird Lane	1			John Vear	Head	M	46		Machine Minder (Cotton Mill)	Worker		Lancs; Oldham	
					Elizabeth Do.	Wife	M		46				Do. do.	
					William Do.	Son	S	23		Woollen Weaver	Worker		Yorks; Bradford	
					Sophia Do.	Daur.	S		18	Cotton Spinner	Worker		Do. do.	
					Margaret Bell	M-in-law	Wid.		74	Retired Laundress		At home	Carnarvon; Conway	Imbecile
					Mary Vear	Boarder	S		26	Cotton Mine	Worker		Lancs; Oldham	
					James Smith	Boarder	Wd.	30		Railway Engine Stoker	Worker		Germany (British subject); Northampton	
7					Walter Johnson	Son		10 mo.					Northampton; Camelo	
					James Do.								Isle of Man	
8	Do.	1			Edward Martin	Head	Wd.	55		Shoemaker	Own account	At home	London; Newington	
	Do.				Hannah Do.	Daur.	S		22	Dressmaker	do.	do.	Do. do.	
	Do.				John Do.	Son	S	49		Stationer	Worker	do.	Do. do.	

End of the Enclosure of ... Parish of ... Novembeby, St. George

The next Schedule to be entered on the following page

Total of Schedules of Houses and of Tenements with less than Five Rooms	Total of Males and of Females...
4 1 1 3	13 12

NOTE.—Draw your pen through such words of the headings as are inapplicable.

Figure A3.12 1901 enumerator's return

188

Appendix 4 Geographical and administrative areas in the census

The following is a guide to types of administrative and geographical units. For a more extensive treatment of such areas, and a dynamic online guide to changing boundaries, see <http://www.visionofbritain.org.uk> (30 Sept. 2004).

Administrative county *see* **County**

Ancient county *see* **County**

Borough
There is agreement neither on what constituted a borough in the Middle Ages, nor on how many there were. Some towns had ancient charters, others claimed the right by prescription, some were incorporated and some had several claims to the title. Among the distinguishing marks of a borough were the possession of its own offices and institutions, which included some degree of exemption from the county's jurisdiction, special schemes of taxation, the right to hold fairs and markets and the right to representation in Parliament.

The 1832 Reform Act took away the right to parliamentary representation from some boroughs, extended the parliamentary limits of others and created boroughs with parliamentary status. This destroyed the identity between municipal and parliamentary boroughs. The Municipal Corporations Act of 1835 officially established boroughs with municipal powers, either by inclusion in the schedule to the act or by later charter. Towns of exceptional importance were made county boroughs, either by inclusion in the original schedule in the 1888 Local Government Act or by later charter. This status carried complete exemption from the jurisdiction of the surrounding or adjacent administrative county. Some important boroughs returned more than one MP to Parliament.

Chapelry
A territorial division of a parish. The ancient parish can be seen as the area served by a parish church. With the rise of population, additional churches were built within the parish, and parts of the latter came to be assigned by custom to these secondary churches under the name of chapelries.

City
An important urban settlement with the rank and title 'city' conferred by royal authority. The term is commonly associated with cathedral towns but there is no necessary correlation. Birmingham, for example, became a city in the nineteenth century but did not have a cathedral.

Civil parish *see* **Parish**

County

The ancient counties, sometimes called the geographical counties, are geographical entities whose origins lay in the period before the Norman Conquest in 1066. They were either Anglo-Saxon kingdoms whose size made them suitable administrative units when England was unified in the tenth century, or artificial creations formed from larger kingdoms.

The counties of England were able to send two knights of the shire to represent them in Parliament. As a result of the 1832 Reform Act, and subsequent legislation, the areas which formed the basis of parliamentary representation (the parliamentary counties) were redrawn and were no longer co-terminus with the ancient counties.

The 1834 Poor Law Amendment Act grouped parishes together into Poor Law unions for the purpose of Poor Law administration. These often included parishes in two or more ancient counties. These unions were the basic building blocks of the registration districts. The registrar-general created an artificial Poor Law or registration county for census purposes, by grouping under one county those unions predominantly comprised of parishes within that ancient county. The registration counties and the ancient counties do not, therefore, necessarily coincide.

A new system of administrative counties was established by the 1888 Local Government Act. These counties were made up of municipal boroughs, and urban and rural sanitary districts. They sometimes coincided with the existing ancient counties but when an urban sanitary district extended into two counties, the whole of the district was accepted as within that county which contained the largest portion of the population of the district according to the census of 1881. Certain ancient counties were subdivided. The three ridings of Yorkshire, for example, each became administrative counties.

County borough *see* **Borough**

Ecclesiastical parish *see* **Parish**

Extra-parochial places

Certain geographic areas were not organised as parishes and hence were called extra-parochial. There were a number of reasons for this arrangement, including association with the crown (Windsor Castle), with a religious house before the Dissolution, or with a cathedral chapter, or with other corporate bodies such as inns of court. These areas enjoyed virtual exemption from taxation; from maintaining the poor, since there was no overseer; from the militia laws because there was no constable to make returns; and from repairing the highways because there was no official surveyor.

In 1857 the privileges of these areas were curtailed by an act 'to provide for the relief of the poor in extra-parochial places'. This decreed that places named extra-parochial in the *1851*

Census Report were to be deemed parishes for this purpose and to have overseers of the poor appointed. In the case of very small areas, the place was annexed to an adjoining parish, if the consent of the owners and occupiers of two-thirds (in value) of the land was obtained. In the case of places not specified as extra-parochial in the *Census Report* the act was merely permissive and, therefore, largely inoperative. An act of 1868 declared that every extra-parochial place existing on 25 December 1868 should be added to the next adjoining civil parish with which it had the longest common boundary. Some lighthouses and small islands, which were not contiguous with any parish, were overlooked in the act and remained extra-parochial. There were still many places extra-parochial from ecclesiastical parishes which enjoyed special privileges under church law or custom.

Hamlet
Subdivision of a parish; a settlement smaller than a village.

Hundred
Subdivision of ancient counties which can already be found in Domesday Book. It was supposed to have originally comprised land capable of supporting 100 families. By the late nineteenth century it had lost all administrative importance.

Improvement commissioners district
From 1748 onwards *ad hoc* authorities known as improvement commissioners were set up by local acts of Parliament in urban areas to deal with the paving, lighting and cleansing of streets. Some of these authorities were given police powers. They consisted of owners of freehold property above a specified value, or of persons elected by the local ratepayers, with an *ex officio* element, for example local justices of the peace. Improvement commissioners were abolished by the 1894 Local Government Act.

Lathe
An ancient division of the county of Kent, containing several hundreds or liberties. Each lathe had a lathe-reeve or under-sheriff.

Liberty
A district analogous to an extra-parochial place, only of a larger extent, in which the normal course of law as it affected the hundred did not apply.

Local board district
The 1848 Public Health Act provided for the establishment of a local board of health, elected by the ratepayers, in every urban area where the inhabitants requested it, or where there was a high death rate. The boards were abolished by the 1894 Local Government Act.

Metropolis
The City of London enjoyed independence as a county by itself from early times. As the population spilled out beyond the City's original limits of about a square mile, there was no

single government unit to exercise authority over the enlarged area. The 1855 Metropolis Management Act created a Metropolitan Board of Works to undertake sanitary works for an area which by then included parts of Middlesex, Surrey and Kent, without altering jurisdictions in any other matters.

The area of the metropolis (with minor boundary changes) became a separate county in 1889 when the general system of administrative counties was established. As a result of the 1899 London Government Act the London Administrative County was subdivided into metropolitan boroughs.

Municipal borough *see* **Borough**

Municipal ward *see* **Ward**

New parish *see* **Parish**

Parish
It is very difficult to define the term 'parish'. Originally the parish was more a collection of rights than a specific area. Before the seventeenth century the parish existed for ecclesiastical purposes as the area under the jurisdiction of a clergyman with the cure of souls. With the establishment of the Elizabethan Poor Law in 1597, the parish began to acquire secular functions, in this case the relief of the poor. Parishes which existed before 1597, and which thereafter had secular as well as ecclesiastical functions, were called 'ancient parishes'.

'Civil parishes' were administrative units which only had secular functions, and were commonly defined as areas for which a separate poor rate could be assessed. The existence, alteration or abolition of these units had no effect on the ecclesiastical arrangements of the locality. Many civil parishes were areas at first subordinate to a mother church which had come in time to enjoy independence, such as hamlets, tithings, townships, chapelries and liberties. If a separate Poor Law rate was levied in the subordinate unit, it could be called a 'hamlet', 'township', and so on, and/or a 'parish'. In order to avoid confusion the 1866 Poor Law Amendment Act required that these areas should be called 'parishes'. Many extra-parochial places had already become civil parishes in 1857.

From 1597 onwards 'ecclesiastical parishes' were established for purely ecclesiastical purposes. They were more numerous than civil parishes, especially when efforts were made to build new churches in urban areas where the population was increasing. Many ecclesiastically subordinate areas within parishes, such as chapelries, were raised to parochial rank, and many formed which had no previous status. In the nineteenth and twentieth centuries a number of statutory provisions allowed the creation of many different types of ecclesiastical or 'new' parishes. It was not unusual for a parish to be refounded to gain privileges and rights conferred by newer statutes.

Parliamentary borough *see* **Borough**

Parliamentary borough division
The 1885 Redistribution of Seats Act created single-member constituencies, and it was necessary to divide up multiple-member boroughs.

Parliamentary county *see* **County**

Parliamentary county division
From 1832 onwards a number of statutes divided the counties established for parliamentary purposes, for example East and West Kent.

Poor Law union
Under 'Gilbert's Act' of 1782 certain parishes were, with the consent of their inhabitants, combined into unions for Poor Law purposes. This partial re-organisation was made more general in England and Wales by the 1834 Poor Law Amendment Act, which vested the management of poor relief in boards of guardians whose sphere of responsibility extended to all the parishes which made up their union. In forming these unions consideration was given to local convenience and to the preservation of existing parishes, rather than to administrative consistency. Many unions were thus partly in two or more ancient counties.

Rape
A division of the county of Sussex, containing several hundreds or liberties. The term may have been derived from 'hrepp' or rope, the Norman method of dividing the land.

Registration county *see* **County**

Registration district
When civil registration was established in England and Wales by the 1836 Births and Deaths Registration and Marriages Acts, the Poor Law union areas were generally adopted as registration districts. A superintendent registrar of births, deaths and marriages was appointed for each.

Registration division
For the purpose of statistical investigation in England and Wales, registration districts thought to possess common characteristics were grouped into registration divisions. Before 1851 there were 27 such areas, which were usually made up of counties or groups of counties. In some cases, however, the pre-1851 divisions included parts of counties. Division IX, for example, comprised Norfolk and the northern part of Suffolk. The pre-1851 divisions were not used for census purposes. In 1851 (with the exception of the area around London) whole registration counties were grouped into 11 divisions:

I LONDON, comprising the portions of Middlesex, Surrey and Kent within the limits of the registrar-general's bills of mortality.

II SOUTH-EASTERN DIVISION, comprising Surrey and Kent (outside the London division), Sussex, Hampshire and Berkshire.

III   SOUTH-MIDLAND DIVISION, comprising Middlesex (outside the London division), Hertfordshire, Buckinghamshire, Oxfordshire, Northamptonshire, Bedfordshire and Cambridgeshire.

IV   EASTERN DIVISION, comprising Essex, Suffolk and Norfolk.

V   SOUTH-WESTERN DIVISION, comprising Wiltshire, Dorsetshire, Devonshire, Cornwall and Somersetshire.

VI   WEST-MIDLAND DIVISION, comprising Gloucestershire, Herefordshire, Shropshire, Staffordshire, Worcestershire and Warwickshire.

VII   NORTH-MIDLAND DIVISION, comprising Leicestershire, Rutland, Lincolnshire, Nottinghamshire and Derbyshire.

VIII   NORTH-WESTERN DIVISION, comprising Cheshire and Lancashire.

IX   YORK DIVISION, consisting of Yorkshire.

X   NORTHERN DIVISION, comprising Durham, Northumberland, Cumberland and Westmorland.

XI   WELSH DIVISION, comprising Monmouthshire, South Wales and North Wales.

Registration sub-district
Registration districts were divided into sub-districts consisting of combined parishes or localities in which resident registrars were appointed for the registration of births, marriages and deaths.

Rural district *see* **Sanitary district**

Rural sanitary district *see* **Sanitary district**

Sanitary district
The Public Health Acts of 1874 and 1875 created new authorities with responsibilities in public health. Urban areas, already included in municipal boroughs or other bodies such as towns with improvement commissioners, were to form urban sanitary districts, the number of which was gradually enlarged in succeeding years. The rest of the country was divided into rural sanitary districts which were co-terminus with Poor Law unions, less the areas in urban sanitary districts. The system was abolished by the 1894 Local Government Act, which transformed urban and rural sanitary districts into general-purpose urban districts and rural districts within the framework of administrative counties.

Tithing
Sub-division of a parish, generally for Poor Law purposes.

Town

A settlement more regularly built than a village and having more complete and independent local government. This term could be applied to cities and boroughs having special privileges and titles but also to smaller settlements which might be indistinguishable from villages except, perhaps, that they had the right to hold periodic markets or fairs.

'Town (not being a city or borough)' *see* **Town**

Township

Sub-division of a parish, generally for Poor Law purposes.

Urban district *see* **Sanitary district**

Urban sanitary district *see* **Sanitary district**

Village

Sub-division of a parish, generally for Poor Law purposes; a centre of habitation in a country district.

Wapentake

Rather than being made up of hundreds, some northern and eastern counties settled by Danish invaders prior to 1066 were divided into wapentakes. The term was perhaps derived from an Old Norse word meaning a waving or brandishing of weapons as a means of signifying consent to a decision taken by the assembled inhabitants.

Ward

Sub-divisions of parliamentary constituencies for electoral purposes.

Ward of urban district *see* **Ward**

Appendix 5 Geographical data sought on each page of the enumerators' books

Each page of the enumerators' returns had spaces or boxes at the top for information on the administrative units covered therein. Some of these units were, of course, mutually exclusive, and the enumerators were expected to strike out those which did not apply.

1841

1 City or borough
2 Parish or township

1851

1 Parish or township
2 Ecclesiastical district
3 City or borough
4 Town
5 Village

1861

1 Parish [or township]
2 City or municipal borough
3 Municipal ward
4 Parliamentary borough
5 Town [not being a city or borough]
6 Hamlet, tithing, etc.
7 Ecclesiastical district

1871

1 Civil parish [or township]
2 City or municipal borough
3 Municipal ward
4 Parliamentary borough
5 Town [not being a city or borough]
6 Village or hamlet, etc.
7 Local board [or improvement commissioners district]
8 Ecclesiastical district

1881

1 Civil parish [or township]
2 City or municipal borough
3 Municipal ward
4 Parliamentary borough
5 Town or village or hamlet
6 Urban sanitary district
7 Rural sanitary district
8 Ecclesiastical parish or district

1891

1 Administrative county
2 Civil parish
3 Municipal borough
4 Municipal ward
5 Urban sanitary district
6 Town or village or hamlet
7 Rural sanitary district
8 Parliamentary borough or division
9 Ecclesiastical parish or district

1901

1 Administrative county
2 Civil parish
3 Ecclesiastical parish
4 County borough, municipal borough or urban district
5 Ward of municipal borough or of urban district
6 Rural district
7 Parliamentary borough or division
8 Town or village or hamlet

Appendix 6 Summary tables in the enumerators' books

1841

1   Number of males and females in vessels on inland navigable waters, in mines or pits, in barns or sheds, in tents or in the open air, or not enumerated as inmates of any dwelling house.

2   The probable number of males and females temporarily present or temporarily absent from the district, and the cause thereof.

3   Number of persons emigrated to the colonies or foreign countries since 31 December 1840.

1851

1   Number of separate occupiers, houses (inhabited, uninhabited, being built), males and females recorded on each page of the nominal returns.

2   As in first table but for each named parish or township. Persons to be divided into those in and out of houses.

3   Estimated number of males and females in vessels on inland navigable waters, in barns or sheds, in tents and in the open air.

4   Number of males and females temporarily present.

5   Number of males and females temporarily absent.

1861

1   Number of males and females temporarily absent, and the reasons for their absence.

2   Number of males and females temporarily present, and the reasons for their presence.

3   Number of schedules, houses (inhabited, uninhabited, being built), males and females in each named parish or township, or parts thereof. Persons to be divided into those in and out of houses.

4   Number of above on each page of the nominal returns.

1871

1   Number of males and females temporarily absent, and the reasons for their absence.

2   Number of males and females temporarily present, and the reasons for their presence.

3   Number of schedules, houses (inhabited, uninhabited, being built), males and females in each named civil parish or township, or parts thereof.

4   Number of the household schedules filled in by the enumerator.

5   Number of elements in (3) on each page of the nominal returns.

1881

1   Number of males and females temporarily absent, and the reasons for their absence.
2   Number of males and females temporarily present, and the reasons for their presence.
3   Number of schedules, houses (inhabited, uninhabited, being built), males and females in each named civil parish or township, or parts thereof.
4   As above for other administrative areas.
5   Number of elements in (3) on each page of the nominal returns.

1891

1   Number of schedules, houses (inhabited, uninhabited, being built), tenements of less than five rooms, and males and females in each named civil parish or township, or parts thereof.
2   As above for other administrative areas.
3   As above but for each page of the nominal returns.

1901

1   Number of schedules, houses (inhabited, uninhabited, being built), tenements of less than five rooms, and males and females in each named civil parish or township, or parts thereof.
2   As above for other administrative areas.
3   As above but for each page of the nominal returns.

Appendix 7 Examples of documents used in the process of census-taking

Instruction books

Examples of the instruction books circulated to the registrars and enumerators prior to census day can be found in various TNA record series: 1841, RG 27/1, pp. 18–35; 1851, HO 45/3579; 1861, RG 27/3, Items 11–14; 1871, RG 27/4, Item 29; 1881, RG 27/5, Item 27; 1891, RG 27/6, Item 6. At the time that these records were transferred to TNA, the volume in the RG 27 series for 1901 was recorded as being 'Wanting'. The instructions for the officers taking the 1901 census in the Islands in the British Seas (the Isle of Man and the Channel Islands) can be found in RG 19/23.

Memorandum books

Blank examples of these memorandum books can be found in TNA record series RG 27: 1861, RG 27/3, Item 17; 1871, RG 27/4, Item 28; 1881, RG 27/5, Item 26; 1891, RG 27/6, Item 70.

Household schedules

Examples of the household schedules can be found in various TNA record series: 1841, RG 27/1, pp. 56–7; 1851, HO 45/3579; 1861, RG 27/3, Item 2; 1871, RG 27/4, Item 5; 1881, RG 27/5, Item 5; 1891, RG 27/6, Item 68; 1901, RG 19/11.

Institutional books

Examples of the institutional books can be found in various TNA record series: 1841 and 1851, HO 107; 1861, RG 27/3, Item 18; 1871, RG 27/4, Item 23; 1881, RG 27/5, Item 21; 1891, RG 27/6, Item 68; 1901, RG 19/11.

Merchant ships' schedules

Examples of the merchant ships' schedules can be found in various TNA record series: 1851, HO 45/3579; 1861, RG 27/3, Item 40; 1871, RG 27/4, Items 8 and 9; 1881, RG 27/5, Items 8 and 9; 1891, RG 27/6, Item 67; 1901, RG 19/11. A ship's schedule does not appear to have been produced in 1841. The instructions to the customs officers relating to the filling out of these schedules can be found in various TNA record series: 1861, RG 27/3, Item 42; 1871, RG 27/4, Item 36; 1881, RG 27/5, Item 34; 1891, RG 27/6, Item 23; 1901, RG 19/21. The instructions for 1851 do not appear to have survived.

Royal Navy ships' schedules

Examples of the Royal Navy ships' schedules can be found in TNA record series RG 27: 1861, RG 27/3, Item 45; 1871, RG 27/4, Item 24; 1881, RG 27/5, Item 22; 1891, RG 27/6, Item 76. No schedule appears to have been issued in 1841. There is evidence that one was used in 1851 but no examples appear to have survived. Examples of the 1901 Royal Naval schedule can be found in pieces at the end of the returns for 1901 (RG 13/5325–5335).

Enumerators' books

Examples of the enumerators' books can be found in the relevant census series for 1841–1901.

Appendix 8   Examples of documents used in abstracting occupational data from the returns

5-	15-	Total under 20	OCCUPATIONS.	Total 20 &upds.	20-	25-	45-	65 & upwards	All Ages
			XX. Oil Miller, Oil Cake Maker, Dlʳ Oil and Colourman Floor Cloth, Oil Cloth Manuf: Japanner India Rub:, Gutta Percha Manuf: Dlʳ Waterproof Goods, Maker, Dealer Others						
			2. Willow, Cane, Rush, Basket Wʳ Dlʳ **Hay, Straw,** Chaff Cutter, Dlʳ (not plali) Thatcher						
			3. Timber, Wood Merchant, Dealer **Sawyer** Lath. Wooden Fence, Hurdle Maker Wood Turner, Box Maker **Cooper,** Hoop Maker, Bender Cork, Bark, Cutter, Manufacturer Others						
			4. **Paper Manufacture** Envelope Maker **Stationer, Law Stationer** Card, Pattern-Card Maker Paper Stainer Paper, Box, Bag Maker Ticket, Label Writer Bill Sticker and others						
			XXI. Coal Miner Ironstone Miner Copper Miner Tin Miner Lead Miner Miner in other, or undefined, minerals Mine Service Haulier						
			2. Coal Merchant, Dealer **Coalheaver,** Labourer Coke, Charcoal, Peat, Cutt:, Burn:, Dlʳ Gas Works Service						
			3. **Stone Quarrier**						

Figure A8.1 A portion of the occupational abstracting sheet for men, 1881
(TNA, RG 27/5, Item 73 – top right-hand section)

CIG

Cigar Case Maker—LEATHER CASE MAKER. **13: 2.**
CIGAR MANUFACTURE. **12: 3.**
Cigar Tube Maker—TOBACCONIST. **12: 3.**
Cinder — Burner, Filler, Sifter — COKE DEALER. **15: 2.**
Cinder—Dealer, Merchant, Shipper—COKE DEALER. **15: 2.**
Circulating Library Keeper—BOOK AGENT. **10: 1.**
Circus Keeper—EXHIBITION SERVICE. **3: 7.**
Cistern Manufacturer. **10: 14.**
City Missionary—MISSIONARY, &c. **3: 1.**
City Treasurer—MUNICIPAL OFFICER. **1: 2.**
(M)CIVIL ENGINEER. **3: 9.**
CIVIL SERVICE. **1: 1.**
Civil Service of East India, Bengal, Bombay, Madras—E. I. & COLONIAL SERVICE. **1: 3.**
Civil Service Pensioner—CIVIL SERVICE. **1:1.**
Clasp, Buckle—Maker. **15: 13.**
Classics—TEACHER, &c. **3: 8.**
CLAY LABOURER. **15: 3.**
Clay—Merchant, Agent. **15: 3.**
Cleaner—COTTON MANUFACTURE. **11: 3.**
Cleaner—DYER, SCOURER. **10: 17.**
Cleaner—LACE MANUFACTURE. **11: 3.**
Cleaner—SILK MANUFACTURE. **11: 2.**
Cleaner—WOOLLEN CLOTH MANUF. **11: 1.**
Cleaner—WORSTED MANUFACTURE. **11: 1.**
Cleaner Piecer—SILK MANUFACTURE. **11: 2.**
Cleaner Steward—SILK MANUF. **11: 2.**
Clear Starcher—LAUNDRY KEEPER. **11: 5.**
Cleater (Mill-hand)—FLAX, LINEN—MANUFACTURE. **11: 3.**
Cleaver—LATH MAKER. **14: 2.**
(M)CLERGYMAN. **3: 1.** (*See Instruc., No. 20 & 33.*)
Clergyman (if Schoolmaster) — SCHOOLMASTER. **3: 8.**
Clerical Agent—*Lay Officer.* **3: 1.**
Clerical Robe Maker—*Robe Maker.* **11: 5.**
Clerical Student—*Theological Student.* **3: 1.**
Clerk (not otherwise desc.)—COMMERCIAL CLERK. **6: 1.**
Clerk to Army Agent—COMMERCIAL CLERK. **6: 1.**
Clerk—Assurance Company, Fire and Life Insurance, Investment Society, Land and Building Society, Loan and Co-operative Society, Provident Society, Savings Bank (not Government)—INSURANCE SERVICE. **6: 1.**
Clerk, Bank—BANK SERVICE. **6: 1.**
Clerk to Catholic Chapel—CHURCH OFFICER. **3: 1.**
Clerk of Cemetery—*Bur. Grd. Serv.* **3: 1.**
Clerk to Chamber of London—*Commercial Company's Service.* **6: 1.**
Clerk to Club House—*Club Ho. Serv.* **5: 1.**
Clerk of Coal Mine—COAL MINE SERV. **15: 1.**
Clerk to Colliery—COAL MINE SERVICE. **15: 1.**
Clerk to Commissioners—DIST. OFFI. **1: 2.**
Clerk to Corporation—MUNICI OFF. **1: 2.**
Clerk to County, District—Officer. **1: 2.**
Clerk to County Treasurer—Clerk to County Officer. **1: 2.**

CLE

Clerk to Dock Company—HARB. SERV. **7: 4.**
Clerk of Farm—FARM BAILIFF. **8: 1.**
Clerk to Fishmongers' Company—*Officer of Public Corporate Company.* **1: 2.**
Clerk to Governess' Instit.—*School Serv.* **3: 8.**
Clerk (Gov. Telegraphs)—CIVIL SERV. **1: 1.**
Clerk (Hat and Bonnet Merchant)—STRAW PLAIT MANUFACTURE. **11: 5.**
Clerk in Holy Orders (if Schoolmaster)—SCHOOLMASTER. **3: 8.**
Clerk in Holy Orders—CLERGYMAN. **3: 1.**
Clerk, Ho. of Parlimnt.—CIVIL SERV. **1: 1.**
Clerk, Inland Revenue—CIVIL SERVICE. **1: 1.**
Clerk to Iron Manuf.—IRON MANF. **15: 14.**
Clerk to Ironworks—IRON MANUF. **15: 14.**
Clerk to Magistrates—SOLICITOR. **3: 2.**
Clerk of Market—MUNIC. OFFICER. **1: 2.**
Clerk in Merch. Offi.—COM. CLERK. **6: 1.**
Clerk, Navig. Comp.—STEAM NAV. SERV. **7: 4.**
Clerk—NAVY OFFICER. **2: 2.**
Clerk—NEEDLE MANUFACTURE. **10: 10.**
Clerk in Newsp. Offi.—NEWSPAPER AGENT. **10: 1.**
Clerk of Official Assignee—OFFICER OF LAW COURT. **1: 2.**
Clerk, Orderly Room—SOLDIER. **2: 1.**
Clerk of Peace. **1: 2.**
Clerk of Peace's Clerk—*Clerk to County Officer.* **1: 2.**
Clerk, Public Office—CIVIL SERVICE. **1: 1.**
Clerk of Race Course—*Race Cse. Serv.* **3: 7.**
(M)CLERK, RAILWAY. **7: 1.**
Clerk, Royal Mint—CIVIL SERVICE. **1: 1.**
Clerk to Sheriff—*Clerk to County Officer.* **1: 2.**
Clerk—SILK MANUFACTURE. **11: 2.**
Clerk to Smelting Company—IRON MANUFACTURE. **15: 14.**
Clerk (Solicitor's)—LAW CLERK. **3: 2.**
Clerk, Telegraph Company's—TELEGRAPH SERVICE (not Gov.) **7: 6.**
Clerk of Theatre—*Theatre Service.* **3: 7.**
Clerk to Union—UNION OFF. **1: 2.**
Clerk of Works—SILK MANUFACTURE. **11: 2.**
Clerk of Works—SURVEYOR. **10: 14.**
Clerk of Works, R.E.—CIVIL SERVICE. **1: 1.**
Clerk (not otherwise desc.)—COMMERCIAL CLERK. **6: 1.**
Clicker—SHOEMAKER. **11: 5.**
Clinical Clerk—MEDICAL ASSISTANT. **3: 3.**
Cloak Warehouseman—*Shawl Manuf.* **11: 3.**
CLOCKMAKER. **10: 7.**
(M)CLOG MAKER. **11: 5.**
Clog Iron Mak.—CLOG MAKER. **11: 5.**
Clogger—SHOEMAKER. **11: 5.**
Cloth Agent—CLOTH MERCH. **11: 1.**
Cloth—Bleacher, Boiler, Brusher—WOOLLEN CLOTH MANUFACTURE. **11: 1.**
Cloth (Bolting) Maker. **11: 4.**
Cloth Button — Maker, Worker — BUTTON MAKER. **11: 5.**
Cloth Cap Maker—HATTER. **11: 5.**
Cloth—Cleaner, Clipper—WOOLLEN CLOTH MANUFACTURE. **11: 1.**
Cloth Cut-hooker—COTTON MANUFACTURE. **11: 3.**
Cloth Cutter—WOOLLEN CLOTH MANUFACTURE. **11: 1.**

*Cloth Makers are frequently called "Clothiers" in Yo[r]... Clothier" elsewhere will be generally understood to mean "...

Figure A8.2 A page from the 1871 occupational dictionary
(TNA, RG 27/4, Item 85, p. 84 right-hand column, and p. 85 left-hand column)

CHR

	Order.	Sub-order.
Chrome Furnace *Man*— DYE, PAINT MANUF : -	**14,**	1
Chromo *Artist*— - - }LITHOGRAPHER -	**9,**	2
Chromo-Lithographic *Printer*— }		
Chronometer *Maker*— }WATCH MAKER, &c. -	**10,**	3
Chronometer Case *Maker*— }		
Church *Cleaner*- - - CHARWOMAN -	**4,**	2
Church *Decorator*— - - PAINTER, &c. -	**11,**	1
Church *Keeper*— CHURCH, &c. OFFICER -	**3,**	1
CHURCH OFFICER, SERVANT— - - -	**3,**	1
Church Bell *Hanger, Tuner, Wheel Maker*— } BRASS, BRONZE MANUF : }	**21,**	12
Church Furniture *Maker*—HOUSE AND SHOP } FITTINGS MAKER }	**11,**	2
Churchwarden- - - CHURCH, &c. OFFICER -	**3,**	1
Churer— - - - - CHARWOMAN -	**4,**	2
Churn *Maker*— - - - COOPER -	**20,**	3
CIDER DEALER— - - - - -	**16,**	2
Cicerone— - - - OTHERS IN SERVICE -	**4,**	2
Cigar *Maker, Finisher, Roller, Sorter*—TOBACCO } MANUF : }	**15,**	—
Cigar Box *Maker*— - - BOX MAKER -	**20,**	3
Cigar Book *Maker*—TOBACCO PIPE, &c. MAKER -	**15,**	—
Cigar Case *Maker*— TOBACCO PIPE, &c MAKER -	**15,**	—
Cigar Light *Vendor* (Street) COSTERMONGER -	**22,**	1
Cigar Tube *Maker*—TOBACCO PIPE, &c. MAKER -	**15,**	—
Cigarette Machine *Maker*—TOBACCO PIPE, &c. } MAKER }	**15,**	—
Cigarette *Maker*— TOBACCO MANUF : -	**15,**	—
Cinchona *Planter*— OTHERS IN AGRIC : -	**7,**	1
Cinder *Burner, Dealer, Filler, Merchant, Shipper,* } *Sifter*—COKE, &c. BURNER }	**21,**	2
Cinder *Man*— } IRON MANUF :		
Cinder *Burner, Filler, Tipper* }IRON MANUF : -	**21,**	8
(Ironworks)— }		
Circular *Addresser, Folder* - TICKET, LABEL } WRITER }	**20,**	4
Circular Comb *Maker*— - SPINNING MACH : -	**10,**	1
Circular *Hand*— - - HOSIERY MANUF : -	**18,**	—
Circulating Library *Keeper*— - PUBLISHER, &c. -	**9,**	1
Circus, &c. *Proprietor, Keeper, Showman* } PERFORMER, &c. }	**3,**	8
Cistern *Maker* (zinc)—ZINC GOODS MANUF : -	**21,**	10
Cistern *Manuf:* (undef :)— HOUSE AND SHOP } FITTINGS MAKER }	**11,**	2
Citrate of Magnesia *Maker*— MANUF : CHEMIST -	**14,**	3
City Treasurer— MUNICIPAL, &c. OFFICER -	**1,**	2
CIVIL ENGINEER— - - - - -	**3,**	6
Civil *Guard* (Prison)— - PRISON OFFICER -	**1,**	1
Civil Service *Artizans* and *Labourers* to be referred to their special trades.		
CIVIL SERVICE (MESSENGERS, &c.)— - -	**1,**	1
CIVIL SERVICE (OFFICERS AND CLERKS)— - -	**1,**	1
Civil Service *Pensioner*— - NO SPECIAL OCC : -	**24,**	—
Clamp *Maker*— - - TOOL MAKER -	**10,**	2
Clamper- - - SPINN : MACH : MAKER -	**10,**	1
Clanser— - - - COAL MINER -	**21,**	—
Clapper *Carrier* (advertisement)— - OTHERS -	**20,**	4
Clarionet *Maker, Turner, Key Maker, Finisher* } —MUS : INST : MAKER }	**10,**	6
CLASP MAKER- - - - - -	**21,**	12
Clay *Carrier, Getter, Picker, Scraper*— BRICK, } &c. MAKER }	**21,**	3
CLAY LABOURER, DEALER— - - - -	**21,**	3
Clay *Miner*— - - CLAY LABOURER -	**21,**	3
Clay *Mixer*— - - - CHINA MANUF : -	**21,**	4

CLA

	Order.	Sub-order.
Clay *Modeller* (Image)— - FIGURE MAKER -	**11,**	3
Clay Pipe *Maker, Importer, Dealer*—TOBACCO } PIPE, &c. MAKER }	**15,**	—
Clay Pot *Turner*— - EARTHENWARE MANUF : -	**21,**	4
Cleaner (to special trade when stated or determinable).		
Cleaner (Undefined)— - - - ARTIZAN -	**22**	2
Cleaner *Piercer, Steward*— SILK, &c. MANUF : -	**17,**	2
Cleaning Rod *Maker*— - - GUNSMITH -	**10,**	5
Cleanser— - - - - COAL MINER -	**21,**	1
Clear *Starcher*— - WASHING, &c. SERVICE -	**4,**	2
Clearer (Cotton)— - - COTTON MANUF : -	**17,**	3
Clearer (Silk)— - - SILK, &c. MANUF : -	**17,**	2
Clearing House (Bank) *Clerk*— BANK SERVICE -	**5,**	2
Clearing House (Railway) *Clerk*—OTHER RAIL : } OFF : }	**6,**	1
Cleaver (Diamond)— - - GOLDSMITH, &c. -	**21,**	7
Cleaver (Fur)— - - FURRIER, &c. -	**19,**	2
CLERGYMAN (ESTABLISHED CHURCH) - - -	**3,**	1
Clerical Robe *Maker*— - - TAILOR -	**18,**	—
Clerk *in all trades—See exceptions* in Instruc- } tions, page 3, § 4 - COMM : CLERK }	**5,**	1
Clerk in Holy Orders— - - CLERGYMAN -	**3,**	1
Clerk of Market- - MUNICIPAL, &c. OFFICER -	**1,**	2
Clerk of the Peace (and Clerks and Assistants)— } OTHER LOCAL OR COUNTY OFFICIAL }	**1,**	2
Clerk of Works— - - BUILDER -	**11,**	1
Clerk to Board of Guardians— MUNICIPAL, &c. } OFFICER }	**1,**	2
Clerk to Church and Chapel— CHURCH, &c. } OFFICER }	**3,**	1
Clerk to Commis- } sioners - - } MUNICIPAL, &c. OFFICER -	**1,**	2
Clerk to Union— - - }		
Clicker (Leather)— - SHOE, &c. MAKER -	**18,**	—
Clicker (Printer's)— - - PRINTER -	**9,**	1
Clinker *Drawer, Grinder, Crusher, Burner*— } PLASTER, CEMENT MANUF : }	**21,**	3
Clipper (Bolt)— - - BOLT, &c. MAKER -	**21,**	12
Clipper (Lace)— - - - LACE MANUF : -	**17,**	3
Clipper (Leather)— - - CURRIER -	**19,**	2
Clipper (Wool)— - WOOLLEN CLOTH MANUF : -	**17,**	1
Clipper and Singer— - - GROOM, &c. -	**8,**	—
Cloak *Merchant*— - - SHAWL MANUF : -	**18,**	—
Cloakroom (Railway) *Attendant*— OTHER RAIL- } WAY OFFICIALS }	**6,**	1
CLOCK MAKER - - }		
Clock *Winder, Jobber,* } - CLOCK MAKER, &c. - } *Cleaner, Dresser* }	**10,**	3
Clock Material *Maker*— }		
Clock Line *Maker*— - - ROPE MAKER -	**17,**	4
Clog *Clasper*— - PATTEN, CLOG MAKER -	**18,**	—
Clog *Dancer*— - - - PERFORMER -	**3,**	8
CLOG MAKER— - - - - -	**18,**	—
Clog Iron *Maker*— } PATTEN, CLOG MAKER - }	**18,**	—
Clogger— - - }		
Closer (Hand and Machine) — SHOE, &c. MAKER -	**18,**	—
Closet *Fitter*— - - PLUMBER -	**11,**	1
Cloth *Booker*— - COTTON MANUF : -	**17,**	3
Cloth *Carrier, Looker*— - COTTON MANUF : -	**17,**	3
CLOTH DEALER— - - - - -	**17,**	1
Cloth *Maker* (Saddle)— - SADDLER, &c. -	**12,**	2
Cloth *Picker* (Jute)— - - JUTE MANUF : -	**17,**	4
Cloth *Printer* (undefined)— - - DYER, &c. -	**17,**	5
Cloth *Scourer*— - WOOL DYER, PRINTER -	**17,**	1
Cloth *Warehouseman, Agent*—CLOTH, &c. DEALER -	**17,**	1

P 2

Figure A8.3 A page from the 1881 occupational dictionary
(TNA, RG 27/5, Item 69, p. 115)

Appendix 9 Statistical analysis of census returns for selected 1901 communities

Table A9.1 Place of birth of population in 1901 communities (%)

	East Tuddenham	Salford	Senghenydd	Spitalfields
Place of enumeration	49.4	51.3	17.7	26.1
Rest of England and Wales	49.9	42.7	79.4	30.6
Scotland	0.5	0.5	0.3	0.3
Ireland	0.2	4.4	0.4	0.6
Outside Great Britain & Ireland	0.0	0.9	0.1	40.4
Not given	0.0	0.2	2.1	2.0
Total Population	**415**	**1975**	**2756**	**3503**

Source: 1901 Census

Table A9.2 Place of birth of household heads in 1901 communities (%)

	East Tuddenham	Salford	Senghenydd	Spitalfields
Place of enumeration	55.0	20.2	11.2	13.8
Rest of England and Wales	44.0	68.0	87.6	28.9
Scotland	1.0	0.7	0.2	0.4
Ireland	0.0	9.0	0.8	0.6
Outside Great Britain & Ireland	0.0	1.6	0.2	55.2
Not given	0.0	0.5	0.0	1.1
Total Number of Household Heads	**100**	**435**	**482**	**723**

Source: 1901 Census

Table A9.3 Occupations of men in 1901 communities as % of occupied men

(for key to Occupational Classification see p. 209, below)

Occupational Classification	East Tuddenham	Salford	Senghenydd	Spitalfields
AG 1	76.3	0.4	2.2	–
AG 2	8.9	–	0.1	–
AG 3	3.0	–	–	2.3
B 2	1.5	8.2	0.2	0.9
M 1	–	0.1	83.1	–
M 2	0.7	–	0.7	–
MF 1	–	6.0	–	0.2
MF 2	–	1.9	0.2	–
MF 4	2.2	2.4	0.4	1.1
MF 6	–	–	–	0.2
MF 7	–	0.1	–	0.8
MF 8	–	0.3	–	–
MF 9	–	0.1	–	–
MF 13	–	1.8	–	3.7
MF 14	–	–	0.8	7.1
MF 15	1.5	–	–	–
MF 16	–	1.6	–	1.2
MF 19	–	38.4	–	–
MF 20	–	0.3	–	–
MF 22	–	1.8	–	–
MF 23	–	–	3.3	45.7
MF 24	–	–	–	0.6
MF 25	–	–	0.1	1.5
MF 26	0.7	1.9	0.6	1.6
MF 28	–	–	–	6.9
MF 29	–	0.1	0.1	–
MF 30	–	0.7	–	1.4
MF 31	–	–	–	0.1
T 1	–	10.1	0.1	3.4
T 2	–	0.1	–	–
T 3	–	0.7	–	–
T 4	–	9.4	3.8	–
T 5	2.2	2.1	0.3	1.2
D 3	–	–	–	0.9
D 4	–	0.4	0.4	0.4
D 5	1.5	2.4	1.9	2.4
D 6	–	–	–	0.5
D 7	–	0.4	0.1	1.5
D 9	–	–	0.1	–

Table A9.3 contd

Occupational Classification	East Tuddenham	Salford	Senghenydd	Spitalfields
D 11	–	0.3	–	1.3
D 12	–	–	–	0.2
D 13	–	–	–	2.0
IS 1	–	0.4	0.1	0.3
IS 2	–	4.8	–	4.2
PS&P 3	–	–	–	0.3
PS&P 4	–	–	0.1	0.1
PS&P 6	–	0.3	–	–
PS&P 8	0.7	–	0.4	0.3
PS&P 9	–	–	0.1	–
PS&P 10	–	–	–	0.1
PS&P 13	–	–	0.3	1.1
PS&P 14	–	0.1	0.1	0.1
DS 1	0.7	0.3	0.1	0.8
DS 3	–	0.7	–	–
PO&I	–	0.7	–	3.3
OTHERS	–	–	0.2	0.6
Number of Occupied Men	**135**	**670**	**972**	**1022**

Source: 1901 Census

Key to Occupational Classification:
AG   Agricultural Sector: 1 Farming; 2 Land Service; 3 Breeding.
B   Building Sector: 2 Operative.
M   Mining Sector: 1 Mining; 2 Quarrying.
MF   Manufacturing Sector: 1 Machinery; 2 Tools; 4 Iron and Steel; 6 Gold, Silver and Jewellery; 7 Earthenware, etc.; 8 Coals and Gas; 9 Chemicals; 13 Wood Workers; 14 Furniture; 15 Carriages and Harness; 16 Paper; 19 Cotton and Silk; 20 Flax, Hemp, etc.; 22 Dyeing; 23 Dress; 24 Sundries Connected with Dress; 25 Food Preparation; 26 Baking; 28 Smoking Products; 29 Watches, Instruments and Toys; 30 Printing and Book-Binding; 31 Unspecified.
T   Transport Sector: 1 Warehouses and Docks; 2 Ocean Navigation; 3 Inland Navigation; 4 Railways; 5 Roads.
D   Dealing Sector: 3 Clothing Materials; 4 Dress; 5 Food; 6 Tobacco; 7 Wines, Spirits and Hotels; 9 Furniture; 11 Household Utensils and Ornaments; 12 General Dealers; 13 Unspecified.
IS   Industrial Service Sector: 1 Banking, Insurance, Accounts; 2 General Labourers.
PS&P   Public Service and Professional Sector: 3 Administration (Sanitary); 4 Army; 6 Police and Prisons; 8 Medicine; 9 Art and Amusement (Painting); 10 Art and Amusement (Music, etc.); 13 Education; 14 Religion.
DS   Domestic Service: 1 Indoor Service; 3 Extra Service (e.g. Charwomen).
PO&I   Property Owning, Independent.
OTHERS   Mostly vague titles that cannot fit in elsewhere.

Table A9.4 Occupations of women in 1901 communities as % of occupied women

(for key to Occupational Classification see p. 209, above)

Occupational Classification	East Tuddenham	Salford	Senghenydd	Spitalfields
AG 1	–	–	1.0	–
AG 2	–	–	–	–
AG 3	–	–	–	0.5
B 2	–	–	–	–
M 1	–	–	–	–
M 2	6.7	–	–	–
MF 1	–	–	–	–
MF 2	–	4.8	1.0	–
MF 4	–	–	1.0	0.5
MF 6	–	–	–	–
MF 7	–	–	–	–
MF 8	–	–	–	–
MF 9	–	–	–	–
MF 13	–	–	–	0.8
MF 14	–	–	–	–
MF 15	–	–	–	–
MF 16	–	3.1	–	–
MF 19	–	71.8	–	–
MF 20	–	–	–	–
MF 22	–	–	–	–
MF 23	–	–	34.0	43.5
MF 24	–	–	–	–
MF 25	–	–	–	0.5
MF 26	–	4.8	1.0	–
MF 28	–	–	–	7.4
MF 29	–	–	–	–
MF 30	–	–	–	0.5
MF 31	6.7	–	–	–
T 1	–	–	–	–
T 2	–	–	–	–
T 3	–	–	–	–
T 4	–	–	–	–
T 5	–	–	–	–
D 3	–	–	–	–
D 4	–	1.4	6.2	1.3
D 5	–	0.3	10.3	2.3
D 6	–	–	–	1.0
D 7	–	1.7	3.1	2.3
D 9	–	–	–	–

Table A9.4 contd

Occupational Classification	East Tuddenham	Salford	Senghenydd	Spitalfields
D 11	–	1.7	–	–
D 12	–	–	–	3.1
D 13	–	–	–	–
IS 1	–	–	–	–
IS 2	–	–	–	–
PS&P 3	–	–	–	–
PS&P 4	–	–	–	–
PS&P 6	–	–	–	–
PS&P 8	3.3	–	–	0.3
PS&P 9	–	–	–	–
PS&P 10	–	–	–	–
PS&P 13	–	–	4.1	0.5
PS&P 14	–	–	–	0.3
DS 1	70.0	8.5	38.1	15.3
DS 3	13.3	2.4	–	10.2
PO&I	–	–	–	–
OTHERS	–	–	–	9.5
Number of Occupied Women	**30**	**294**	**97**	**391**
% of all women with occupation	**14.7**	**28.9**	**7.5**	**22.4**

Source: 1901 Census

Table A9.5 Age structure of population in 1901 communities

	Under 10 Years (%)	60 years and over (%)	Total Population
East Tuddenham	21.0	12.0	415
Salford	26.4	4.1	1975
Senghenydd	28.8	2.7	2756
Spitalfields	28.5	2.8	3503

Source: 1901 Census

Table A9.6 Sex structure of population in 1901 communities

	East Tuddenham	Salford	Senghenydd	Spitalfields
Men (%)	50.8	47.9	53.4	50.3
Women (%)	49.2	52.1	46.6	49.7
Total Population	**415**	**1975**	**2756**	**3503**

Source: 1901 Census

Bibliography

Manuscript sources

1841 and 1851 Census Returns (The National Archives of the UK: Public Record Office (hereafter TNA), HO 107).

1861 Census Returns (TNA, RG 9).

1871 Census Returns (TNA, RG 10).

1881 Census Returns (TNA, RG 11).

1891 Census Returns (TNA, RG 12).

1901 Census Returns (TNA, RG 13).

Board of Inland Revenue: Valuation Office: Field Books (TNA, IR 58).

Board of Inland Revenue: Valuation Office: Finance Act 1910, Record Sheet Plans: London Region: Tower Hamlets District (TNA, IR 121/20).

Census Returns: Correspondence and Papers (TNA, RG 19).

Crosby Ravensworth Parish Records (Kendal, Cumbria Record Office, WPR/7).

Forms and Instructions for taking the Census (TNA, RG 27).

General Register Office: Letter Books (TNA, RG 29).

Home Office: Registered Files (TNA, HO 45).

John Sutherland's diary and 1861 census book (in the possession of Mrs. Doris Jackson of Birk Nott, Heversham, Cumbria).

London School Board Statistical Committee (Greater London Record Office, SBL 908).

Reference Maps of Registrars' Districts (TNA, RG 18).

Statistical account of the parish of Stonesfield, Oxfordshire (Oxfordshire Record Office, MSS. DD Par. Stonesfield 69).

Treasury Board Papers (TNA, T 1).

Parliamentary Papers

1811 Census Report: Abstract of the Answers and Returns (PP 1812 XI [316 & 317]).

Abstract of the answers and returns made pursuant to an Act, passed in the first year of the reign of His Majesty King George IV, intituled, "An Act for taking an Account ..." Enumeration Abstract, Vol. I, 1831 (PP 1833 XXXVII [149.]).

Minutes of Evidence Taken (Session 1830) before the Select Committee on the Population Bill (PP 1840 XV [396.]).

1841 Census Report: Abstract of the Answers and Returns (PP 1844 XXVII [587.]).

1841 Parish Register Abstract. England and Wales and Islands in the British Seas (PP 1845 XXV [623.]).

1851 Census Report: Tables of the Population and Houses (PP 1851 XLIII [1399.]).

1851 Census Report: Population Tables, I (PP 1852–3 LXXXV [1631.]).

1851 Census Report: Population Tables, II (PP 1852–3 LXXXVIII Pt. 1 [1691–I.]).

1861 Census Report (PP 1863 LIII Pt. 1 [3221.]).

Return Relating to Elementary Education (Civil Parishes) (PP 1871 LV [201.]).

1871 Census Report (PP 1873 LXXI Pt. I [872.]).

1871 Census Report (PP 1873 LXXI Pt. II [872–I.]).

1881 Census Report (PP 1883 LXXX [c.3797.]).

Conditions of the Working Classes. Tabulation of the Statements Made by Men Living in Certain Selected Districts in London in March 1887 (PP LXXI [c.5228.]).

Report of the Treasury Committee on the Census (PP 1890 LVIII [c.6071.]).

1891 Preliminary Census Report (PP 1890 XCIV [c.6422.]).

1891 Census Report (PP 1893–4 CVI [c.7222.]).

Explanatory Letter of the Registrar General of England and Wales Relative to the Census of 1891 (PP 1894 LXIX [Cd.331.]).

Census 1901. Islands in the British Seas (PP 1903 LXXXIV [Cd.1473.]).

1901 Census Report (PP 1904 CVIII [Cd.2174.]).

The Agricultural Output of Great Britain (PP 1912–13 X [Cd.6277.]).

Evidence and Index to the Second Report of the Royal Commission on Public Records, Vol. II, Pt. III (PP 1914 XLVI [Cd.7456.]).

Articles, books and unpublished papers

Anderson, G., *Victorian Clerks* (Manchester, 1976).

Anderson, M., *The American Census: a Social History* (New Haven, Conn., 1988).

Anderson, M., *Family Structure in Nineteenth Century Lancashire* (London, 1971).

Anderson, M., 'Standard tabulation procedures for the census enumerators' books 1851–1891', in Wrigley, E. A. (ed.), *Nineteenth-Century Society* (Cambridge, 1972), pp. 134–45.

Anderson, M., 'The study of family structure', in Wrigley, E. A. (ed.), *Nineteenth-Century Society* (Cambridge, 1972), pp. 47–81.

Anderson, M., 'Households, families and individuals: some preliminary results from the national sample from the 1851 census of Great Britain', *Continuity and Change*, 3 (1988), pp. 421–38.

Anderson, M., 'Mis-specification of servant occupations in the 1851 census: a problem revisited', *Local Population Studies*, 60 (1998), pp. 58–64.

Anderson, M., 'What can the mid-Victorian censuses tell us about variations in married women's employment?', *Local Population Studies*, 62 (1999), pp. 9–30.

Arkell, T., 'Identifying the census enumerators – Cornwall in 1851', *Local Population Studies*, 53 (1994), pp. 70–5; reprinted in Mills, D., and Schürer, K. (eds.), *Local Communities in the Victorian Census Enumerators' Books* (Oxford, 1996), pp. 36–41.

Armstrong, A., *Stability and Change in an English Country Town: a Social Study of York 1801–51* (London, 1974).

Armstrong, W. A., 'Social structure from the early census returns', in Wrigley, E. A. (ed.), *An Introduction to English Historical Demography* (London, 1966), pp. 209–37.

Armstrong, W. A., 'The interpretation of census enumerators' books for Victorian towns', in Dyos, H. J. (ed.), *The Study of Urban History* (London, 1968), pp. 67–86.

Armstrong, W. A., 'The use of information about occupation, pt. 2: an industrial classification, 1841–1891', in Wrigley, E. A. (ed.), *Nineteenth-Century Society* (Cambridge, 1972), pp. 226–310.

Armstrong, W. A., 'The census enumerators' books: a commentary', in Lawton, R. (ed.), *The Census and Social Structure* (London, 1978), pp. 28–81.

Benjamin, A. A., 'Human afflictions: a study of the north Ceredigion census returns, 1851–1871', *Ceredigion*, 10 (1985), pp. 155–60.

Booth, Charles, 'Occupations of the people of the United Kingdom, 1801–81', *Journal of the Statistical Society of London*, 49 (1886), pp. 314–444.

Bouquet, M., *Family, Servants and Visitors: the Farm Household in Nineteenth and Twentieth Century Devon* (Norwich, 1985).

Bristow, B. R., 'Population and housing in nineteenth-century urban Lancashire: a framework for investigation', *Local Population Studies*, 34 (1985), pp. 12–26.

Burton, V. C., 'A floating population: vessel enumeration returns in censuses, 1851–1921', *Local Population Studies*, 38 (1987), pp. 36–43; reprinted in Mills, D., and Schürer, K. (eds.), *Local Communities in the Victorian Census Enumerators' Books* (Oxford, 1996), pp. 47–55.

Chapman, C., *Pre-1841 Censuses & Population Listings in the British Isles* (Dursley, 1994).

Charlton, C., '"Bag in hand, and with a provision of papers for an emergency" – an impression of the 1891 census from the pages of some contemporary newspapers', *Local Population Studies*, 47 (1991), pp. 81–8.

Cobbett, William, *Rural Rides* (Harmondsworth, 1983).

Cochran, W. G., *Sampling Techniques* (New York, 1973).

Coleman, B. I., 'The incidence of education in mid-century', in Wrigley, E. A. (ed.), *Nineteenth-Century Society* (Cambridge, 1972), pp. 397–410.

Conk, M., 'Labor statistics in the American and English census: making some invidious comparisons', *Journal of Social History*, 16 (1982–3), pp. 83–102.

Crafts, N. F. R., *British Economic Growth during the Industrial Revolution* (Oxford, 1987).

Cullen, M. J., *The Statistical Movement in Early Victorian Britain: the Foundations of Empirical Social Research* (Hassocks, 1975).

Davidoff, L., and Hall, C., *Family Fortunes: Men and Women of the English Middle Class 1780–1850* (London, 1987).

Davin, A., 'Working or helping? London working-class children in the domestic economy', in Smith, J., Wallerstein, I., and Evers, H., *Households and the World Economy* (London, 1984), pp. 215–32.

Davin, A., *Growing up Poor: Home, School and Street in London 1870–1914* (London, 1996).

Deane, P., and Cole, W. A., *British Economic Growth, 1688–1959* (Cambridge, 1969).

Drake, M., and Finnegan, R. (eds.), *Sources and Methods for Family and Community Historians: a Handbook* (Cambridge, 1994).

Drake, M., Mageean, D., and Pryce, W. T. R., 'Quantitative techniques', in Drake, M., and Finnegan, R. (eds.), *Sources and Methods for Family and Community Historians: a Handbook* (Cambridge, 1994), pp. 175–202.

Drake, M., and Mills, D. R., 'The census enumerators: a LPSS research project', *Local Population Studies Society Newsletter*, 14 (1994), pp. 1–12.

Drake, M., and Mills, D. R., 'A note on census enumerators', *Local Population Studies Society Newsletter*, 29 (2001), pp. 3–9.

Duprée, M., *Family Structure in the Staffordshire Potteries, 1840–1880* (Oxford, 1995).

Dyos, H. J., *Victorian Suburb: a Study of the Growth of Camberwell* (Leicester, 1977).

Emerson, J., 'The lodging market in a Victorian city: Exeter', *Southern History*, 9 (1987), pp. 103–13.

Engels, F., *The Condition of the Working-Class in England from Personal Observation and Authentic Sources* (Moscow, 1973).

Eyler, J. M., *Victorian Social Medicine: the Ideas and Methods of William Farr* (London, 1979).

Feinstein, C. H., *National Income, Expenditure and Output of the United Kingdom, 1855–1965* (Cambridge, 1972).

Floud, R., *An Introduction to Quantitative Methods for Historians* (London, 1990).

Foster, J., *Class Struggle and the Industrial Revolution: Early Industrial Capitalism in Three English Towns* (London, 1974).

Foucault, M., 'The subject and power', in Dreyfus, H. L. and Rabinow, P. (eds.), *Michel Foucault: Beyond Structuralism and Hermeneutics, with an Afterward by Michel Foucault* (Brighton, 1982), pp. 208–26.

Foucault, M., 'Governmentality', in Burchell, G., Gordon, C., and Miller, P. (eds.), *The Foucault Effect: Studies in Governmentality* (London, 1991), pp. 87–104.

Garrett, E., Reid, A., Schürer, K., and Szreter, S. (eds.), *Changing Family Size in England and Wales: Place, Class and Demography 1891–1911* (Cambridge, 2001).

Gainer, B., *The Alien Invasion : the Origins of the Aliens Act of 1905* (London, 1972).

Gibson, J., and Hampson, E., *Census Returns 1841–1891 in Microform: a Directory to Local Holdings in Great Britain; Channel Islands; Isle of Man* (Birmingham, 1994).

Glass, D. V., *The Development of Population Statistics* (Farnborough, 1973)

Glass, D. V., and Taylor, P. A. M., *Population and Emigration: Government and Society in Nineteenth Century Britain* (Dublin, 1976).

Glass, D. V., *Numbering the People: the Eighteenth Century Population Controversy and the Development of Census and Vital Statistics in Britain* (London, 1978).

Goldstrom, J. M., 'Education in England and Wales in 1851: the education census of Great Britain, 1851', in Lawton, R. (ed.), *The Census and Social Structure: an Interpretative Guide to Nineteenth Century Censuses for England and Wales* (London, 1978), pp. 224–40.

Goose, N., 'Farm service in southern England in the mid-nineteenth century', *Local Population Studies*, 72 (2004), pp. 77–82.

Green, J. A. S., 'A survey of domestic service', *Lincolnshire History and Archaeology*, 17 (1982), pp. 65–9.

Greenstein, D., *A Historian's Guide to Computing* (Oxford, 1994).

Grigg, D., 'Farm size in England and Wales, from early Victorian times to the present', *Agricultural History Review*, 35 (1987), pp. 179–89.

Hacking, I., *The Emergence of Probability* (Cambridge, 1975).

Hacking, I., *The Taming of Chance* (Cambridge, 1990).

Hancock, R., 'In service or one of the family? Kin-servants in Swavesey, 1851–1881, Ryde, 1881 and Stourbridge, 1881', *Family and Community History*, 21 (1999), pp. 141–8.

Harvey, C., Green, E., and Corfield, P., 'Record linkage theory and practice: an experiment in the application of multiple pass linkage algorithms', *History and Computing*, 8 (1996), pp. 78–89.

Henriques, U. R. Q., *The Early Factory Acts and their Enforcement* (London, 1971).

Higgs, E., 'The tabulation of occupations in the nineteenth-century census, with special reference to domestic servants', *Local Population Studies*, 28 (1982), pp. 58–66.

Higgs, E., 'Domestic servants and households in Victorian England', *Social History*, 8 (1983), pp. 203–10.

Higgs, E., 'Counting heads and jobs: science as an occupation in the Victorian census', *History of Science*, 23 (1985), pp. 335–49.

Higgs, E., *Domestic Servants and Households in Rochdale, 1851–1871* (New York, 1986).

Higgs, E., 'Domestic service and household production', in John, A. V. (ed.), *Unequal Opportunities: Women's Employment in England 1800–1918* (Oxford, 1986), pp. 124–52.

Higgs, E., 'Women, occupations and work in the nineteenth century censuses', *History Workshop Journal*, 23 (1987), pp. 59–80.

Higgs, E., 'The struggle for the occupational census, 1841–1911', in MacLeod, R. M. (ed.), *Government and Expertise: Specialists, Administrators and Professionals, 1860–1914* (Cambridge, 1988), pp. 73–86.

Higgs, E., 'The definition of the "house" in the census of 1841', *The Local Historian*, 19 (1989), pp. 56–7.

Higgs, E., *Making Sense of the Census: the Manuscript Returns for England and Wales, 1801–1901* (London, 1989).

Higgs, E., 'Disease, febrile poisons, and statistics: the census as a medical survey, 1841–1911', *Social History of Medicine*, 4 (1991), pp. 465–78.

Higgs, E., 'Occupational censuses and the agricultural workforce in Victorian England and Wales', *Economic History Review*, 48 (1995), pp. 700–16.

Higgs, E., 'The General Register Office and the tabulation of data, 1837–1939', in Campbell-Kelly, M., Croarken, M., Flood, R., and Robson, E. (eds.), *The History of Mathematical Tables: from Sumer to Spreadsheets* (Oxford, 2003), pp. 209–34.

Higgs, E., *The Information State in England: the Central Collection of Information on Citizens, 1500–2000* (London, 2003).

Higgs, E., *Life, Death and Statistics: Civil Registration, Censuses and the Work of the General Register Office, 1837–1952* (Hatfield, 2004).

Higgs, E., 'The linguistic construction of social and medical categories in the work of the English General Register Office', in Szreter, S., Dharmalingam, A., and Sholkamy, H. (eds.), *The Qualitative Dimension of Quantitative Demography* (Oxford, 2004), pp. 86–106.

Hinde, A., *England's Population: a History since the Domesday Survey* (London, 2003).

History and Computing: Special Issue on Record Linkage, 4.1 (1992).

History and Computing: Special Issue on Record Linkage, II, 6.3 (1994).

Holmes, R. S., 'Identifying nineteenth-century properties', *AREA*, 6 (1974), pp. 273–7.

Holmes, R. S., and Armstrong, W. A., 'Social stratification', *AREA*, 10 (1978), pp. 126–9.

Horn, P., *The Rise and Fall of the Victorian Servant* (Dublin, 1975).

Horn, P., 'Child workers in the Victorian countryside: the case of Northamptonshire', *Northamptonshire Past and Present*, 7 (1985–6), pp. 173–85.

Horrell, S., and Humphries, J., 'Women's labour force participation and the transition to the male-breadwinner economy, 1790–1865', *Economic History Review*, 48 (1995), pp. 89–117.

Huff, D., *How to Lie with Statistics* (London, 1991).

Jarausch, K. H., and Hardy, K. A., *Quantitative Methods for Historians: a Guide to Research Data and Statistics* (London, 1991).

Jenkins, G. H., 'The historical background to the 1891 census', in Parry, G., and Williams, M. A. (eds.), *The Welsh Language and the 1891 Census* (Cardiff, 1999), pp. 1–30.

Jones, G. Stedman, *Outcast London: a Study in the Relationship between Classes in Victorian Society* (Harmondsworth, 1984).

Jordan, E., 'Female employment in England and Wales 1851–1911: an examination of the census figures for 15–19 year olds', *Social History*, 13 (1988), pp. 175–90.

Knodel, J., 'An exercise on household composition for use in courses in historical demography', *Local Population Studies*, 23 (1979), pp. 10–23.

Laslett, P., and Wall, R., *The Household and Family in Past Time* (London, 1974).

Lawton, R. (ed.), *The Census and Social Structure: an Interpretative Guide to Nineteenth Century Censuses for England and Wales* (London, 1978).

Lawton, R., 'Census data for urban areas', in Lawton, R. (ed.), *The Census and Social Structure: an Interpretative Guide to Nineteenth Century Censuses for England and Wales* (London, 1978), pp. 82–145.

Laxton, P., 'Liverpool in 1801: a manuscript return for the first national census of population', *Transactions of the Historical Society of Lancashire and Cheshire*, 130 (1980), pp. 73–113.

Lee, R., and Lam, D., 'Age distribution adjustments for English censuses, 1821–1931', *Population Studies*, 37 (1983), pp. 445–64.

Lumas, S., 'Women enumerators', *Local Population Studies Society Newsletter*, 14 (1994), pp. 3–5.

Lumas, S., *Making Use of the Census* (London, 2002).

McHugh, P., *Prostitution and Victorian Social Reform* (London, 1980).

MacKay, T., *A History of the English Poor Law, III* (London, 1904).

Mawdsley, E., and Munck, T., *Computing for Historians: an Introductory Guide* (Manchester, 1993).

Mills, D. R., and Mills, J., 'Occupation and social stratification revisited: the census enumerators' books of Victorian Britain', *Urban History Yearbook 1989* (Leicester, 1989), pp. 63–71.

Mills, D. R., and Pearce, C., *People and Places in the Victorian Census: a Review and Bibliography of Publications Based Substantially on the Manuscript Census Enumerators' Books, 1841–1911* (Cambridge, 1989).

Mills, D. R., and Drake, M., 'The census, 1801–1991', in Drake, M., and Finnegan, R. (eds.), *Sources and Methods for Family and Community Historians: a Handbook* (Cambridge, 1994), pp. 25–56.

Mills, D. R., and Schürer, K., 'Employment and occupations', in Mills, D. R., and Schürer, K. (eds.), *Local Communities in the Victorian Census Enumerators' Books* (Oxford, 1996), pp. 136–60.

Mills, D. R., and Schürer, K. (eds.), *Local Communities in the Victorian Census Enumerators' Books* (Oxford, 1996).

Mills, D. R., 'Trouble with farms at the Census Office: an evaluation of farm statistics from the censuses of 1851–1881 in England and Wales', *Agricultural History Review*, 47 (1999), pp. 58–77.

Mitchell, B. R., *Abstract of British Historical Statistics* (Cambridge, 1962).

Morgan, D. H., *Harvesters and Harvesting 1840–1900* (London, 1982).

Morris, R. J., 'In search of the urban middle class. Record linkage and methodology: Leeds, 1832', *Urban History Yearbook 1976* (Leicester, 1976), pp. 15–20.

Nissel, M., *People Count: a History of the General Register Office* (London, 1987).

O'Brien, P., and Keyder, C., *Economic Growth in Britain and France, 1780–1914* (London, 1978).

Office of Population Censuses and Surveys and General Register Office, Edinburgh, *Guide to Census Reports, Great Britain 1801–1966* (London, 1977).

Parish Registers (London, 1845).

Parkinson, D. H., 'Comments on the underenumeration of the US census, 1850–1880', *Social Science History*, 15 (1991), pp. 509–16.

Perkyns, A., 'Birthplace accuracy in the censuses of six Kentish parishes 1851–81', *Local Population Studies*, 47 (1991), pp. 39–55; reprinted in Mills, D. R., and Schürer, K. (eds.), *Local Communities in the Victorian Census Enumerators' Books* (Oxford, 1996), pp. 229–45.

Perkyns, A., 'Age checkability and accuracy in the censuses of six Kentish parishes 1851–1881', *Local Population Studies*, 50 (1993), pp. 19–38; reprinted in Mills, D. R., and Schürer, K. (eds.), *Local Communities in the Victorian Census Enumerators' Books* (Oxford, 1996), pp. 115–35.

Pooley, C., and Whyte, I. D. (eds.), *Migrants, Emigrants and Immigrants: a Social History of Migration* (London, 1991).

Porter, T. M., *The Rise of Statistical Thinking 1820–1900* (Princeton, N.J., 1986).

Pryce, W. T. R., 'The census as a major source for the study of Flintshire society in the nineteenth century', *Journal of the Flintshire Historical Society*, 26 (1973–4), pp. 114–43.

Pryce, W. T. R., and Williams, C. H., 'Sources and methods in the study of language areas: a case study of Wales', in Williams, C. H. (ed.), *Language in Geographic Context* (Clevedon, 1988), pp. 167–237.

Ravenstein, E. G., 'The laws of migration', *Journal of the Statistical Society of London*, 48 (1885), pp. 167–235.

Razzell, P. E., 'The evaluation of baptism as a form of birth registration through cross-matching census and parish register data: a study in methodology', *Population Studies*, 26 (1972), pp. 121–46.

Roberts, E., *Women's Work 1840–1940* (London, 1988).

Robin, J., *From Childhood to Middle Age: Cohort Analysis in Colyton, 1851–1891* (Cambridge, 1995).

Rowntree, B. S., *Poverty: a Study of Town Life* (London, 1901).

Rowntree, B. S., *Poverty and Progress: a Second Social Survey of York* (London, 1941).

Royle, S. A., 'Social stratification from early census returns: a new approach', *AREA*, 9 (1977), pp. 215–19.

Rushton, P., 'Anomalies as evidence in nineteenth–century censuses', *Local Historian*, 13 (1978–9), pp. 481–7.

Rusnock, A. A., *Quantifying Health and Population in Eighteenth-Century England and France* (Cambridge, 2002).

Samuel, R., 'Comers and goers', in Dyos, H. J., and Wolff, M. (eds.), *The Victorian City: Images and Realities, Vol. I* (London, 1976), pp. 123–60.

Schofield, R. S., 'Sampling in historical research', in Wrigley, E. A. (ed.), *Nineteenth-Century Society* (Cambridge, 1972), pp. 146–90.

Schürer, K., 'The historical researcher and codes: master and slave or slave and master', in Mawdsley, E., Morgan, N., Richmond, L., and Trainor, R. (eds.), *History and Computing III: Historians, Computers and Data – Applications in Research and Teaching* (Manchester, 1990), pp. 74–82

Schürer, K., 'The 1891 census and local population studies', *Local Population Studies*, 47 (1991), pp. 16–29.

Schürer, K., 'Understanding and coding the occupations of the past: the experience of analyzing the censuses of 1891–1921', in Schürer, K., and Diederiks, H. (eds.), *The Use of Occupations in Historical Analysis* (St Katharinen, 1993), pp. 101–62.

Schürer, K., and Diederiks, H. (eds.), *The Use of Occupations in Historical Analysis* (St Katharinen, 1993).

Schürer, K., 'Computing', in Drake, M., and Finnegan, R. (eds.), *Sources and Methods for Family and Community Historians: a Handbook* (Cambridge, 1994), pp. 203–20.

Schürer, K., and Mills, D. R., 'Population and demography', in Mills, D. R., and Schürer, K. (eds.), *Local Communities in the Victorian Census Enumerators' Books* (Oxford, 1996), pp. 72–85.

Sheppard, J. A., 'The east Yorkshire agricultural labour force in the mid-nineteenth century', *Agricultural History Review*, 9 (1961), pp. 43–54.

Snell, K. D. M., 'Agricultural seasonal employment, the standard of living, and women's work in the south and east, 1690–1860', *Economic History Review*, 2nd ser., 34 (1981), pp. 407–37.

Snell, K. D. M., *Annals of the Labouring Poor: Social Change and Agrarian England 1600–1900* (Cambridge, 1985).

Steckel, R. H., 'The quality of census data for historical inquiry: a research agenda', *Social Science History*, 15 (1991), pp. 579–99.

Stephens, W. B., *Sources for English Local History* (Chichester, 1994).

Szreter, S. R. S., 'The genesis of the registrar-general's social classification of occupations', *British Journal of Sociology*, 35 (1984), pp. 522–46.

Szreter, S., *Fertility, Class and Gender in Britain 1860–1914* (Cambridge, 1996).

Thomas, C., 'Rural society in nineteenth-century Wales: south Cardiganshire in 1851', *Ceredigion*, 6 (1970), pp. 388–414.

Thomas, S., 'The enumerators' returns as a source for a period picture of the parish of Llansantffraid, 1841–1851', *Ceredigion*, 4 (1963), pp. 408–21.

Thomas, S., 'The agricultural labour force in some south-west Carmarthenshire parishes in the mid-nineteenth century', *Welsh History Review*, 3 (1966–7), pp. 63–73.

Thomson, D., 'Age reporting by the elderly in the nineteenth century census', *Local Population Studies*, 25 (1980), pp. 13–25.

Tilley, P., 'Creating life histories and family trees from nineteenth century census records, parish registers and other sources', *Local Population Studies*, 68 (2002), pp. 63–81.

Tillott, P. M., 'Sources of inaccuracy in the 1851 and 1861 censuses', in Wrigley, E. A. (ed.), *Nineteenth-Century Society* (Cambridge, 1972), pp. 82–133.

Todd, A., *Nuts and Bolts: Family History Problem Solving Through Family Reconstitution Techniques* (Bury, 2003).

Trinder, B., *The Market Town Lodging House in Victorian England* (Leicester, 2002).

Verdon, N., "'… a subject deserving the highest praise": wives and the farm economy in England, *c.*1700–1850', *Agricultural History Review*, 51 (2003), pp. 23–9.

Victoria History of the County of Middlesex, Vol. II (London, 1911).

Wall, R., Woollard, M., and Moring, B., *Census Schedules and Listings, 1801–1831: an Introduction and Guide* (Colchester, 2004). This guide is Working Paper V in the History Department, University of Essex, Working Paper Series. An updateable version of this will shortly be available at <http://www.histpop.org.uk/pre41/>.

Warwick, M., and Warwick, D., 'Burley-in-Wharfedale in the nineteenth century: a study of social stratification and social mobility', *Local Population Studies*, 54 (1995), pp. 40–55.

Whitehead, F., 'The GRO use of social surveys', *Population Trends*, 48 (1987), pp. 45–54.

Winchester, I., 'What every historian needs to know about record linkage for the microcomputer era', *Historical Methods*, 25 (1992), pp. 149–65.

Woollard, M., '"Shooting the nets": a note on the reliability of the 1881 census enumerators' books', *Local Population Studies*, 59 (1997), pp. 54–7.

Woollard, M., 'The 1901 census: an introduction', *Local Population Studies*, 67 (2001), pp. 26–43.

Woollard, M., 'The employment and retirement of older men, 1851–1881: further evidence from the census', *Continuity and Change*, 17 (2002), pp. 437–63.

Woollard, M., 'The classification of multiple occupational titles in the 1881 census of England and Wales', *Local Population Studies*, 72 (2004), pp. 34–49.

Woollings, B., 'An Orsett census enumerator', *Local Population Studies*, 56 (1996), pp. 54–9.

Wrigley, E. A. (ed.), *Nineteenth-Century Society: Essays in the Use of Quantitative Methods for the Study of Social Data* (Cambridge, 1972).

Wrigley, E. A. (ed.), *Identifying People in the Past* (London, 1973).

Wrigley, E. A., 'Baptism coverage in early nineteenth-century England: the Colyton area', *Population Studies*, 29 (1975), pp. 299–316.

Wrigley, E. A., and Schofield, R. S., *The Population History of England 1541–1871* (London, 1981).

Wrigley, E. A., 'Men on the land and men in the countryside: employment in agriculture in early-nineteenth-century England', in Bonfield, L., Smith, R. M., and Wrightson, K. (eds.), *The World we have Gained: Histories of Population and Social Structure* (Oxford, 1986), pp. 295–336.

Wrigley, E. A., *Poverty, Progress and Population* (Cambridge, 2004).

Index

CPSIA information can be obtained
at www.ICGtesting.com
Printed in the USA
LVHW100923210521
688071LV00004B/4

9 781905 165001